Unions Are Not Inevitable!©

UNIONS

------- *are not* -------

INEVITABLE!©

FOURTH EDITION

Lloyd M. Field, Ph.D.
CHRP, SPHR (USA), FCIPD (UK)

UNIONS ARE NOT INEVITABLE!© by Lloyd M. Field, Ph.D.
Copyright © 2000 by Brock Learning Resources Inc.

All rights reserved. No part of this publication may be reproduced or transmitted in any form or by any means, electronic or mechanical, including photocopy, recording, or any information storage and retrieval system, without permission in writing from the publisher. For information address Brock Learning Resources Inc. Postal Box 305, Waterloo, Ontario, Canada N2J 4A4. Tel. (519) 725-3464   Fax (519) 725-1036

The ideas, suggestions and materials presented in this publication have been solely directed at improving employer-employee relationships through the application of sound human resource management concepts and practices. They are presented with the understanding that neither Brock Learning Resources Inc. nor the author is engaged in rendering legal advice. If legal advice is required, the services of a qualified labor lawyer should be obtained.

ISBN 0-920075-03-7

First Edition: 1981
Second Edition: 1987
Third Edition: 1993

Fourth Edition

Canadian Cataloguing in Publication Data

Field, Lloyd M.
    Unions are not inevitable

4th ed.
0-920075-03-7

1. Personnel management. 2. Industrial relations. 3. Trade-unions.
I. Title.

HD31.F51 2000   658.3   C00-932326-0

Printed and bound in Canada.

With sincere intentions I have written this book in the spirit of the Dharma. The ideals and values expressed in this book belong to many people in my life—family, friends, teachers and clients. To those present and those whose memories live on, I dedicate this book.

Contents

Foreword by Ron Knowles   xiii

Introduction   1

1   Positive Employee Relations   7

What Is Positive Employee Relations? · Unhealthy Conditions Lead to Unionization · The Core Positive Employee Relations Values · Assumptions that Support Positive Employee Relations · The Role of Positive Employee Relations · *Take Action!*

2   Anti-Union vs. Union-Free: A Big Difference   21

Introducing the Sherborne Company · The Cost of Unionization to the Organization · The Cost of Unionization to Leaders · The Cost of Unionization to Employees · *Take Action!*

3   Why Employees Join Unions   29

Major Workplace Dissatisfactions · The Roots of Dissatisfaction · What the Union Offers · Unions Exploit Existing Issues · Defusing Employee Dissatisfaction · Employee Perception Surveys · *Take Action!*

4   The Organizer's Strategy   43

Profile of a Potential Union Organizer · The Truth about the Employer's Role · The Nature of Unions and Organizing Campaigns · Union Tactics · Some Early Warning Signals · How to Respond · Pre-Empting the Union · *Take Action!*

5   Building the Infra-Structure   71

Pro-Active, Not Reactive: A Mantra for Senior Management · Union-Free Means Pro-Employee · A Philosophy that Embraces People as Well as Profit · Management Must "Get It Together" · Employee Relations from the Employee's View · The Significance of the Supervisor · Reinforce the Positive · Supervisors Need Recognition Too · Developing a Positive Employee Relations Program for Your Organization · Be Prepared · *Take Action!*

6   Becoming an Employer of Choice   100

Employer of Choice Status: The Olympic Gold · Qualities of the Good Company · Start by Checking Your Alignment · Internal Marketing — Laying the Groundwork · Internal Marketing — Translating the General to the Specific · Internal Marketing — The Basics · Internal Marketing — What Is at Stake? · The Role of Recognition · Principles of Recognition · Recognition Program Guidelines · Internal Marketing Guidelines · Internal Marketing Opportunities · *Take Action!*

7   Selecting Supervisors   123

Supervisors Are People Managers · Developing People-Management Skills · Finding New Supervisors · Critical "Fit" Factors · Interviewing Supervisory Candidates · *Take Action!*

8   Recruiting and Selecting Employees   134

The Recruitment Process · Is Outsourcing the Hiring Function the Answer? · Job Analysis · Job Description · Finding Good Candidates · Preparing for the Interview · The Interview · Tips for Awkward Situations · Post-Interview Task List · *Take Action!*

9   Training and Managing Supervisors   168

Training Is Essential to Winning Supervisory Commitment · Communication Is Paramount · Linking Communications to Supervisory Training · Supervisory Response to an Organizing Drive · Competency-Based Management Development · Developing Effective Supervisors and Managers · *Take Action!*

| 10 | Communicating Your Message | 199 |

Employee Expectations and Needs · Management Must Take the First Step · A Communications Program — The Basics · Managing Communications · Critical Communication Skills · Ten Communication Do's · Ten Communication Don'ts · *Take Action!*

| 11 | Appraising Employee Performance | 220 |

Why an Appraisal Is Important · Motivational Factors · Creating a Climate for Change · Adult-to-Adult Feedback · Establishing Performance Standards · The Performance Appraisal Discussion · Conducting the Appraisal · *Take Action!*

| 12 | Managing Employee Performance | 258 |

What Does It Mean to "Manage" Performance? · Negative Discipline · Responsible Performance Management · Values and Guiding Behaviors · When Guiding Behaviors Are Not Practiced · What to Do · *Take Action!*

| 13 | Issue Resolution | 285 |

What Happens When Issues Go Unresolved · External Resolution Options · Alternative Issue Resolution Processes · Other Internal Mechanisms · Setting Up an Issues Resolution Program · *Take Action!*

| 14 | Employee Retention | 303 |

Why Good Employees Leave · Career · Relationships · Economics · How Can You Keep Your Best Employees? · *Take Action!*

| 15 | Creating A Decertification Climate | 316 |

Encouraging Decertification · Strategy · Tactics · Eliminating the Old Paradigm · Reclaiming the Positive Organization · Doing Things Differently · Regaining Leadership · From Managing to Leading · A Scenario · *Take Action!*

Epilogue		335

Appendices

A	Employee Perception Survey	339
B	A Supervisor's Guide To Remaining Union-Free Through Positive Employee Relations	353
C	Activity Vector Analysis©	371
D	Let's Talk© — An Employee's Guide to Effective Communications	381
E	Sherborne Employee Handbook	391
F	Life Management Skills Workshop	401

Acknowledgments	407
How to Contact Us	409

List of Tables and Figures

Table 1.1	McGregor's Theory X and Theory Y	18
Table 2.1	Cost of unionization to the company	24
Table 2.2	Cost of unionization to the employees	24
Figure 7.1	Skills needed at different levels of management	124
Figure 7.2	Role suitability	127
Table 9.1	Employee communication techniques	169
Table 9.2	Training and communications schedule	174
Table 11.1	Evolution of performance appraisals	221
Table 11.2	Outcomes that reinforce employee behavior	223
Table 12.1	Elements of a responsible performance management program	262
Table 15.1	What changes are needed?	323

List of Exhibits

Exhibit 4.1	Sherborne letter #1	55
Exhibit 4.2	IBWW bulletin #1	58
Exhibit 4.3	Sherborne letter #2	60
Exhibit 4.4	IBWW bulletin #2	62
Exhibit 4.5	Sherborne information bulletins	64
Exhibit 5.1	Sherborne mission statement	90
Exhibit 5.2	Welcome letter	91
Exhibit 5.3	Goals of the Positive Employee Relations program	93
Exhibit 5.4	Positive Employee Relations policy	95
Exhibit 8.1	Job analysis worksheet	152
Exhibit 8.2	Sample job description	157
Exhibit 8.3	Ideal candidate worksheet	159
Exhibit 8.4	Detailed interviewing guide	160
Exhibit 9.1	Supervisory needs inventory	186
Exhibit 9.2	Generic model of a supervisory training program	188
Exhibit 9.3	Competency-based training and development	191
Exhibit 9.4	War games exercise	195
Exhibit 10.1	Meeting planner and checklist	215
Exhibit 10.2	Communications model	217

Exhibit 11.1	Conducting a performance appraisal	235
Exhibit 11.2	Performance appraisal for employees	237
Exhibit 11.3	Performance appraisal for leadership personnel	244
Exhibit 12.1	Responsible performance management program	267
Exhibit 12.2	Written statement of consequences	277
Exhibit 12.3	Further statement of consequences	279
Exhibit 12.4	Notification of suspension	281
Exhibit 12.5	Issues arising from not practicing guiding behaviors	283
Exhibit 13.1	Issue resolution policy	294
Exhibit 13.2	Request for resolution form	298
Exhibit 13.3	Request for further consideration form	299
Exhibit 13.4	Memo to employee from employee panel	300

FOREWORD

by RON KNOWLES

When the first edition of *Unions Are Not Inevitable!* was published, Lloyd Field could not have known that the relevance of Positive Employee Relations would continue to increase. But that is exactly what has happened. Employees everywhere face a very different working life than the one on which the first edition was based and all too often the result of this new environment is a widening gap in the relations between employees and managers.

Business organizations have been transformed. We all know that in today's marketplace it is a competitive imperative that companies be faster, leaner and more customer-responsive. Technology both enables and requires employees to work faster and smarter. We have revolutionized the workplace. Managers have been trained to empower front-line workers to make decisions and take responsibility for the results. In industry today, mangers really do listen to employees. The improvements in human relations have been genuine and will endure.

There can be no doubt that the development of more effective companies based on greater employee involvement has been a very good and necessary change. But there is a darker underside to all of the organization improvement. Things move so quickly that employees are often "empowered" without corresponding training or access to information or technology. Performance expectations have increased dramatically and that is both exhilarating and exhausting. Perpetual change is exciting and frustrating. The workplace is barely recognizable and even the most positive people are hard-pressed to cope with the pace of change and the ceaseless performance demands. Senior leaders have as much difficulty coping with the challenges as anyone else and sometimes fall back into older ways of thinking and acting. For example, their communication may often be incomplete or occasionally dishonest, instantly undermining all of the good work they do to be effective and inclusive leaders. Much of our feelings about these realities remains unspoken since nobody wants to be seen as negative or resistant to change. Newer and younger employees may simply vote with their feet. When the talented younger employees encounter the inconsistencies of contemporary organizations, they may very quickly say "I'm out of here" and management may never know why. These are the conditions that are creating the widening gap and growing cynicism between companies and their people.

Positive Employee Relations are as important as they have ever been, but for different reasons. The problem is less likely to be unenlightened or exploitive treatment of employees (although amazingly that still happens) than the underlying angst that results from the incredible effort to keep up and stay positive that is required of employees and mangers alike. And that is why this new updated edition of *Unions Are Not Inevitable!* is so timely and so important.

As a manual for union-free management, *Unions Are Not Inevitable!* is impressively complete and comprehensive. It literally does contain everything you could possibly want to know about the subject, right down to the detailed text of employee communiquées. At one level it is a paint-by-numbers plan for staying union-free and, if that is your interest, you will receive greater value than you are expecting. The advice is clear, practical, workable, adult and very wise. It contains every tip, checklist, exercise, template, "do" and "don't" you would ever need. But even a person like me who is not persuaded that staying union free is always in a company's best interests, can benefit from

Lloyd's new edition. *Unions Are Not Inevitable!* is intensely humanistic and value-based. The proposition is that you achieve Positive Employee Relations by creating the conditions under which people can develop "self-respect through self-responsibility." That is worth doing for its own sake. It also has some very important outcomes such as productivity, the ability to adapt to changing external environments and, of course, staying union-free. Lloyd makes no bones about the fact that staying union-free is an outcome—a result of how well management does its job of helping people achieve their potential as psychologically independent people.

The book is at its best when it sets out the seven core values on which Positive Employee Relations rests. The suggested values represent a very advanced level of understanding of what counts in the workplace. Lloyd's advice is slightly unexpected and very, very challenging. Would you have imagined that the workplace was a place where you should expect to find a "spirit of partnership" or a "solid belief in decency"? Or that Positive Employee Relations require that these egalitarian principles be taken seriously as a matter of the most urgent practicality? The book gives you a great deal in the form of practical advice, but it also demands a great deal of its readers, that we hold ourselves as leaders to a very high standard of principled behavior. And if the book is somewhat hard on unions, it is harder on managers.

Over the years I have found all the prescriptions and advice on the nature of leadership and employee relations unclear, sometimes contradictory and far less helpful than I needed. It is hard to have confidence about what we should do if even the experts cannot agree. This book sets out perhaps the clearest definition of leadership I have seen and does so in a manner that is crystal-clear and very detailed. The respective roles of leaders, managers and supervisors are each analyzed and described in detail and in a way anyone can follow and use as a guide. Lloyd's experience very definitely shows and tells managers what they should and should not do in great detail and with the confidence that comes from his career-long interest in these issues.

My own experience has taught that, in the long run, the workplace does need to be fit for humans, and if it isn't organizations will pay a high price in the areas they care most about — productivity, return-on-investment and the ability to compete successfully. This realization has been surprisingly long dawning on many managers. But the realization is only the first step. Building the required relationships and environment is very hard to do and tougher to sustain. *Unions Are Not Inevitable!* reflects a profound understanding of how to do it. But you will also find yourself persuaded that Positive Employee Relations is a goal far more important than the interests of a particular company or group of employees.

Ron Knowles, MBA, FCMC
Director, Western Management Consultants of Ontario
Author of *Coming to Our Senses: Reclaiming
 the Dignity of Organization Life*

Unions Are Not Inevitable!©

INTRODUCTION

This book is about Positive Employee Relations. This phrase has at least two generally accepted interpretations. First, it is a euphemism for remaining union-free through preventative labor relations. Second, it simply means what it says — positive rather than negative relationships with employees, regardless of their role or level in the organization.

I use the phrase predominantly in its latter meaning throughout this book. Remaining union-free is not the result of a single event. While winning a certification or election vote may well be cause for celebration, we must not lose sight of the fact that there was a reason for the vote in the first place. *The goal is not to have the need for a vote.* By establishing solid, reciprocal and positive relationships with our employees, there should be no reason for employees to seek the intervention of a union. In the vast majority of cases, a trade union merely responds to the dissatisfaction perceived in the workplace. This dissatisfaction becomes the platform on which the union builds its organizing or marketing campaign. Consequently, the goal of Positive Employee Relations is to establish policies and practices that encourage employees to talk about their concerns, issues, complaints, etc. (the "stuff" of which dissatisfaction is made), with their leaders in order to obtain responsible, reasonable and fair resolution.

An organization's Positive Employee Relations approach usually requires management to make at least two significant changes. First, to base business decisions (including all human resource decisions) on a set of values or beliefs that speak to our capacity for *self-respect and self-responsibility*. And second, to develop a fresh perspective about what the term "employee" connotes — and replace the notion of the "hired hand" or "alive equipment" with that of the "internal customer or vendor."

If we successfully manage to change to value-based decision-making, the second change will, in all likelihood, follow naturally. The remedy for unionization rests sharply on the point of value-based behavior. If we continue to put profits before people, the union movement will continue to sell its message to receptive customers — your employees. At the operational level, our managerial mindset appears to place *people* and *profits* in conflict. But they should be in harmony and alignment. *People make profits; not the other way around.* When referring to *people*, I use the term inclusively. From entrepreneurs to cafeteria staff, from presidents to custodians, and from receptionists to team members on the assembly line, the mental and physical efforts of *all* these people earn the profits.

Understanding and acting upon this point — that *people make profits* — causes our thoughts and behaviors about others in the workplace to change. Enlightened leaders will realize that *inspiring* others is more respectful and beneficial than *controlling* others. Honesty, trust and integrity will be recognized as the key values on which to build successful long-term relationships. Relationships with internal customers (employees) will be seen as just as important as those with external customers. These two stakeholder groups have a symbiotic relationship. One cannot exist without the other. A strike or lock-out, for example, rarely benefits either stakeholder.

Remaining union-free also requires that entrepreneurs, presidents, chairmen and boards of directors face tough questions regarding their human resources. For example, consider how the business community views the imposition of timelines such as the requirement to meet legislated regulations for filing tax returns. The norm is for the organization to have an "annual paradigm." This annual ritual is then divided into twelve roughly equal components with their own practices for variance-to-income and variance-to-expenditure ratios. The bottom line — *profit* — is always analyzed in terms of dollars earned rather than in terms of human innovation, achievement and productivity.

This assumption is supported by the false notion that a business has a twelve-month life cycle, renewable annually. The fact that this is not the truth does not preclude it from being perceived as a fundamental reality by many managers. By accepting this illusion we initiate policies and practices that relate to profits and annual shareholders' returns in an effort to reduce expenditures in the fourth quarter and increase the recording of income (from all possible sources) in the same period. Everyone's happy — management and shareholders — correct?

Well, maybe not. Too often the employee group (and in the recent past, various management groups) have taken a *hit* on this issue. For most organizations, payroll costs are among the top three most expensive operating factors. If we can reduce them to the lowest possible number, we can maximize profits. Higher profits lead to all the "good things" businesses are in business for, right?

Let's imagine that a single element of the annual assumption were to change. *If* governments accepted some form of human resource accounting that encouraged management to show employee commitment, creativity and innovation in a manner that approximates business goodwill, patents and copyright processes, many business leaders would be eagerly exploring creative ways to maximize return-on-investment by viewing their human resources as an asset. Admittedly, that's a big "if." But what a phenomenal paradigm change that would be! However, for the present, neither government nor the business community have seriously addressed this "if."

Could we engage our human resources in creative ways that address their individuality, their minds and their thoughts? Of course we could! It is just a matter of shifting the paradigm about employees (at all levels of the organization) from "alive expenses" to talented and respectful resources. Must we wait for the government to sanction such initiatives?

If we *don't* make such a paradigm shift, the trade union movement will continue to sell its services to your employees, services that include negotiating wages, benefits and working conditions with you, the employer. For good measure they throw into their "service mix" an advocacy role. And, every time management acts unfairly (from the union's perspective), they initiate a response or grievance. The more grievances they can justify, the more they validate their worth to your employee groups.

As leaders of organizations and as individual shareholders who venture into the stock market, we support this situation by insisting on viewing payroll as an expense and not as an investment. And, if this is not problematic enough, we then impose a twelve-month timeline juxtaposed to the benefits of strategic or long-term planning.

If the old adage that "management gets the union it deserves" is true, then this also speaks to the paradigm shift. If we believe and think *excellence* in everything we do, we behave as excellent leaders. Yes, a lot of training, development and mentoring is required to make this happen. But without new thoughts and new behavior there will be no new examples of excellence. And excellence, like every aspect of our personal and business life, is always in a state of change or transition.

A strong correlation exists between excellence in leadership and Positive Employee Relations. To earn employees' trust and respect we must encourage employees to think about self-respect, personal responsibility, self-advocacy, choices, ownership for decisions, etc. This presents an immense opportunity for organizations, an opportunity that has always existed. Unfortunately, the vast majority of leaders and entrepreneurs have simply not seen it. Why? Maybe because their perspectives are still geared to the monthly financials, the daily quantity shipped or orders fulfilled, and not the human values and systems that *result* in numbers that look good.

You either believe this or you don't. If you do, remaining union-free is a natural consequence; if you don't, you will likely fight the union battle regularly. Think of it this way: the advent of unions followed the rise of the free enterprise system. Maybe we started off on the wrong foot. Maybe we didn't really understand Adam Smith's message. Regardless, in today's economy — global, fast, service- and technology-driven, with a wildly fluctuating stock market — the only common denominator is the humanness we share with others. When, as leaders, we stop advocating for the trust and respect of all our employees, we create an opportunity for dissatisfaction, mistrust and mis-information to take root. Unions thrive on such opportunities.

Implementing the values that underpin sound and respectful employee-employer relationships is difficult and time consuming and, as a result, requires investment capital. This approach is not a quick fix. There are no short-cuts when dealing with people. Any good relationship requires effort and commitment on the part of both parties. But you can be sure that the efforts that go into creating and maintaining a healthy, productive employee-employer relationship will produce benefits for everyone involved. As my father counseled me, whatever is worth doing is worth doing well.

This book presents detailed exhibits, concrete examples and a step-by-step process to help you plan and implement a Positive Employee Relations program that will make a substantial difference to your organization and to the employees who contribute in so many ways to its success.

1
POSITIVE EMPLOYEE RELATIONS

Let's start by clarifying what this book *isn't* about.

This is *not* a book about union-bashing, union-busting or even union-hating. Rather, my concern is with developing Positive Employee Relations, which, I believe, are consistent with the best interests and ideals of North American employees *and their employers*. Throughout this book I will refer to "union-free" to denote an optimal system of human resource management, knowing full well that many pro-unionists will interpret "union-free" to mean "anti-union." Nothing could be further from the truth!

Furthermore, as we develop the philosophy and practices of Positive Employee Relations, it would be easy to misinterpret my basic motives. I am not proposing a set of business practices based on treating people well because they are people and deserved to be well treated. This goes without saying, but it is not my basic motivation in writing this book.

Enterprises are in business to make money. There it is, out in the open. It may sound crass or make you feel uncomfortable, but it shouldn't. All businesses exist to make money. It's not the only reason, but it is a universal one. Many entrepreneurs start their own business to tap into their creative talents or energies, or to satisfy market demands or just to produce a better product or supply a superior service. But all businesses that stay in existence do so because they make money. Making a profit may not be the reason an organization was started, but it is the reason that it still exists today.

It is important to acknowledge this up front, because many criticisms of Positive Employee Relations focus on monetary issues. "It's too expensive to cater to all our employees' needs. If we did that, we'd be out of business." But in reality, failing to treat your employees like adults with important needs and valuable insights, and neglecting to take the pulse of your organization, can be *far more expensive in the long run*. Employees are often the best source of information about how to run the business most profitably. As well, dissatisfied employees will often seek out a third party (a union) to make sure that their concerns are heard and acted upon. And, as we will see, the presence of a union on your shop floor, in your retail store or in your computer center takes a significant bite out of your bottom line.

WHAT IS POSITIVE EMPLOYEE RELATIONS?

Positive Employee Relations is a holistic approach to managing an organization's human resources. If implemented with commitment, it can eliminate the need that employees have for trade union representation. Positive Employee Relations addresses both *what* leaders do and *how* they do it when it comes to *managing people*. Creating a Positive Employee Relations environment starts with the premise that *all* employees (and their families) — not just the management staff — are stakeholders in the business.

This book is intended to demonstrate both the value of a Positive Employee Relations program, as well as the steps you need to follow in order to implement such a program. To do this, numerous exhibits and appendices have been included that can be used as a guide for your own practices. To make these illustrations more meaningful, a fictitious organization and union have been created. In the next chapter, you will be introduced to Sherborne Company.

UNHEALTHY CONDITIONS LEAD TO UNIONIZATION

Before developing and implementing a Positive Employee Relations program for this fictitious organization, however, let's first examine the conditions that can lead to unionization. In and of themselves they are not remarkable, and indeed may sound familiar to you. The company may experience problems in these ways:

- reduced productivity
- quality rejects
- unscheduled downtime
- equipment/mechanical sabotage
- accidents
- tense work environment
- uncertain decision making among management
- poor communications with staff
- dissatisfied employees
- absenteeism/lateness
- numerous employee complaints and concerns
- need for disciplinary actions
- excessive employee turnover
- decreased commitment from staff and management
- fatigue, stress among both staff and management.

If these conditions were present in our company, it would clearly have a negative effect on our bottom line — remember, that's still our primary focus. What is less clear is how we move our company from this state to our preferred (and, possibly, decertified) state. What is required is a change in thinking throughout the entire company. A new paradigm must evolve that places Positive Employee Relations in the forefront. In doing this, you will have taken the first steps on the road to creating a positive organization.

THE CORE POSITIVE EMPLOYEE RELATIONS VALUES

At the heart of this new paradigm are the values of your company. Values are the core principles and beliefs of the organization. Values identify what is important to members of the group (the employees) in carrying out their work. Values must be *real-time* values: they must be statements of what the organization *currently* values. A senior management team may state that it wishes to change its values, but it cannot espouse a value it does not currently practice.

Values answer the question of what is important to us. Values are not meant to be what we should do; rather they should inspire, motivate and energize us. Values can replace rules in a Positive Employee Relations environment. If a decision fits the values, then it is the right decision.

▶ Values are the belief systems of the organization. If the values expressed in the boardroom differ from those held by employees delivering your product or services, this difference can lead to points of disconnection, disharmony and, eventually, customer dissatisfaction.

Values should, in most hierarchic organizations, be led from the top — that is, by the senior management group.

Consistency, based on a solid exploration of the corporate values, is critical. All senior managers must understand the values equally well and apply them in ways that are consistent with their own leadership styles. In whatever way is appropriate, each leader must inspire and "walk the talk," based on the values shared with all employees. A disconnect at the senior level will have wide-ranging consequences further down the organizational structure.

Two additional points of consideration. First, the company's values should flow logically from one to the other. One value statement should not be in conflict with another. Inconsistency on such core issues can only lead to mis-communications, disharmony or discredit to the whole process. Second, values should be beliefs that everyone in the organization can understand and contribute towards. It is the synergy coming from all organizational levels that makes the difference between an average group and a great group. The more positive the values embraced by a company, the more employees will feel encouraged to share these values.

▶ Positive values bind the organization together.

The following are the Seven Core Values for Positive Employee Relations for the Sherborne Company:

1. Spirit of Partnership
2. Solid Belief in Decency
3. Commitment to Self-Knowledge and Development
4. Respect for Individual Differences
5. Health, Safety and Well-being
6. Appreciation that Change Is Inevitable
7. Passion for Products and Process.

The role of the front-line leaders

The values of any organization are communicated to employees by both the words and actions of management. Since employees have most of their day-to-day contact with managers and supervisors, it follows that the organization must ensure that these people are able to accurately deliver the correct message. However, many supervisors come from non-supervisory backgrounds. They were once employees and, because they were the most skilled at their task, they were promoted. In all likelihood, their ascendancy to management had nothing to do with their "people skills." But too few organizations take this into account when promoting employees to the rank of supervisor, and they neglect to provide their new supervisors with the necessary training for their new role. In fact, many old-paradigm organizations are so focused on production that they don't even evaluate the "people performance" of their managerial and supervisory personnel.

▶ Supervisors who lack people management skills can be considered pro-union.

That is, they are most comfortable working within a rules-based, black-versus-white environment. For technically oriented supervisors it's always easier when the rules are spelled out in a collective agreement. Unfortunately, these are the people who will be communicating the values of your organization. The more you establish the right conditions for employees to exercise self-responsibility, the more you alter the role of the supervisor. Existing supervisors may well feel threatened or upset, and your Positive Employee Relations message may not get through to employees.

Before your values can be communicated, you must make sure that you have the right messenger. Be realistic. The changes you want to make may be too much for some of your leadership people. You may need to re-evaluate their role in the organization.

Revising supervisory thinking

We will return to the selection and training of supervisors in Chapters 7 and 9. But for now, the following five steps outline how you should proceed in turning your pro-union *foreman* into a *supervisor* of Positive Employee Relations:

1. Define the roles, activities and acceptable behaviors for supervisors who do a "great job" at dealing with employees (and who, in effect, offer employees more than the union).
2. Deliver training to support these preferred behaviors.
3. Provide feedback to all supervisors.
4. Reward supervisors who:
   • resolve problems at, or before, the first stage.
   • train employees who are promoted by other managers.
   • achieve departmental productivity, quality or other goals using persuasion or influence rather than the power of their position.
   • show maturity in their dealings with all employees by treating employees as adults, not children.
5. Apply corrective action to supervisors who do not fit the new model. Be willing to follow up with termination, if necessary.

▶ Never accept poor performance from anyone, especially a leader!

Responding to issues in a Positive Employee Relations environment

Now let's look at each of the Seven Core Values and examine how different training and work experience produce different behaviors. In this example, the foreman's behavior reflects years of experience working in a unionized environment, while the supervisor's behavior reflects experience with Positive Employee Relations.

1. Spirit of Partnership
- Both employees and managers are recognized as adults — they simply perform different roles.
- Employees and managers are players on the same team.
- Every role is integral to the success of the department/business.
- Who solves a problem is not the issue; only that it is solved. Recognize that employees often have critical information otherwise unavailable to management.

Example:	*Foreman's Response:*	*Supervisor's Response:*
When faced with a problem:	Tells employee what to do.	Supervisor and employee decide together. Both have input. "What do you think we should do?"

2. Solid Belief in Decency
- All employees inherently deserve respect.
- Employees are treated holistically, in a manner that acknowledges that their business/professional lives are interconnected with their personal/social lives.
- Managers are honest and "walk the talk."
- Openness is the ground rule for all relationships.

Example:	Foreman's Response:	Supervisor's Response:
Discussing a sensitive issue:	Believes you have to stretch the truth, even if it involves lying, to protect the company or the employee. It's just part of the job.	Supervisor is known for his/her integrity. People are more important than work. There is no need for "work around" solutions if you talk honestly and openly.

3. Commitment to Self-knowledge and Development
- Organization makes substantial investments in training.
- Employees are encouraged to learn, apply new ideas.
- Employees are encouraged to take risks and responsibility.
- Mistakes are viewed as learning experiences; not as punishable offences.

Example:	Foreman's Response:	Supervisor's Response:
Training	Shows employee how to do the job, then leaves him/her alone. Follow up is sporadic as foreman is too busy with other tasks. Unwilling to share experience because knowledge is seen as power.	Training occurs on an on-going basis. Knowledge is recognized as part of the job, part of the company's culture. Supervisors share their experiences and train employees to solve their own work-related problems.

POSITIVE EMPLOYEE RELATIONS

4. Respect for Individual Differences
- There are no "second-class" employees.
- This is a workplace devoid of discrimination and harassment.
- An employee's personal life, values and culture are important to the employee as an individual.

Example:	*Foreman's Response:*	*Supervisor's Response:*
Apparent inter-cultural conflicts; easier tasks go to one group and are perceived as not being shared equally.	Has no diversity training experience. Makes no effort to appreciate the difficulty of the non-English speaking employees. Willingly establishes production targets to encourage competition among groups.	Bases decision on group discussion. Makes every effort to have multi-lingual employees translate for those with limited English fluency. Collaboratively works to achieve mutual respect among group members. Views diversity as an opportunity for synergy.

5. Health, Safety and Well-being
- Workplace safety is a basic employee right.
- Employee can stop any work process or activity that is unsafe.
- The employee assistance program is regularly promoted.
- Corrective action is taken when work is too repetitive, computer screens are too small, etc.

Example:	*Foreman's Response:*	*Supervisor's Response:*
When an employee reports an injury:	Comments that employee complains too much. ("The job is physical and the employee knew that.") Physical risks are just part of the job. Lost time due to accident is just a subterfuge to take time off work.	Supervisor feels no job is worth hurting yourself for. Takes whatever action is necessary to get medical attention. Investigates to remove any systemic factors that contributed to the accident.

6. Appreciation that Change Is Inevitable
- Employees are trained to embrace change as a natural event.
- Employees are shown how requirements from customers can change frequently, thereby changing their role or responsibility further down the process.
- Employees have variety and flexibility in their work.
- There are smooth transitions in the event of layoffs or relocations.

Example:	Foreman's Response:	Supervisor's Response:
When a new process is introduced:	Leaves employees out of the loop until the last possible moment. Will make it as much as possible like the old process, so employees don't sabotage it.	Supervisor asks employees to help plan the changes and prepare for them. Employees are recognized for trying new ways to resolve change-related problems.

7. Passion for Products and Process
- Managers and employees live the values in the workplace in how they perform the actual work.
- Managers and employees become personally involved and responsible for the success of the organization.
- Continuous improvement and competitive advantage are by-products of shared values and collaborative effort.
- Profit is the result of doing everything else right.

Example:	Foreman's Response:	Supervisor's Response:
A poor-quality shipment is about to be sent out:	Realizes there is a 75 percent chance it won't be caught by the customer. Decides to let it go, then quickly moves on to a new crisis.	Employee advises supervisor that a quality error was just found on product about to be shipped. Supervisor asks employee what to do. Both agree to correct the problem immediately. Reputations are more valuable than the time needed to rework.

ASSUMPTIONS THAT SUPPORT POSITIVE EMPLOYEE RELATIONS

Managers intending to develop a Positive Employee Relations program must have some understanding of human and organizational behavior. A wealth of information may be found under the broad headings of behavioral sciences and organizational development by authorities such as Maslow, McGregor, Herzberg, Meyers, Likert and Skinner. Much excellent research has been conducted in this field within the last four decades. For the most recent work, see Alderfer, Erez, Zidon, Mintzberg, Drucker, Pascale and Handy.

McGregor's Theory X and Theory Y

The thoughts of Douglas McGregor and his friend Abraham Maslow underpin the principles of Positive Employee Relations advocated in this book. McGregor's theories on assumptions regarding human nature are particularly relevant. In *The Human Side of Enterprise*, he concluded that organizations are structured and managed, for the most part, on the basis of certain assumptions that he formulated into Theory X and Theory Y.

McGregor insisted that his theories did not attempt to describe people *as they are* but merely to describe the *assumptions* that managers may have about their employees.

▶ The danger with assumptions is that, once established, they are often treated as facts and regularly become self-fulfilling.

Managers tend to operate their departments on the basis of such assumptions. It is interesting to note, as McGregor did, that managers almost universally deny their assumptions. A great many managers who vehemently deny that people lack integrity, are lazy, don't want responsibility and don't want to achieve, run their departments as though every word of Theory X were the gospel truth.

TABLE 1.1 — McGregor's Theory X and Theory Y

THEORY X	THEORY Y
People by their very nature:	People by their very nature:
Lack integrity.	Have integrity.
Are fundamentally lazy and desire to work as little as possible.	Work hard toward objectives to which they are committed.
Avoid responsibility.	Assume responsibility within these commitments.
Are not interested in achievement.	Desire to achieve.
Are incapable of directing their own behavior.	Are capable of directing their own behavior.
Are indifferent to organizational needs.	Want their organizations to succeed.
Prefer to be directed by others.	Are not passive and submissive.
Avoid making decisions whenever possible.	Will make decisions within their commitments.
Are not very bright.	Are imaginative and creative.

In creating a blueprint for Positive Employee Relations, this book assumes Theory Y to be true for almost all individuals. That is, that employees will take initiative and prefer to be self-directed. Those who do not are likely responding to our society's inability to touch the lives of all its citizens.

THE ROLE OF POSITIVE EMPLOYEE RELATIONS

The motivations behind the creation of a pro-active human resource system are as selfish as they are egalitarian. In approaching our employees as legitimate stakeholders in the organization, we hope to engage both their labor and their intelligence. Employees who are fundamentally satisfied with their work will, in my experience, be more productive for themselves and their employers. By reducing the factors related to employee dissatisfactions, we unleash creativity and commitment: two important success factors to which a union has no response.

If we, as employers and managers, do not satisfy the needs and aspirations of our employees, we can expect our employees to seek out a third party who will recognize and respond to those needs. The goals of organizations and the goals of employees do not have to be in opposition. They are so only when our values and our assumptions about employees and organizations are in conflict.

The premise behind this book is that prevention is not only the best course of action, but that it may be the only avenue open to creating long-term, harmonious employee-management relations. It's the only avenue that makes good business sense. Positive Employee Relations is a philosophy that is unencumbered by hierarchical, tradition-laden management practices or labor legislation. Positive Employee Relations does not evoke visions of labor tribunals and the judicial system — it speaks to the responsibilities shared by leadership and employees to ensure that their organizations are satisfying "communities" which in turn provide products and services for a reasonable return-on-investment.

TAKE ACTION!

1. Understand and learn to recognize the unhealthy conditions that can lead to unionization.
2. Identify and examine your company's values, or core principles and beliefs.
3. Recognize the importance of front-line supervisors, and take steps to ensure that they are acting in conformity with the organization's values.
4. Examine your assumptions about employees. What behaviors do they lead to?

2
ANTI-UNION VS. UNION-FREE: A BIG DIFFERENCE

So you're on board! You want to build a Positive Employee Relations program. You're going to hire only leaders who share this vision. And you're going to put in place an enlightened set of human resources practices that are in line with the philosophy of Positive Employee Relations. You believe strongly that heading in this direction will be in the best personal and financial interests of all your organization's stakeholders, including the employees.

The last thing you need is a union to get in the way. In fact, staying union-free is one of your key objectives. So it's no surprise that you have strong feelings about this subject. Or is it? In examining why you and your management team don't want a third-party intervening in your workplace, you are likely to bump up against the adversarial paradigm of labor-management relations that actually *fosters* pro-union sentiment among your employees and is the anathema of a strong Positive Employee Relations program.

Let's examine what it means to be "anti-union." Such a concept is generally against the principle of "free association" that is embedded (in one form or another) in our governments' charters of rights/bills of rights, etc. Taking a public "anti-union" stand is illogical at best and illegal at worst. Going into any union campaign with management talking about an "anti-union" stand will only lead to embarrassment, tarnished credibility and a financial penalty imposed by the labor board. In some jurisdictions, such a position, if proven by the union, will lead to automatic union certification or representation.

From another perspective, being anti-union is a short-term strategy that leads to long-term pain. Anti-union usually implies the following sentiments:

> "No union is ever going to take over my company!"
> "I don't care what the employees want, this is our company and management will run it our way."
> "They have no rights here and I'll go to the limit to keep them out."

The reality is that unions are interested in your employees, not your company. Why? Unions want to provide services to your employees for a fee — union dues. The prime service they market is consistency and "fairness" based on the principle of seniority. To achieve this they need to negotiate a collective agreement with management. Any additional powers or influence they gain over time rests with their ability to capitalize on management's mistakes or weaknesses, especially management's predicament when facing a conflict between the "value of profit" versus the "value of employees."

Being anti-union is in direct opposition to being union-free. Positive Employee Relations is built on the view that employees have integrity, deserve respect and can make a difference in the success of the business. Telling employees that we are anti-union is, in effect, telling them that they cannot exercise rights granted them as citizens. Moreover, an anti-union stand is, by definition, negative. By focussing on the negative, we deflect valuable brain power, creativity and energy that could be used positively to resolve the people-versus-profits values conflict.

INTRODUCING THE SHERBORNE COMPANY

Our imaginary company, Sherborne Company, manufactures and markets the "world-famous Sherborne Widget." The company has just celebrated its thirtieth anniversary by successfully listing on a major stock exchange. Originally a family-run business, Sherborne is now in the process of recruiting a number of professional managers to run the operation as the founding members move into retirement. The company is a one-plant operation with approximately 500 employees.

The manufacturing processes are also in transition, moving from semi-skilled assembly lines to automated job tasks and, in some cases, robotics. As a result of pressure applied by some of Sherborne's customers, the company is in the process of implementing a continuous improvement program. The Sherborne Widget is marketed in North America through the company's own sales force, while export sales are handled by a number of manufacturers' agents throughout Mexico, Europe and Asia.

Currently, the employee population is not represented by a union. In the early years of Sherborne Company there were fewer employees, but each one felt a personal responsibility to the company's founders. The owners, in turn, made every effort to know and appreciate each employee. But as the Sherborne Widget gained market share, the nature of business on the shop floor changed. Supervisors grew increasingly concerned with productivity numbers and less focused on the individual needs of employees. The original workforce, who often acted out of loyalty to the company's founders, retired and new employees, who didn't have those same loyalties, began to resent being used by their supervisors to meet challenging production targets.

Recently, as the new production processes — especially robotics — have been introduced, these feelings have been exacerbated. As this adversarial relationship becomes institutionalized, management fears that the workforce has begun to feel more like workers than employees. Though management has yet to confirm these suspicions, there is also a fear that employees are increasingly interested in unionizing. Within the last two months, three different supervisors have discovered discarded literature from the International Brotherhood of Widget Workers (IBWW) on company premises.

THE COST OF UNIONIZATION TO THE ORGANIZATION

The managers at Sherborne Company are convinced that they don't want a union intervening in their relationship with their employees. But why?

Traditionally, it is difficult for managers and supervisors to express the precise nature of their non-union sentiments. The reasons usually given — the union will get in the way, it'll only slow things down, routines will become regimented by union-negotiated breaks and workplace conditions — are rooted in the same adversarial attitudes that made the union attractive to employees in the first place.

As we will discuss, these attitudes (and often the people who promote them) must be re-aligned or re-assigned before the organization can move forward. A Positive Employee Relations program will require every member of the management team to put these adversarial notions aside and treat employees as adults rather than as uncooperative children. This is in everyone's best interests and will create the conditions where a unionized workplace is the least attractive alternative.

There are, however, bona fide reasons why your organization should strive to create the conditions where unionization is of no appeal to employees. The most basic reason is that *unionization is costly.*

In more than one private study conducted in the United States, tracking a five-year period following unionization of their workforces, it was found that *operating costs increased by more than 25 percent of the gross payroll and benefit cost.* See Tables 2.1 and 2.2 for examples of how much unionized companies and employees pay annually. For Sherborne Company, with a gross payroll of $18 million, unionization would result in an increase in operating costs of $4.5 million.

TABLE 2.1

COST OF UNIONIZATION TO THE COMPANY (25% of gross payroll)	
Payroll	25% annually
$5 million	$1,250,000
$10 million	$6,250,000
$25 million	$2,500,000

TABLE 2.2

COST OF UNIONIZATION TO THE EMPLOYEES (2.5 hrs monthly)
100 Employees x $15/hr. x 2.5 hrs. x 12 mos. = $45,000 (annually)
200 Employees x $18/hr. x 2.5 hrs x 12 mos = $108,000 (annually)
300 Employees x $20/hr. x 2.5 hrs. x 12 mos. = $180,000 (annually)

Higher costs, lower productivity, reduced flexibility

The increased costs of unionization are *not* associated with individual wages and benefits. Rather, they result from:

- narrowly defined jobs that may require two people to perform what previously was one job.
- restrictive production practices, where work assignment flexibility is limited by seniority.
- the departure of high achievers, who do not want their merit pay opportunities eliminated.
- an inability to take appropriate and timely disciplinary action, including termination of employees, if warranted.
- strikes, slowdowns and other non-productive, union-initiated actions.

Clearly, the money lost in the additional costs of a labor agreement is due primarily to *lower productivity*. What's more, some labor relations professionals peg the increased costs in a unionized company at more than 25 percent — even as high as 35 to 50 percent. This additional ten to 25 percent is not due to lower productivity, but is the result of:

- the company's lack of flexibility regarding staffing, relocation and work assignments.
- the establishment of an adversarial working environment where a win-lose attitude is prevalent.
- customer losses due to reduced quality and/or production standards.
- the grievance resolution program that consumes time and money at an insatiable rate.
- time devoted to labor-management relations and costly bargaining procedures.
- fees that management pays for legal and management consultants.

If higher costs and lower productivity are factors most often identified by managers who do not want a unionized environment, then the above list highlights the third factor in non-union sentiment: *reduced management flexibility*. The inevitable change in employee-employer relationships that accompanies unionization may cost far more than financial statements can show. Management will lose:

- the ability to deal with people on a one-on-one basis — a union is a collective.
- advantages resulting from frequent, open, unencumbered discussion with employees.
- the privilege of determining individual wages, including the opportunity to reward individuals or teams who have made a substantial contribution.
- the freedom to select people for promotion on the basis of performance, as opposed to seniority.
- the ability to settle disciplinary problems without the politics and posturing of self-serving union officials.
- the freedom to transfer people to other jobs without running the seniority-and-bumping obstacle course.

THE COST OF UNIONIZATION TO LEADERS

Before managers and supervisors can successfully communicate the organization's Positive Employee Relations program, they need to have a clear idea of what would happen if a union drive were successful.

On a day-to-day basis, the loss of flexibility that comes with a labor contract is felt most keenly by front-line supervisors and managers. In a union-free environment, human resource policies on issues such as transfer, training, recognition, discipline and so forth are carried out by front-line supervisors. Hence, there is a significant amount of pressure placed on the supervisor to carry out the company's policies fairly and consistently. Many supervisors at this point may ask themselves, "Why bother? With a collective agreement in my pocket, I won't have to worry about all this." But if the union does win a certification, the job of the supervisor will change dramatically.

The union, through the stewards, acts as a blocker to front-line supervisors in many situations, influences the supervisors' working conditions, interferes with interpersonal relationships, and drives up the hours of work. It puts supervisors in ambiguous roles by usurping many of their previously held functions.

In a fully unionized workplace, no supervisor may require an employee to perform tasks that are not part of the employee's job. The "it's not my job" syndrome has frustrated, enraged and immobilized many supervisors, who may find it easier to adjust a temperature gauge personally rather than to ask the first person in sight to do it. In one unionized nursing home a bottle fell and shattered, but the broken glass that was a danger to patients could be cleaned up by no one but the housekeeping person, who was absent at the time.

Flexibility is throttled in a unionized environment. Some years ago, in a uranium mine in northern Quebec, supervisors and mine operators had worked out a mutually satisfactory plan for allowing employees to conduct personal business on a work day and make up the lost shift the following week. But when the union objected that some employees (to make up the shift) were working longer than the specified number of hours in a week, the practice was discontinued. After that, employees simply forfeited a day's pay if they had to miss a shift for personal reasons.

THE COST OF UNIONIZATION TO EMPLOYEES

While it is clear to most leaders that their organization will suffer from the presence of a union, it is less obvious that the employee population will also suffer. After all, didn't they want the union in the first place? Weren't they the ones looking for someone to safeguard their interests? Someone to ensure job security and fight for better wages and working conditions?

In reality, a union can only guarantee your employees (its members) three things:

1. That they will pay union dues.
2. That they will have the right to strike or be locked out.
3. That they will have access to formal grievance procedures.

As for everything else regarding the labor-management relationship, the union will have to *negotiate* with management.

The tangible costs of unionization to employees are easily calculated. Union dues and fines will be stipulated in the union constitution or in the "terms and conditions" of managing the union local. They are often based on a certain number of hours per month at the employee's hourly rate of pay. These figures can result in substantial additions to the union's coffers (see Table 2.2). At Sherborne Company, the employee population earns an average of $18 per hour. If the IBWW certification drive is successful, the IBWW constitution states that union members owe 2.5 hours of pay per month in dues. For Sherborne's 500 employees this would work out to union contributions of $270,000 per year. If a three-year agreement is signed, the employees have just added $810,000 to the union's bank account. What's more, employees will have to sacrifice their whole pay if they ever vote to go out on strike.

But the consequences to employees of opting for a union go beyond monetary issues. The reality is that a union's presence in the workplace — with a collective agreement that guides all labor-management action — creates a rigid and adversarial environment. Management becomes the enemy and there is no freedom to be an individual. The contract can stipulate that advancement is based on seniority, not performance. Incentive pay will disappear because it contravenes the terms of the contract. And, finally, there will be no room for management to consider individual employee needs on a case-by-case basis.

We have already seen that unionization increases an organization's operating costs. But the tragedy is that these dollars are not passed on to employees. With few exceptions, employees within a given industry earn about the same rate of pay whether they are unionized or not. Many non-unionized companies keep their wages in line with those of unionized companies, and most partially unionized organizations match non-union wages within their collective agreements. Though this money is not passed along to employees, the organization still must bear these increased costs, which are eventually passed along to consumers. Once the union is in place, *union members lose, management loses and ultimately, the consumer loses.*

TAKE ACTION!

1. Assess the real costs of unionization to the organization and to the employees.
2. Remember that remaining union-free is the application of good management practices; it is not about being anti-union.

3
WHY EMPLOYEES JOIN UNIONS

The leadup to unionization can take at least two forms. Working conditions can become so oppressive that employees may feel they have no choice but to seek the protection of a union. But even if a work situation does not reach this stage, employers can leave themselves vulnerable to unionization; the union message often finds interested ears among disgruntled employees.

The reasons why people decide to sign a union membership cards are as varied as the people involved. However, some issues appear to have almost universal validity. Ongoing dissatisfaction with unresolved workplace issues invariably leads to frustration.

▶ Unresolved employee dissatisfaction will lead to frustration and alienation that, in turn, will provide organizing opportunities for unions.

MAJOR WORKPLACE DISSATISFACTIONS

Almost all workplace dissatisfactions fall into one of the following broad categories:

- job security
- workplace environment
- leadership's attitudes and practices
- lack of appreciation
- human resource practices
- wages and benefits
- lack of promotion or advancement opportunities.

Job security

Two examples illustrate the problem: (1) Employees become aware that the company's lay-off practices have not been handled fairly; (2) A long-term employee is terminated and there is a communications vacuum surrounding his/her departure. The issue in both examples is the same: lack of planned communications surrounding significant events. Employees surmise: *If it could happen to those people, why not me?* Most employees, most of the time, do not give the employer the benefit of the doubt. We must go out of our way to earn their trust.

Workplace environment

Daily physical evidence that the workplace is dirty, unsafe, crowded, is poorly heated or has inadequate lighting, tools and equipment. From a social perspective, the workplace is unfriendly, co-workers are hostile and there is no sense of pride in the products produced or the services delivered. The message conveyed by the environment is that management does not care — economical concerns have a higher value than the hygiene needs of employees.

Leadership's attitudes and practices

In most workplaces the supervisor (or front-line manager) *is* the company in the eyes of employees. Supervisors are perceived as having incredible power and influence in the organization. Far too often, however, supervisors are promoted from their previous position with little consideration for how well their competencies and behavior will fit with the new position. Without the proper training, many supervisors fall into bad habits: administering policies inconsistently, playing favorites, missing opportunities to praise employees on a job well done. In the eyes of disgruntled employees, the supervisor's loyalty, commitment and knowledge won't be enough to offset his or her shortcomings.

Lack of appreciation

Most workplace cultures focus on the short term versus the long term, control over employees versus trust in their capabilities and integrity, and managing versus inspiring. Performance appraisals are not part of the routine. Hence, recognition and appreciation are not built into the culture. In fact, just the opposite is the case. When something goes wrong, how long does it take for the supervisor to deliver the bad news? Some employees would claim, "at the speed of light." This has many negative consequences, probably the most critical being that those employees whose achievements deserve positive feedback never receive it — driving them further into the camp of the discontented.

Human resource practices

There are times when we ask the human resources team to do the impossible, such as: (1) Ensure that our Positive Employee Relations program is healthy and vibrant; and (2) Find 20 new employees within 48 hours. Unless there are 20 previously interviewed, tested and reference-checked candidates waiting in the wings, the second task is impossible to perform thoroughly. To find 20 "warm bodies" may not be difficult, but to find candidates who fit the culture, have the correct values, technical skills and compatible beliefs about customer and quality is unlikely. Since products must be shipped, the 20 "bodies" are hired with the rationale that the poor performers can always be removed during the probation period. This is *not* a good Positive Employee Relations strategy and, in the long term, not a good strategy to ensure productivity and quality.

Wages and benefits

Surprisingly, this is the least common reason for employees to sign membership cards. Why? Because most organizations have made some effort to keep wages and benefits in line with their community and their industry. Compensation data is usually available from the local human resource association, industry association, etc. For some technical or professional positions, similar data is available from the professional society itself. Employers who are paying minimum wage because of the nature of their business are likely paying wages similar to that of their competition. (Under these circumstances, wages and benefits become a significant factor leading to unionization.)

Lack of promotion or advancement opportunities

Employees who feel that they are stuck in a job with no potential for growth will eventually feel dissatisfied.

Workplace dissatisfaction is about employee perceptions. If your employees *believe* something to be true about your organization or its policies, then for all intents and purposes it is true. To a dissatisfied employee, a union offers the perception of control, a feeling of belonging and opportunities for growth and change.

▶ Employee perceptions are realities and unions will try to exploit these issues in their organizing drive.

Whether based in facts or not, employee perceptions are realities and unions will try to exploit these issues in their organizing drive. The supervisor's role is to manage employee perceptions. If, for example, a company's disciplinary policies are clearly outlined and communicated and then applied consistently and fairly by the supervisor, employees won't perceive their treatment to be unjust.

▶ Companies win the battle of perceptions on the strength of their past performance.

THE ROOTS OF DISSATISFACTION

Should your employees want to unionize, the impetus, in all likelihood, will be related to one or more of the issues listed above. A broader perspective of employee dissatisfaction would also include some of the following concerns:

- poor job design (tasks that are monotonous and uninspiring because the decision-making component has been removed), leading to employee frustration and anxiety.
- lack of leadership, including inconsistent and/or unclear direction from management.
- autocratic supervisory practices that demand obedience, submissiveness and, in turn, lead to lack of commitment, alienation, favoritism and turnover.
- an overall organizational climate that promotes mediocrity, where employees are almost encouraged to get away with as much as they can.
- an organizational communication system in which employees (who provide the products/services that keep the company in business) are the last to be told of changes in product lines and schedules, new ideas being generated through research and development efforts, new markets that have been opened up, changes planned in plant layout and so on.

Usually, the only parts of the employee-employer relationship that are detailed in writing are those that address pay, benefits, hours of work, vacation entitlement and the like. Potentially more contentious issues remain unrecorded, perhaps because they are difficult to capture in words. These include job descriptions, performance standards and policy/procedure statements concerning discipline, issues resolution, performance appraisal, recognition and so forth.

▶ **When human resource matters (such as policies and procedures) are left unwritten, they become major sources of frustration for all involved.**

Both the employee and his/her supervisor independently form an opinion as to the meaning, scope, implications and consequences of unwritten practices. Over time, these perceptions become realities to the individuals involved. Once the perceptions are fixed in the mind of the employee and the supervisor, the potential for conflict exists.

Many organizations have a process for resolving such conflicts. If, for example, an employee does not agree with a particular disciplinary action taken by his/her supervisor, the employee may lodge a complaint using the company's complaint procedure or open-door policy. Implicit in upward communication practices such as the open-door policy are two important components: first, that the employee is a mature adult who can speak for him/herself; and second, that the employee will be given a fair hearing.

When management responds favorably to the employee's complaint it is, in effect, reinforcing the employee's perception of being correct and of having some power to influence management.

However, should management not favor the employee's point of view, one of the following outcomes is likely:

- The employee will withdraw the complaint and accept management's view as to why the complaint is not valid.
- The employee will leave the company and seek employment elsewhere.
- Where alternate employment does not exist or is not desirable, the employee may turn to a union to gain more clout or power over management.

When turned down by management — that is, when the employee's complaint is not resolved to his/her satisfaction — the employee will continue to perceive management as unfair and will infer that he/she has little influence over the workplace.

An individual employee will likely have little impact on unionization unless the employee can gather the support of other like-minded or dissatisfied employees. Collectively, they will be successful only if they believe, and can persuade others to believe, that a union will lead to more influence or power and hence a change in the issues that are causing dissatisfaction.

WHAT THE UNION OFFERS

Employees' dissatisfaction may easily go undetected by management but will probably be identified quickly by an outside observer such as a union organizer. The ability of the organizer to spot weaknesses is similar to that of an external auditor who, being objective, will see more quickly the flaws in a company's financial systems and records.

As for the employees, while their general dissatisfaction may be building to the point where they will be receptive to a union organizer, they probably have great difficulty in estimating the strength of their feelings. Here, an astute and experienced union organizer can act as a catalyst by voicing unrealized frustrations and assuring the employees that their concerns are valid, that they really are badly treated. The following list summarizes what unions will purport to offer to disgruntled employees:

- job security and due process
- fairness and consistency in administration
- predictability of the future
- adequate problem-solving and grievance procedures
- pay and benefits that meet or exceed industry standards
- standardized promotion practices.

The union organizer recognizes that some employees have job-related frustrations and uses this knowledge to his/her own ends. Management can do the same. But management must anticipate the employees' dissatisfaction before it ever gets to the courting stage between employees and the union. Conducting an employee perception survey (sometimes called an attitude or opinion survey; see the end of this chapter and

Appendix A) every 12 months will indicate problem areas and allow management to beat a potential union drive to the punch.

UNIONS EXPLOIT EXISTING ISSUES

The organizer will probably begin developing the campaign from inside your organization and then will develop a strategy using issues that already exist, enlisting some of your employees to spread the word.

Don't assume that in order to appeal to the employees' feelings of insecurity, an organizer will base the strategy on questionable claims. Union organizers don't have to dig for material to weave into an organizing campaign. Supervisors and managers, in the course of their duties, frequently make magnificent blunders that bring joy to the heart of any union supporter. The organizer may uncover evidence of the following:

Favoritism

The astute union organizer will not fail to emphasize the protection the union will give to the individual against a supervisor who shows favoritism, makes unreasonable demands or harasses employees.

In most organizations employees will perceive, rightly or wrongly, certain actions of their supervisors to be unfair. For example, one group may feel that the supervisor has allocated available overtime work to a few favorites rather than spreading it evenly among all qualified employees. If the company cannot produce actual records to refute the employees' claim or does not have a fair system for assigning overtime to those who sign up, the union's argument gains weight, not only with these employees but with others who may feel that the same thing could happen to them.

Unfair treatment/discrimination

Unions will, understandably, play to the hilt any circumstance in which an individual employee has been, or is thought to have been, unfairly treated. How can the organizer lose with an argument that goes like this: "If it can happen to old Charlie, it can happen to you, unless you have us to protect you!"

Lack of representation

The organizer will remind employees that if one of them is unfairly disciplined by a supervisor, they have no recourse to representation. The organizer would point out that the union (when and if certified) would champion the alleged infraction through the grievance procedure and ultimately to independent arbitration and, at the same time, would protect the employee against retribution by the company.

Vulnerability

Unions legitimately can, and often do, remind employees that in the absence of a union contract, the generous fringe benefits and good wages they enjoy may be reduced or rescinded by management without discussion. This argument is particularly effective in highly industrialized sectors where employees often have a basic distrust of management for this very reason.

Lack of seniority privileges

As with wages and benefits, the issue of seniority appeals to employees' insecurities. Again, the organizer will point out that in the absence of a union contract, the company can ignore seniority in matters of layoff, recall, transfer and promotion. This argument is of particular interest to long-serving employees, employees with lower skill levels and employee groups with low turnover.

DEFUSING EMPLOYEE DISSATISFACTION

Nothing defuses employee dissatisfaction better than sincere communication, especially when it leads to positive action. Employees are willing to talk if management is willing to listen. As a consultant, I am frequently asked to conduct employee perception surveys in organizations where management perceives a communications breakdown. Usually this breakdown involves employees who have indicated discontent and the prospect of unionization looms on the horizon. After spending as little as three or four hours in direct communication with employees we usually have the issues — both symptoms and problems — on the table.

Management shouldn't expect a machine operator to walk over to a supervisor and tell him he's only 50 percent productive because the set-up engineer placed the machine control panel too high. But as a management consultant, if I'm called in to unclog the communications network, I can say to a group of employees: "What the hell's wrong with this outfit?" And somebody will likely say: "Dammit, the trouble around here is that management spends more time taking courses and reading books on industrial engineering than it does listening to us, the employees who run the machines."

I can't count the number of times I've heard employees say: "I've tried time and again to tell my supervisor (or the front office) what's wrong around here, but she doesn't listen — so I've given up. To hell with them all. When this place gets screwed up badly enough, then maybe they'll listen." In no time, a consultant hears the whole story, reports to the disbelieving president, who then makes inquiries and finds out that there really *is* a problem.

Why must a consultant be called in to an organization to do what rightly falls into a manager's domain? The employee population will not open up unless the right climate has been established. Hire an outsider (consultant, university professor, etc.) to conduct the employee perception survey the first time; then managers and supervisors, with a little training and guidance, can keep the dialog going on indefinitely.

▶ The number one cause of unionization is leadership's attitudes and practices towards employees.

But managers must take the first step in communicating and asserting the organization's value systems. Supervisors must be secure in the knowledge that employee dissatisfaction can be reported and that something will be done about it. When it is apparent that a supervisor has management's support, the supervisor becomes the most effective liaison between top management and the employee. The supervisor is empowered and management has gained key support in communicating its values. An all-employee orientation program should be put into place to educate the workforce about the validity of organizational goals, and inform management of employee needs and requests that are keeping the organization from achieving its goals.

In one of our employee education programs, we begin by encouraging employees to discuss the free enterprise system, labor economics and, later in the program, the union movement in general. We share with them information from a union organizer's handbook because many of them have never realized that recruiting members is as important to unions as selling hamburgers is to McDonald's. The success of both depends upon softening up the prospective client by appealing to the client's needs and then asking the client to part with his money.

While our approach is preventative, it is important to understand that it focuses not on how we can prevent *unionization* but rather on how we can prevent the *deterioration of employee relations* in the workplace, since such deterioration might eventually lead to unionization.

Don't wait until government has to legislate improved working conditions or lobby groups succeed in winning changes to human rights legislation. When you get legislation, you get bureaucracy and inflexibility. Make sure that Positive Employee Relations practices are part of your values and make sure everyone lives them.

EMPLOYEE PERCEPTION SURVEYS

How can we satisfy employee needs before they become union issues? If you have resources for only one project, rely on the employee perception survey. Let me share with you our approach to this survey and how it can be immensely helpful to your Positive Employee Relations program.

Management approval is essential before starting this communications process. Questions will arise during the employee sessions that management must be prepared to answer. Otherwise, issues may surface that, if left unresolved by management, could become material for a union organizing campaign.

The survey should consist of a series of questions to which yes/no, agree/disagree or multiple choice answers are required. The design of the survey need not be complex or expensive; your human resources department will no doubt have sample surveys to share with you.

The pre-survey communications plan consists of distributing a copy of the survey to senior management, explaining that the purpose of the survey is to gain employee input on a variety of issues. Management will be asked to study the questions and make a commitment to discuss frankly with employees the issues that are likely to surface as a result of the survey. If the management group is in agreement, a letter outlining the purpose of the survey, and signed by a senior manager, is then sent to all employees three to four weeks in advance of the survey.

Two weeks before the survey is to be conducted, post a schedule showing the date, time, department and survey code on the employees' departmental bulletin boards.

About one week in advance of the survey, send a final communication to employees about the survey and its purpose, stressing that participation is voluntary, that the identity of participants will be kept confidential, and that only groups, not individuals, will be identified. This memorandum is usually sent by the consultant as a way to further reinforce the confidentiality issue.

During the survey session, which takes place on company time and lasts about 45 minutes, the consultant introduces the survey — its purpose, process and feedback mechanism. The consultant then asks the group not to discuss the questions outside the room as this could influence the answers of people who have not yet participated in the survey and affect the survey's outcome.

After all groups have been surveyed and coded, the answers are statistically summarized according to the various groups. But at this point we have only scratched the surface. Now we select up to ten critical issues arising from the survey responses that will be shown to the employees at special focus group meetings. These sessions, in which we solicit feedback from those surveyed, last 60 to 90 minutes.

No management personnel are admitted during the feedback sessions; the only non-employee participant is the consultant.

The employees are first shown the results of their group's survey, and then those of the entire employee population. The consultant then begins with a non-threatening question that appears early in the survey, such as "Why did 75 percent of this group answer 'no' to the question about the company cafeteria? What's wrong with the cafeteria?"

The consultant's dialog usually runs something like this: "Please help me. I need to know what this means. Is the food greasy? Is the menu limited? Do you have to wait in line too long? I have to write a report and make recommendations to your management. Is it okay if I write down your answers?" Out will come issues such as sanitation problems, price increases and food quality. Then the consultant moves into the core questions, for example, questions referring to grievance procedures, disciplinary matters, fairness and equity in the workplace, etc.

The survey question "Do you get satisfaction on grievances around here?" usually rates a high percentage of negative answers. So the consultant starts probing. Someone provides an example of unfair treatment. Frequently, an internal union organizer (or would-be shop steward) will show his/her hand, lured by the prospect of a captive employee audience. All the issues the internal organizer is using in his/her campaign are likely to emerge during this session.

We recommend that the employee perception survey be conducted every 12 months in order to keep management up to date on the issues that matter to employees. It also provides a meaningful vehicle for feedback to the employee population.

The survey's aim is not to obtain statistics but to identify issues that will form the basis for future communications. It is definitely not intended to be a witch hunt. Management must *not* confront an organizer or malcontent revealed during the survey feedback sessions. This would destroy the likelihood of employee cooperation in future sessions and credibility would be lost forever. The consultant will identify the key issues for management so that management can use the information to improve (or commence) its Positive Employee Relations program.

▶ *Knowing* your employees' perceptions neutralizes the union organizer and gives you a distinct advantage. *Acting* upon these issues reduces the risk of unionization.

It is essential that someone outside the organization conduct the first round of surveys. A year or so later, groups selected at random should be asked if it is necessary to bring in a consultant, or if an employee (who may or may not be in management) could conduct the survey.

The purpose of the entire exercise is to gather information that will help management to satisfy the needs of its employees. Once the two-way communications line is established and employees know they can speak freely, they must be given the opportunity to do so regularly.

Undertaking an employee perception survey is an irreversible process. Managers add to employee dissatisfaction when they refuse to listen to complaints. Union organizers are quick to recognize and verbalize employees' growing feelings of dissatisfaction and to act on their findings. By using perception surveys, managers can learn of problems before they become fuel for union organizers.

Appendix A includes a complete employee perception survey and a sample of the supporting pre-survey communications.

TAKE ACTION!

1. Carefully examine the seven categories of major workplace dissatisfaction, in light of your organization and its practices.
2. Be aware of the weaknesses in your organization — these will be the primary focus of a union organizer.
3. With the help of a consultant, administer an initial employee perception survey. The key steps are as follows:

- Identify the issues to be addressed.
- Set objectives/procedures.
- Obtain management committee approval.
- Select an external consultant.
- Develop the survey instrument.
- Administer the survey questionnaire.
- Process and analyze survey data.
- Interpret the results with employees.
- Provide results to management.
- Identify and implement steps to resolve problems.

4 THE ORGANIZER'S STRATEGY

If employees come to regard unionization as their only option, your company becomes extremely vulnerable. The employee group will be watching management's moves with a critical, probing eye. And they will also have an opportunity to hear the union organizer's message firsthand. To anticipate and respond to the moves of a union organizer, management should be fully aware of current techniques and strategies used in recruiting union members.

PROFILE OF A POTENTIAL UNION ORGANIZER

In understanding how a union campaign progresses, your managers and supervisors will better recognize those employees within your company who are potential union organizers. With the help of a very credible psychological assessment tool, our consulting firm has developed a behavioral profile of a potential union organizer. While this profile is only a generality — not every union organizer will exhibit all these characteristics — the vast majority will follow this pattern. Someone who successfully champions "dissatisfaction" as a sales presentation for the union cause is likely to:

- demonstrate strong leadership abilities and be forceful.
- easily and comfortably approach other people.
- be persuasive, convincing and perhaps even Machiavellian.
- be impatient, reactive and want to get on with things quickly.
- be somewhat independent, with his/her own agenda.

Many of these characteristics (primarily the first three) will also be found in your better supervisors. But a dissatisfied employee who exhibits these characteristics can be a dangerous employee, especially if there is no mechanism in place for communicating and resolving dissatisfaction.

▶ Unaddressed, this dissatisfaction never goes away, it just goes underground, where it can develop a particularly strong root system.

THE TRUTH ABOUT THE EMPLOYER'S ROLE

If you fear that your employees may be considering unionization, you may feel angry or even betrayed by them. It's important to remember that employers have the responsibility to safeguard the interests of their employees, and that you face consequences for not doing so. Keep in mind the following:

- You, the employer, initiated and concluded an employment agreement with each of your employees.
- Employees are stakeholders in your organization.
- Employee concerns are legitimate and must be addressed.
- Employees who exhibit these characteristics (as per the profile) will act on their dissatisfaction if their concerns remain unaddressed.

THE NATURE OF UNIONS AND ORGANIZING CAMPAIGNS

Unions are for-profit businesses. They do not exist solely to serve as agents of social justice, even though legislation in some jurisdictions allows unions to keep their financial data confidential and union dues to be tax deductible.

▶ Unions are for-profit businesses.

As seen through the eyes of non-unionized employees, a union is an outsourced advocacy service. Paid for by the employees, it negotiates wages, benefits and a grievance procedure. Seen in this light, it is clear that unions are in the business of providing a service to employees when the employer does not. This is a private enterprise, not a social action group.

▶ Unions are an advocacy service paid for by employees.

But how does this "service" enter your organization in the first place? The vast majority of organizing campaigns start *inside* a company, not through an external initiative of the union. An employee or group of employees who are dissatisfied contact a union employee. That union official, or business agent, then meets with the employee(s) to determine:

- the viability of the dissatisfaction. Is it a broad-based sentiment that would result in a successful certification drive?
- whether the employee(s) could be trained to be the internal organizer(s) or organizing committee. If this is the case, the union will run a number of weekend training programs on "how to organize a campaign."
- what problems and issues should be noted. These will become the basis of the campaign. The union will want it to appear that these issues are relevant to the entire employee population. It will prepare and distribute to the entire employee population leaflets that highlight union solutions to these issues and the union's ability to succeed in negotiations with management where individuals would normally fail.

Once started, the organizing campaign is run by the internal organizing committee, who is coached by the business agent/union organizer. The union can run the campaign by mail and, in some jurisdictions, can distribute leaflets on-site outside of work hours (for example, in the lunch room). Unlike the employer, the union can call off-site meetings in a social setting, visit the employees' homes, and post information to the internet. And, if not properly supervised, your company's own intranet may be used to make contact.

It is crucial to remember that the organizing campaign will focus on issues generated by dissatisfied employees, *not* issues necessarily important to the trade union. This is often the key to success for the union: its message is customized and specific to the workplace in question and it offers solutions. Employees "sitting on the fence" in a certification vote can often be swayed by union rhetoric because it appeals to what they believe are their own issues.

UNION TACTICS

The union organizer's communications strategy will probably involve the following tactical steps:

- input from the employee group
- customized messages
- employee involvement
- emotional appeal
- relentless effort.

Input from the employee group

The union organizer will rely on input from the employee group. A strategy will be built around issues raised by employee complaints or by management's lack of awareness or sensitivity. Regardless of how the union organizer "develops" the employee concern, the focus will be on employee issues, not union issues. Historically, this has not been a strategy used by management. Management typically communicates issues that are of concern to the management or supervisory group or to the company in general, without relating these issues to employees.

The union organizer, however, reasons: "If I get the attention of the employee group by talking about the issues that are important to them, they will be more receptive and responsive to my union message." It's a strategy the unions have found to be extremely effective.

Customized messages

The union organizer will focus on the experiences of the group involved. While the union organizer may not talk about specifics and specific individuals, the message will be a personal one. It will relate to the employees as individuals and not as "workers."

Employee involvement

The union organizer will use the employee involvement approach by presenting an instance in which management has been lax. For example, perhaps management's failure to install safety guards on machinery has resulted in severe injury to an employee. Then employees will be asked how management (in general) can be persuaded or legally bound to install new safety equipment. The strategy here is relatively straightforward. Employees will be asked to make suggestions and recommendations on how management can be made to do this or that. In workplace environments where, for example, human blood is handled and the risk of infection is high, the safety "story" is made all that more emotional and frightening.

The union organizer may ask employees for their recommendations on how to solve a particular problem. Their ideas will then be discussed and a "best solution" will emerge. At this point, the *employees have been involved in problem identification, have discussed available options, and have helped select the most appropriate option*. The employees will now perceive the recommended solution as their own and if management is not prepared to enter a discussion of this solution, management will be seen in a negative, non-credible light. The union organizer's strategy will have worked and management will have missed an opportunity to pre-empt the union organizer.

Emotional appeal

The union organizer's communications program will have an emotional aspect. Union organizers will talk at the employees' level about employee needs and concerns, appealing to both emotion and intellect. They know how to stir employee emotions — and thereby win commitment to the union cause. And they apply Maslow's Theory of Human Needs by playing to the employees' needs for basic survival issues as well as to their need to be part of a group.

Organizational or corporate communication has not yet reached the same level of artistry as that achieved by many unions. Managers too often try to make their communications, particularly written communications, impersonal and objective. They try to keep individuals and subjective issues out of the picture. The employee can't help but compare the two types of input: the corporation's cold, objective, efficient approach with the union's subjective, engaging, emotional appeal.

Relentless effort

Union organizers never stop trying. Regardless of the outcome of a union drive, they can always claim victory. For example, if successful in organizing the employees, they are clearly the winner. On the other hand, if they attempt to win 100 percent support for their issue but come in at only 35 percent, that too can be demonstrated as a 35 percent success. Compared to the original zero percent, 35 percent is undoubtedly a success. Furthermore, it demonstrates a positive influence over the group.

Management has a lot to learn in this particular area. So often, after surviving an organizing campaign, the employer will avoid confronting the issues raised by the campaign, fearing that to do so might lead to a win/lose situation. There is a palpable feeling of relief among some organizations, a belief that the company can now get back to the business of making products or providing services.

Instead of attempting to gain strength by finding a way to succeed in what might be termed an adverse situation, the employer pulls away. For example, even if supervisory attitudes and behaviors were a major factor in a union garnering 40 percent support, managers are often reluctant to address these issues. The feeling that employees shouldn't tell management how to deal with management — that the tail is wagging the dog — pervades many organizations. Rather than deal with genuine employee concerns raised by the organizing drive, management focuses on how to undermine the credibility of the concerns. The possibility for communicating meaningfully with employees is decreased and perhaps even eliminated.

Regardless of the interpretation, employees are judging the behavior of the employer. From the employees' point of view, management's action is seen as uninformed, untrustworthy or, at best, naive. The employer's failure to communicate is seen as a vote of non-confidence.

▶ Even if an organizing campaign fails, the union can try again soon, so the employer may have won only the first battle.

SOME EARLY WARNING SIGNALS

An organizing campaign is usually an internal process, orchestrated by an outside professional organizer but built on issues that employees consider important. A well-run campaign will usually not surface until many union authorization or membership cards have been signed — and senior management may be the last to know.

All levels of management must learn to notice and interpret the signs of union organizing. Watch for some of the following:

- lack of eye contact
- information evaporates
- unusual groupings
- complaints change
- use of labor terminology
- customized handouts

- store fronts or websites
- strangers on site
- home visits
- unusual information requests.

Lack of eye contact

Although subtle, this can be an important sign. Imagine a plant manager walking the shop floor, greeting people, as he/she normally would do. Astute managers recognize when people are looking away or avoiding direct eye contact. The moment a social bond is broken, when employees have begun seriously considering union advances, they will be more likely to avoid direct eye contact with managers.

Information evaporates

In a normal work environment, information always flows in established patterns and talk from the shop floor usually reaches the supervisor. When dissatisfaction among employees has led to feelings of alienation, people are less likely to talk to the supervisor. Managerial personnel must be aware of communication patterns so that they can discern changes.

Unusual groupings

Watch for a change in the number, composition and size of informal groups at lunch, coffee breaks or buzz sessions. If, when the supervisor joins the group, an embarrassing silence ensues, followed by small talk, it probably indicates that the supervisor has interrupted a conversation that the employees prefer not to share. In addition, be aware of congregations of employees whose jobs are unrelated and who have little in common, in out-of-the-way places. Supervisors should be "tuned in" to notice if their friendly greetings result in rapid shifts in conversation. They should also note changes in congregation sites.

Complaints change

Adept supervisors notice an increase in the number or nature of employee complaints or grievances, and obvious change in employees' attitudes toward the supervisor, expressed either formally or informally. If employees who formerly took their concerns to a supervisor now operate with a signed petition, the level of concern is increased.

Use of labor terminology

Listen for a shift in the employees' use of language, especially the presence of labor terminology that has never had a place in your organization. Often phrases such as "We have a *right* to this" and "We want to *grieve* this management decision" signal the presence of a union organizer or business agent among your employees.

Customized handouts

A more obvious sign is the existence of union propaganda in the work area, such as leaflets, notices posted surreptitiously and the wearing of pro-union insignia. These will often exhibit the union's attempts to customize its message to your workplace.

Store fronts or websites

These are public signals, accessible to the community at large, that a union has targeted your workplace. The address of the store front and website will usually be marketed in the customized handouts.

Strangers on site

Obviously, allowing strangers on to your worksite encourages all kinds of security problems, one of which is unionization. The union will work hard to reach your employees, especially on your second and third shifts when management is most likely to be absent from the plant. It's important that your perimeter security is at its most vigilant during these periods.

Home visits

The union has every right to visit your employees in their homes. There is nothing you can do about this. But you should be aware of any "grapevine" information that indicates home visits are taking place.

Unusual information requests

Be aware of specific and persistent requests for detailed information on company policies and programs, such as the details and rationale of compensation or retirement plans or statistics about company employees and terminations. These requests are often a sign of an organizer trying to gather data on issues that the union will want to negotiate later.

HOW TO RESPOND

It's one thing to be attuned to the ten warning signs of union activity listed above; it's another to know what the appropriate response is. Do not interpret any of these warning signs, if observed, as proof that your employees are about to form or join a union. They are merely signs that management's policies have not been as proactive or successful as hoped for. Once you've come to this understanding, follow these steps:

- Do not terminate or discipline those you perceive to be the "organizers" or in favor of a union.
- Gain an understanding of what has changed.
- Evaluate all human resources incidents of the past six months.
- Tread carefully!

Do not terminate or discipline

If you do so, you will only have created a martyr for the union cause. Additionally, there is no justification in law or in the principles of sound Positive Employee Relations to support this course of action.

Gain an understanding of what has changed

These warning signs signal a heightened degree of employee dissatisfaction. Managers should investigate the causes of this change through surveys, focus group meetings, walking the shop floor, asking questions, etc.

Evaluate all human resources incidents of the past six months

Check the records of all hires, terminations, disciplines and job transfer requests that have been filed within the last six months. Is there a pattern? Is a manager, supervisor or human resources person not treating employees fairly?

Tread carefully!

If the warning signs indicate a serious level of employee dissatisfaction, take your managers and supervisors aside and explain to them management's and the employees' rights during a union organizing campaign.

You do not want to overstep your rights (and be accused of an unfair labor practice) but you want to ensure that union literature is honest (you can communicate to employees the content of labor legislation, so that untrue claims — e.g., union "guarantees" of job security — can be refuted). Please refer to Appendix B, A Supervisor's Guide to Remaining Union-Free through Positive Employee Relations.

PRE-EMPTING THE UNION

When an organizer conducts a campaign, the strategy is more flexible, more employee-oriented and more emotional than management's typical approach. The organizer invites "audience" participation and gives, or appears to give, serious consideration to the suggestions elicited.

By acting immediately, management can pre-empt the union's strategy. Communicate to your employees. Involve them as legitimate stakeholders in your organization.

▶ If you respect and treat your employees as you would your customers and other stakeholders, you will never need a third party to negotiate your working relationship.

The following exhibits will provide the reader with an example of correspondence that might transpire during a union organizing campaign. For these exhibits, our fictitious employer, the Sherborne Company, and our imaginary union, the International Brotherhood of Widget Workers, have been used. To follow the typical escalation in the rhetoric, I suggest that you read the correspondence sequentially from Exhibit 4.1 through 4.6.

EXHIBIT 4.1

SHERBORNE COMPANY
15 BOND ST., WINDRUSH, ONTARIO

November 5, 20 —

To All Employees:

It has come to my attention that the International Brotherhood of Widget Workers is conducting an organizing campaign at Sherborne. As your employer, we wish to take this opportunity to inform you of your rights during an organization attempt by a trade union. It *is not* our intention to engage in an exchange of inflammatory accusations with anyone. It *is* our intention to keep you positively informed of your legal rights and to keep the record straight on the facts.

Facts you should know are these:

1. If more than 40% of the employees sign Application for Membership Cards, the Labor Board will call for a Representation Vote; and if 50% plus one of those who vote support the union then all employees are in the union. And, paying union dues. [Note: the 40% figure applies in Ontario. Each jurisdiction has its own requirements regarding certification.]
2. Your right to be represented or not to be represented by a union is established in the Ontario Labor Relations Act. That Act is enforced by the Ontario Labor Relations Board.
3. The Act states that no trade union shall seek by intimidation or coercion to compel any person to become a member of a trade union. It also provides that an employer is free to express his views as long as he does not use coercion, intimidation, threats, promises or undue influence. Therefore, employees are protected by law to act freely in rejecting or accepting a union.

4. A decision to be represented by a union *limits your right* to talk directly to your management group on your *own* behalf.

It is a common organizational tactic of trade unions to tell employees that all (or at least most) of their co-workers have signed cards in order to induce you to join the crowd. We suggest that you think for yourself and not be misled by false statements and misinformation.

Here are some questions you should be asking or considering:

1. Are you aware that a union does not bring automatic wage and benefit increases?
2. Are you aware that a union can only negotiate — it cannot guarantee wage adjustments, job security, etc.
3. If no agreement is reached, will there be a strike? How long will it last?
4. Will the union pay your wages while you are on strike?
5. Do you realize that the union will want Sherborne to deduct your monthly payments to the union *from your paycheck*? Do you know how much these dues might be? Where does your money go?

We would prefer to maintain a work environment that gives recognition to *each individual's* qualifications, performance, suggestions and problems. To this end, we believe that the interests of each employee, as well as Sherborne, are best served through handling employee relations matters on an individual basis rather than through representation by a third party.

As a reminder, let us review *a partial list* of what you currently receive *without having paid any union membership fees and monthly dues*:
1. Fair wage rates and incentive system.
2. Group life insurance.
3. Extended health care including prescription drugs, etc.
4. Semi-private hospital service.
5. Accidental death and dismemberment coverage.
6. Long-term disability pay.

7. Group dental insurance plan.
8. Matching contributions to the retirement savings plan.
   Note: The premiums for the above are fully paid for by Sherborne.
9. Ten (10) statutory holidays paid by the company.
10. Vacation   - 2 weeks after 1 year.
                   - 3 weeks after 5 years.
                   - 4 weeks after 12 years.
11. Shift premiums.
12. Overtime pay (time and a half and double time on holidays).
13. Christmas party and gift completely paid for by Sherborne. Also annual children's picnic and the annual golf tournament.
14. Jury duty — no loss in pay if you are called to serve on jury duty.
15. Paid time off in the event of a death in your immediate family.

We do not intend to interfere with you in your decision of whether or not to join a union. However, this is an important decision and one which deserves your serious consideration. We hope this letter will be of some assistance to you in making your decision as to whether or not a third party can improve the working relationship that we have here at Sherborne.

Again, we urge you to *check the facts yourself and do not be misled.*

Yours sincerely,

W.H. Burford
General Manager

EXHIBIT 4.2

International Brotherhood of Widget Workers

AN INVITATION TO A BETTER FUTURE

You work hard at your job. And it pays off for the company.
But what about you?

What can you do if you are unfairly laid off,
suspended or fired?
Is your job secure?

What can you do if your job is threatening your health?
Is your workplace safe?

What can you do to make sure everybody
is treated fairly at work?
Is there favoritism or discrimination at your company?

What can you do to get a raise?
Are your wages enough for all your hard work?
Do you have decent benefits?

When you really need it,
who will speak for you?

It's better with a union
When you're a union member, your rights are guaranteed in a contract. When you're a union member, you have expert help from lawyers, health and safety professionals and experienced negotiators who will help you get the best deal possible. When you're a union member, you will get the respect you deserve.

And when people like you need a union, they turn to North America's fastest-growing union — the **International Brotherhood of Widget Workers.** We represent workers in every industry and in every type of job — from manufacturing and mining to offices, services industries and hotels.

Choosing the IBWW means your voice will be heard in the most democratic union in North America. You will develop your own bargaining proposals, vote on your own contract and elect your own local officers. Each member also has a vote in the election of regional and national officers.

And in the IBWW, you'll get the training and education to put that democracy into action.

It's your right — it's the law

Your right to join and participate in a union is protected by law. It's illegal for an employer to discriminate against you (in any way) because of your union support.

The first step

For more information on what the IBBW can do for you and your fellow workers, contact the representative below. It's your first step toward a better future.

Jim Brown, Business Agent
999-111-0000
International Brotherhood of Widget Workers

EXHIBIT 4.3

SHERBORNE COMPANY
15 BOND ST., WINDRUSH, ONTARIO

November 10, 20__

Miss Rose Patel
100 Flower Lane
Windrush, Ontario

Dear Rose,

UNIONS DON'T GUARANTEE — THEY JUST *PROMISE*

Fact 1
You will continue to receive lots of information from the union promising many things. Don't be misled! Union promises must eventually come to the bargaining table where they are negotiated and the negotiations will be finalized only when Sherborne and the trade union sign a collective agreement. Likewise, the union will have to negotiate a list of requests from management.

Fact 2
Find out what you get in return for the union dues that you will have to pay. Remember, the trade union *does not* pay your salary nor, by the same token, does it do anything toward generating the income that is used to pay your salary and benefits and provide for working conditions.

Fact 3
You will, no doubt, be told that with a trade union you will have job security that you don't have now. We believe that this doesn't make sense. You and your fellow employees will have job security as long as work is performed efficiently and as long as Sherborne continues to grow. The presence or absence of a union has nothing to do with the question of job security.

Fact 4

You now have the right to deal with management on a one-to-one basis — a stronger position than through a third party. Remember, the union will be charging you a legal monthly fee to deal with Sherborne. Do you really need to spend your hard-earned money to have someone talk to us?

Fact 5

Labor relations history tells us that pro-union employees generally come out to vote while non-union employees do not. This frequently means that many employees lose the election because they don't come out to vote. To win the vote the union only needs 50% plus 1 of those who show up to vote. *Remember this a secret ballot.* So come out on December 8 and MAKE YOUR VOTE COUNT!

VOTE NO!

Yours very truly,

W.H. Burford
General Manager

EXHIBIT 4.4

International Brotherhood of Widget Workers

Answers to your questions
What prevents an employer from interfering with its employees' right to join a union?

The Labor Relations Act protects the right of employees to join a union. It states that no employer may interfere with the formation or selection of a union. Among other things, this means that an employer cannot try to influence its employees unduly.

It is illegal for an employee to be fired or penalized for being a union supporter. The Labor Relations Board can order an employee's reinstatement with back pay and interest.

How can a union help me?
Wages are usually not the number one reason why people want a union. Many issues that affect you and your family are so complex that you sometimes would rather forget about them.

In recent organizing campaigns, employees raised their concerns about job security, pension, job postings, favoritism and problems with workers' compensation. Most people want a union so they could have their own copy of a signed collective agreement, so as to know where their boundaries are. Boundaries and guidelines in the workplace are just as important as knowing where your neighbor's property line starts and ends. You and your neighbor might get along great and you both agree that you can extend your flower garden two feet on his property. Your neighbor decides to sell his house because he wants to profit by $20,000. Your new neighbor surveys the property and decides to put stakes outlining his property and also decides to tear out your flower bed because it's on his property.

Remember, the rules can change at any time if you do not have a signed collective agreement.

Workers today are faced with some complex issues and in the union movement we continually stress the importance of education. By educating workers they are better equipped to handle the problems and concerns that they have to face in the workplace.

Do you know that under recent changes to the Labor Relations Act the government has given you more rights? Do you know that with the new employment equity legislation and the seniority provisions of a IBBW collective agreement you could move further ahead?

In its social teachings, the Catholic Church firmly maintains that labor unions have an essential role to play in preventing the violation of the dignity of human work and serving as a "mouthpiece for the struggle for social justice." Without unions, working people have no collective voice in our industrialized society. Through labor unions, workers are able to strive for just wages, decent working conditions, appropriate social benefits and a democratic voice in the workplace.

Through labor unions, workers are also able to press for changes in public policy and participate in a broader social movement for the building of a just society. In effect, the Church maintains that labor unions are an "indispensable element of social life." For these reasons, Church teaching encourages Catholic workers to become actively involved in their own unions and urges the Catholic community as a whole to support the essential role that labor unions have to play in society.

If you are curious to know more about our union, call:

Jim Brown, Business Agent
International Brotherhood of Widget Workers
999-111-0000

EXHIBIT 4.5

SHERBORNE COMPANY
15 BOND ST., WINDRUSH, ONTARIO

December 4, 20__

Miss Rose Patel
100 Flower Lane
Windrush, Ontario

Dear Rose,

There are only four (4) business days before the Labor Relations Board conducts the union Certification Vote. Your vote is important. You will be given the unique opportunity, on December 8, to cast a secret ballot to determine whether or not you want to have an outside party come into Sherborne to represent you.

It's important that you think through your decision carefully before you cast your vote. You have the right to do so. We hope you will exercise this right.

To help you make your decision, we have prepared a series of information bulletins that answer 13 critical questions. We will distribute these bulletins over the next two business days. Please read them. If you have any questions, talk to us about them.

The election should be won because of decisions people make before casting their ballot. Good decisions are based on good information. Make sure you have as much clear and precise information about the IBWW as you do about Sherborne.

REMEMBER: COME OUT TO VOTE!

Yours very truly,

W.H. Burford
General Manager

EXHIBIT 4.6

SHERBORNE COMPANY
15 BOND ST., WINDRUSH, ONTARIO

EMPLOYEE INFORMATION BULLETIN #1

Question: How does Sherborne feel about the union?

Answer: We do not believe that a union will advance the interests of employees at Sherborne. On election day (December 8) we ask you to vote "NO."

Question: What difference does it make to Sherborne and our future if the union is certified?

Answer: A big difference! Among other things, if the union gets in and Sherborne and the union cannot agree on a collective agreement, there is always a possibility that our business and your pay could be stopped because of a strike. Ask yourself how our customers would react to a threatened or actual interruption of deliveries of the Widget product line.

Today, we enjoy a family feeling and a sense of working together toward a common goal. To replace this with shop stewards and grievance committees would make Sherborne a very different place.

SHERBORNE COMPANY
15 BOND ST., WINDRUSH, ONTARIO

EMPLOYEE INFORMATION BULLETIN #2

Question: If I am approached by anyone concerning the union certification vote, do I have to listen to them?

Answer: No. You do not have to listen to anyone, including the union organizers, unless you want to. You are free to make up your own mind.

If there is any attempt by the union or its organizers to intimidate or threaten you or your fellow employees, please let any member of management know and we will ensure that proper procedures are followed.

Please remember that it is a common union tactic to suggest that you are the "last one to sign the Union Membership Card."

SHERBORNE COMPANY
15 BOND ST., WINDRUSH, ONTARIO

EMPLOYEE INFORMATION BULLETIN #3

Question: Isn't having the union the best way to guarantee my job security?

Answer: No. The only way any of us can have job security is if Sherborne continues to grow and remain competitive in our new international markets.

Question: What faith should I place in union promises?

Answer: If the union were to represent the employees of Sherborne, it would only get the right to negotiate with Sherborne. The union cannot guarantee anything because it cannot force Sherborne to give anything that we are unable to give.

SHERBORNE COMPANY
15 BOND ST., WINDRUSH, ONTARIO

EMPLOYEE INFORMATION BULLETIN #4

Question: Why is the union so interested in my vote?

Answer: The answer is clear! Your membership means more money for the union, in the form of initiation fees and membership dues. Have you asked the union how much your dues will be if it gets in? Maybe you should find out before it's too late!!

Normally, union dues amount to two or three hours of wages per month *plus* any initiation or administration fee. In addition, most union constitutions have provisions to charge members a fine (approximately $25) for violating union rules. Again, we recommend you obtain and review a copy of the union constitution.

SHERBORNE COMPANY
15 BOND ST., WINDRUSH, ONTARIO

EMPLOYEE INFORMATION BULLETIN #5

Question: If I do not want to pay union dues or become a union member, what are my obligations if the union gets in?

Answer: If the union gets in, you will almost certainly be forced to pay union dues as a condition of employment. When the union requests compulsory deduction of dues from employees' paychecks, the law requires the employer to make such deductions. In addition, unions most often insist on compulsory membership in the union as a condition of employment. If the union is successful in that demand, they could force the termination of any employee who chooses not to join the union, or who is expelled from the union for any reason.

SHERBORNE COMPANY
15 BOND ST., WINDRUSH, ONTARIO

EMPLOYEE INFORMATION BULLETIN #6

Question: If I have signed a union card, do I have to vote for the union?

Answer: No. You may vote for or against the union *whether or not* you signed a union card. The vote will be conducted by the Ontario Ministry of Labor, and will be by *secret ballot*. No one will ever know how you voted.

Question: Why is it so important that everyone eligible to vote casts his or her ballot?

Answer: Because the vote will be decided by a simple majority of those who vote. If you want this choice, exercise your democratic right and vote. If you want the choice to be *yours*, you must vote; otherwise, the choice will be *theirs*.

Only those people who vote count! For example, if only ten people show up to vote and six vote for the union, all employees are then covered by the union contract.

SHERBORNE COMPANY
15 BOND ST., WINDRUSH, ONTARIO

EMPLOYEE INFORMATION BULLETIN #7

Question: How will the union certification vote be conducted?

Answer: The vote will be conducted by the Ontario Labor Relations Board and will be by secret ballot. You may vote for or against the union whether or not you signed a union card. **No one will ever know how you voted.**

SHERBORNE COMPANY
15 BOND ST., WINDRUSH, ONTARIO

EMPLOYEE INFORMATION BULLETIN #8

Question: If the union gets in, can I still deal with Sherborne as an individual?

Answer: No. If the union gets in you will be governed by a union contract and union constitution. Sherborne could not deal with you on an individual basis in matters relating to wages and working conditions.
  Remember: Get a copy of the union constitution! It's your responsibility and right.

Question: Why can't we try the union out for a while, and if we do not like it, get rid of it?

Answer: No employee should think he or she can try out a union and get rid of it if he or she feels like it. Employees can only get rid of a union under very limited circumstances and then there is a very complex legal procedure involved. Once the union is in, it is generally in to stay!

SHERBORNE COMPANY
15 BOND ST., WINDRUSH, ONTARIO

EMPLOYEE INFORMATION BULLETIN #9

Question: If the union is not successful in being certified to represent the Sherborne employees, will there be any type of discriminatory action taken against employees who supported the union?

Answer: No. It is not a policy of Sherborne to take action against any employee for exercising free democratic choice. It is also unlawful for Sherborne — or the union — to take any action against you for exercising your free choice.

TAKE ACTION!

1. Learn to recognize the characteristics of an employee who has the potential to be a union organizer.
2. Be aware of the early warning signals of union organization. Do not discipline or terminate any employees if you suspect they may be involved in union organizing.
3. Be prepared to defend your union-free position. The most effective way of doing this is by *treating your employees as you would your customers and other stakeholders.*

5

BUILDING THE INFRA-STRUCTURE

There is one thing about which an employer can always be certain: if an organization fails to recognize and address the needs of its employees and acknowledge their contributions, there will be a union poised to fill the vacuum that has been created. A Positive Employee Relations program eliminates that vacuum, making unionization redundant. But it requires a deep commitment on the part of senior management, a commitment to do more than pay lip service to the principles of Positive Employee Relations. And this requires a pro-active approach.

PRO-ACTIVE, NOT REACTIVE: A MANTRA FOR SENIOR MANAGEMENT

The attitudes and practices resulting from a reactive management style — one that erodes rather than enhances the employees' job scope, working conditions and interpersonal relationships — feed the climate of unionism.

▶ **Pro-union sympathies are a result of negative experiences within organizations.**

You can rest assured that employees, either supervisory or non-supervisory, are not by definition pro-union and anti-company. *If they become so, it is as a result of their experiences within the organization.* How can the organization defuse the threat of unions? By anticipating potential trouble spots and working wholeheartedly to prevent their growth.

Unions have known for a long time that the hint of a strike is often enough to modify the behavior of management. But reactive modifications tend to be viewed with skepticism. However, if management sincerely adopts the philosophy that its most important resource is its human resource, then the organization minimizes the threat of a strike and the union loses a powerful organizing tactic and potential negotiating strategy.

It is too much to expect that employees will rally around a company that takes an anti-union stand. But they will become *pro-company* if they see their supervisors and managers supporting policies consistent with good employee relations: opening channels for two-way communication, involving employees in decision making and demonstrating a sympathetic and humane awareness of the employees' point of view.

▶ **Why must management wait until it is boxed in to realize that employee involvement in business problem identification and resolution is not only normal but *good business*?**

Employee involvement should be at the heart of management's Positive Employee Relations program. To assume that employees are not interested in business decision making, that they are incapable of making meaningful suggestions and that their only interest is self-interest, will only fuel the frustration and anxiety that breed employee discontent.

If management has a business problem related to production, administration or even relocation, why not involve the employee group (your ever-present audience) in solving the problem? Whatever your decision, it is the employees who will have to carry it out. How much better it would be if they are given a chance to discuss the alternatives and are told why one solution was chosen over another. Being involved, they are more likely to feel committed to the chosen solution.

There are two likely explanations of why management historically has not involved employees in business decisions. First, managers tend to be unaware that employee involvement is a viable or useful strategy. Second, they generally feel uncomfortable and/or incapable of handling the employees' suggestions. They are afraid that if they say "no," the employees will become alienated. In this regard they are wrong. Wrong because, if employee suggestions are considered among all the alternatives and choices are made in an open, participatory environment, employees will still feel part of the decision-making process. Saying "no" to employee suggestions won't necessarily lead to alienation. But not involving employees at all sows the seeds of unionization.

UNION-FREE MEANS PRO-EMPLOYEE

Typically, management's reasons for resisting unionization range from hard-headed economic considerations to paternalism based on questionable motives. The following three points are often presented to support management's position:

- Unionization costs an employer between 25 and 35 percent of gross annual payroll (excluding wages or benefit plan increases to employees).
- Unionization curtails management's freedom to manage.
- All-powerful unions victimize gullible employees who should be protected for their own good.

The first two points are valid. The third, a benevolent concern for the welfare and interests of employees, frequently disguises management's selfish motives. For reasons both real and imaginary, managers are reluctant to have to deal with employees through a third party. Many owners and managers have had little or no experience with unions and, as a result, base their decision on nuggets gleaned from the "locker room." On the other hand, there are managers who have lived through the demoralizing effects of having their employees working-to-rule or going on strike.

Today, thankfully, we understand that economic ends cannot be achieved when there is distrust and conflict. The reasons for employee dissatisfaction and lack of commitment are likely to undermine, sooner or later, the economic survival and growth of the organization.

If an organization wishes to remain union-free it may apply short-term "preventative labor relations practices" that appear to be correcting the problems. This is invariably misguided. For example, it may ask legal counsel to prepare an employee handbook that reads like a collective agreement/union contract so as to dupe the employees into a false sense of security. But temporary solutions like these fail miserably when the company gets busy and reverts to its true values. The employees realize they have been taken in and their level of distrust increases accordingly. If it is to retain its union-free status, the organization must manage its human resources with an approach that is *at least* as enlightened and committed as that used to manage its physical and financial assets.

Management must concentrate its resources on a limited number of strategically focused result areas. (It is difficult to achieve organizational excellence if there are too many goals.) The unifying goal should be to develop an optimal working environment in which the idea of unionization has no attraction, an environment in which management encourages and rewards employee development and has high expectations of every member of its workforce.

Management must reassess its goals, placing a concern for human resources high on the priority list.

▶ Management's approach should be positive rather than negative — pro-people, rather than anti-union; pro-active, rather than reactive.

A PHILOSOPHY THAT EMBRACES PEOPLE AS WELL AS PROFIT

To maintain a union-free environment, an organization's underlying management philosophy should be constantly reassessed. It is an accepted management axiom that the sole factors in any business are survival and growth. Unfortunately, this is sometimes interpreted by leaders to mean survival and growth *at any cost*. This short-term approach, which frequently leads to a dehumanized work environment, has created critical long-term labor relations problems for many companies.

Business must make a profit, but it must also give equal time to satisfying the needs and aspirations of its employees. A human resource philosophy must embrace these equally important goals. We cannot attain one without attending to the other. As you begin to develop a program of Positive Employee Relations, you must take every opportunity to communicate and reinforce the nature and goals of policies that support the program.

However, this philosophy must be taken out of the abstract. It should be articulated clearly and thoroughly. Exhibit 5.1 illustrates the Sherborne Company's Mission Statement, a balance between economic and human resource goals.

MANAGEMENT MUST "GET IT TOGETHER"

This brings us to one of the most critical points in our Positive Employee Relations program. We must not only say we are going to be fair in our human resource programs, but we must *demonstrate fairness in the development and day-to-day implementation of these policies.* And this is achieved through words *and* actions.

▶ If management's actions don't support the words, the Positive Employee Relations program will be empty.

Once a Positive Employee Relations program has been communicated to employees, they will be watching very closely to see how the ideas translate into actions. It's all very well for the company to express its desire to deal directly with them, without intermediaries, but it will only be through actual performance — in carrying out its program — that the company will gain credibility in the eyes of the employees and *earn* its union-free status.

If we compare the workplace to a theater in which management is on stage and employees are in the audience, we can better understand the dynamics that take place when management announces a Positive

Employee Relations program. The audience perceives two themes: survival and growth of the organization, and fair treatment of the employee population. They will try to determine which has greater weight. They will be aware that Theme A sometimes conflicts with Theme B. They will watch as the main character shifts from hero to villain from one act to the next. They will try to determine whether the players are truly living their parts or merely acting them. The audience may enter the theater in a skeptical mood. To make the audience "suspend their disbelief," the players must speak the truth.

Members of the audience may compare the performance to one staged by a previous employer or judge it on the basis of what they know (either from personal experience or hearsay) about the benefits of unionization.

▶ Employees will compare the actions of their current employers to the promises of a union organizer.

Above all, the audience will be sensitive to whether the actors are playing their roles with *conviction*. They will be alert to any signs that this is not the case. At some point, management makes an appeal for audience support by inviting audience participation. Eventually, if everyone plays their respective roles with integrity, they cease to be roles. The Positive Employee Relations program becomes less of a performance and more of a reality as it becomes fully integrated into the organization's culture.

A management program is a definite plan of intended *proceedings*; a program of Positive Employee Relations is something more. *It is a way of life*. Carefully considered, specific procedures must be *initiated* and then *maintained*.

Exhibit 5.2 is an example of a welcome letter to a newly hired employee that reflects the philosophy of numerous companies committed to programs of Positive Employee Relations.

EMPLOYEE RELATIONS FROM THE EMPLOYEE'S VIEW

While the goals of management and employee can be harmonized, management *must take the initiative* because every new employee brings a residue of distrust or uncertainty to the job. The magnitude of that concern will vary from one employee to another, but it will be present. It stems from previous unfair employment experiences (overtime not paid, passed over for promotion without any explanation, recognition not given for good ideas, etc.) and sometimes it can be traced back to the dinner table, where family members talk about their workplace experiences. If the new employer does not recognize this issue, determine its magnitude and take a pro-active position to address it, the residue will never be balanced with a new and more positive reality for the employee.

To achieve this, management must take a hard look at every procedure used in recruiting, selecting, placing, retaining, training and compensating employees. In doing so, management will begin to see employee relations from a new perspective: that of the employee. This is the perspective required to develop human resource practices that will respond professionally and sensitively to such concerns as:

- Am I in the right job?
- Can I handle this job?
- How will I know if I'm doing well?
- How do I get a promotion?
- How do I tell my supervisor what is annoying me?
- Will anyone listen?
- What are my chances of getting a larger paycheck this month?
- Should I borrow money to buy a new car? (Is my job secure?)
- Are working conditions safe? (Is my employer meeting the spirit as well as the letter of safety and occupational health legislation?)
- If I don't produce, will they fire me?

In considering such concerns, management can begin to articulate to employees the company's Positive Employee Relations program. Exhibit 5.3 details the goals of such a policy, while Exhibit 5.4 details its philosophy and process. Note that they are written in a traditional tone that can easily be adapted to the language of continuous improvement. Together, they comprise the complete policy statement. When working toward goals that are mutually beneficial to employees and management, employee relations must be recognized as a high-priority objective and given the appropriate long-term attention it deserves.

THE SIGNIFICANCE OF THE SUPERVISOR

While Chapters 7 and 9 will address the selection and training of supervisors, it is important at the outset to recognize the degree to which the supervisor's words can lead to greater employee understanding of corporate objectives, policies and plans, and can increase motivation, productivity and commitment. However, the supervisor must know and believe in the messages and signals from management that are to be passed on to the workforce. Company communications, like myths, vary according to the viewpoint of the teller. Make sure the front-line supervisor is in step with management's philosophy.

A Positive Employee Relations policy must be lived — not just communicated in a company-wide memo. And this must be done well before a union organizing campaign surfaces. When an explicit company viewpoint is absent, employees often assume the company has taken a neutral position regarding unions. This assumption has led employees to sign union authorization cards because they thought management did not care one way or the other. This should *never* happen.

Management's position can be clearly stated in its Positive Employee Relations policy, which may be circulated in a variety of ways: in an employee handbook and other in-house publications, in a pre-interview recruiting package, on the corporate intranet or on bulletin boards.

▶ Ultimately, it will be the supervisor's job to demonstrate by word, deed and *attitude* that the company means what it says.

REINFORCE THE POSITIVE

Behavior modification is based on the theory that behavior is largely shaped by environment. As such, it has a powerful application to Positive Employee Relations. The theory, usually associated with Harvard psychologist B.F. Skinner, posits that an individual's actions can be modified by controlling the response to those actions. Rather than probing the reasons behind actions, behavior modification theory concentrates on changing the actions themselves.

Reinforcement, or a calculated response to a behavior, may be positive or negative; its purpose is to increase the tendency for a desired behavior to occur. The frequency and timing of the reinforcement has a significant influence on how quickly the desired behavior will be learned and how long it will last. Depending on the work situation and the employee's values, the following reinforcements may be effective: bonuses or incentives, the freedom to choose aspects of one's job, training others, and increased responsibility and influence.

An organization can apply positive reinforcement to encourage behaviors consistent with its Positive Employee Relations program. It can train managers and supervisors in the art of building the employees' self-esteem while at the same time increasing efficiency. When the organization has determined the performance it requires and has set specific goals for each employee, formal performance reviews should be conducted in which job performance and work-related behaviors are closely monitored. Employees are given detailed feedback on the effectiveness of their performance with reference to past performance and performance standards.

The supervisor systematically reviews the feedback on each employee and reinforces the positive aspects of the employee's behavior, usually by praising improved performance. Supervisors are encouraged to develop methods of reinforcement that neither exaggerate nor undervalue the importance of the employee's efforts. (See Chapter 11 for more information on performance reviews and appraisals.)

SUPERVISORS NEED RECOGNITION TOO!

In too many companies, training the supervisor means training to keep production up and costs down. Promoted on Friday, the supervisor arrives at work on Monday and begins to supervise people who were peers the previous week. Unfortunately, nobody told the new supervisor that the most delicate aspect of a supervisor's job is *achieving results through people.*

The promotion may have been based on past performance appraisals. But rarely do these appraisals ask questions related to the candidate's human resource management skills. Instead they focus exclusively on meeting production or service schedules and the quality and quantity of work.

How much positive recognition is given to a supervisor for running a department in which the grievance or absenteeism level is below the company norm? In most organizations, such recognition rarely happens. So we find the supervisor — with all good intentions — doing what he/she has been asked to do; that is, keep production up and costs down. It's taken for granted that, as a former rank and file employee, the supervisor now knows how to work with people. *Nothing can be further from the truth!*

Professional, well-seasoned managers frequently question their own ability to manage. If your company's Positive Employee Relations program is to succeed, it depends on strong support from your supervisors. Recognize, then, that the new supervisor will grasp for any assistance you can offer in the mysterious art of human resource management.

DEVELOPING A POSITIVE EMPLOYEE RELATIONS PROGRAM FOR YOUR ORGANIZATION

A sound Positive Employee Relations program gains a sure footing when senior management is committed, and supervisors are appropriately selected and trained. Once these are firmly secured, you can begin to address the following checklist of components essential to the success of any Positive Employee Relations program:

- basic philosophy
- statement of policy
- employment
- training
- compensation
- safety
- managing performance
- communications
- supervisors
- evaluating the climate
- following up.

Basic philosophy

Adopt a sincere, values-based approach that will enable the company to benefit owners, employees and society at large. Express management's commitment to a Positive Employee Relations program.

Statement of policy

State objectives clearly. Make a highly visible and credible statement against which all parts of the Positive Employee Relations program can be tested.

Employment

Review and, if necessary, revise application forms and interviewing procedures to bring them in line with human rights and employment equity/ equal employment opportunity legislation. From the beginning of the employment relationship, every effort should be made to match employees with jobs, acquaint employees with their fellow employees and work environment, explain procedures for advancement and outline job responsibilities and standards of performance. Explain complaint and grievance procedures, company policies and general employee relations practices. (On recruitment issues, see Chapter 8.)

Training

Avoid hit-or-miss training. Teach employees to work efficiently so they are able to direct and improve their efforts on the job. Encourage employees to meet attainable goals. Appraise their performance and potential frequently. (On appraisal issues, see Chapter 11.)

Compensation

Determine pay rates and benefits on the basis of survey data for similar job responsibilities in similar industries in the community. Compensation should also be based on *equal pay for work of equal value*. Wage discrimination based on gender is senseless and unfair, as well as illegal. A job evaluation program assessing the worth of all jobs to the company should be used.

Safety

Treat safety as a fundamental consideration and a major responsibility.

Managing performance

Be fair and consistent. No intrigue, no rumors. (See Chapter 12 for a thorough look at policies and procedures related to managing performance.)

Communications

Keep supervisors informed of management decisions so that they are prepared to explain announcements. Schedule communications to prevent rumors. Make decisions known through meetings, publications, bulletin boards, interviews and committees. (See Appendix D for a unique and effective employee-supervisor communications program: Let's Talk©.)

Supervisors

Select those who can develop the ability to convey management's philosophy sincerely. Keep supervisors fully informed at all times. (See Appendix B.)

Evaluating the climate

Use perception surveys and follow-up on the results. Analyze frequency, origin and type of employee comment and complaint. Watch work flow, absenteeism and turnover. Watch for evidence of discontent and low morale. Discuss indicated problems frankly with front-line supervisors. (See Appendix A for a sample employee perception survey.)

Following up

This Positive Employee Relations program is perpetual. Review human resource policies. Make sure wages and benefits are consistent with those paid in similar industries throughout the community. Make the company's position known and ensure that all employees know how to (and in fact do) communicate their problems to management.

BE PREPARED

When faced with a union organizing campaign it would be folly not to double (and sometimes triple) check some of your practices. The expanded checklist that follows details steps to be taken *to reduce your susceptibility during a union campaign.* But don't wait for a union campaign! These steps should be part of any ongoing Positive Employee Relations program whether or not there is any obvious sign of union activity:

- Create a human resources database.
- Create a wage and salary database.
- Market your benefits.
- Seek employee feedback.
- Know the opposition.
- Insist on consistent and fair policies.
- Communicate — then communicate again.

Create a human resources database

- Prepare computerized lists of employees' names, addresses, phone numbers; include names of spouse/partner, children, etc.
- Include employees' names by department, facility locations, shift, length of service, employee versus supervisory/management status.

Create a wage and salary database

- Computerize all wage and salary administrative plans. Make data available by job grade, salary range, employees' names, etc.
- Annually (more often if needed) review the compensation structure to ensure competitiveness in the marketplace. Make adjustments when needed (not 12 months later).
- Document, in employee-friendly language, all policies and procedures related to pay practices. For example, overtime, call-in-pay, cost-of-living adjustments, merit pay, etc.
- Review database to ensure that there are no inequities that could become opportunities for union organizers.
- Annually (more often if needed) participate in local and industry wage and benefit surveys. Determine how current and competitive your programs are. Deficiencies should be addressed promptly.
- If there is no survey conducted in your geographic area, initiate one. Have a locally based consultant or human resource professor conduct the survey to ensure confidentiality and correct data-reporting practices.
- Be aware that wage and benefit deficiencies will be used by union organizers to illustrate the organization's unfairness or worse, its greed.

Market your benefits

- Record and publish all of the organization's benefit programs. Regularly market the benefits to your employees (and possibly their spouse/partner). Consider installing computerized kiosks to provide employees with instant, personalized benefits information.

- Clarify what you are required to pay in your jurisdiction versus what you are actually providing. For example, employer contributions may be required to support a national social insurance/security program. A retirement or pension plan can be built on top of the national program; such a retirement plan is a benefit and should be marketed accordingly.
- Including *all* your benefits means going beyond insurance-type programs. Include social and recreational activities, educational/tuition assistance, subsidized cafeteria or food service, etc.
- It is not uncommon to see that the cost of *all* the benefit programs, as a percentage of wages, can amount to 25 percent plus. This is a substantial amount and the organization's marketing efforts should show that for every $10 in direct wages, there is another $2.50 or more in indirect costs to support the employee and his/her family.

Seek employee feedback

- The two most frequently used processes are employee perception surveys and focus groups. For either method to be successful, adhere to the following guidelines:
- Include employee input when developing the questions.
- Ask how employees would like to receive the feedback (if possible, avoid handing out/distributing printed copies of the results package).
- Involve employees in following through on changes that result from the feedback.
- Collect feedback data by department so that action plans can be initiated in the correct work areas.
- Do not require employees to sign the surveys. Surveys should be completed, at work, in areas that can be supervised. This ensures that you know who actually completed each survey, while ensuring anonymity regarding who completed which survey.
- *Do not* conduct any form of employee feedback process if the organization is unwilling to address each and every issue. In responding to any issue there are at least three options:

i) Yes, we can and will correct this now.
ii) No, that cannot be corrected because...
iii) We don't know, but will get back to you in [a specific period of time].

Know the opposition

- Participate in, or initiate, a bi-monthly meeting of senior managers (for example, human resource manager, plant/factory manager, etc.) to discuss union activity in your labor market (the geographic base from which you draw employees) and in your industry.
- Union data is frequently made available by the national government and/or provincial/state labor departments/agencies, from manufacturers'/business/trade associations, and from human resource associations. A key manager should be in the network to receive all this information, then report back at regular management meetings.
- The more "intelligence" you have about the union movement, particularly in your industry and geographic area, the better. No one, to my knowledge, lost a union organizing campaign because they had too much information about the specific union and the personalities involved.

Insist on consistent and fair policies

- The organization's value system becomes the basis for all human resource practices. This is the only reasonable way to achieve respect, fairness and consistency in the workplace. (This assumes that these beliefs are part of the organization's value system.)

▶ **The number one cause of unionization is untrained leadership.**

- Either provide meaningful training that results in participative and collaborative leadership behavior from each supervisor/manager or find them employment elsewhere. To state that the management

team embraces Positive Employee Relations and knowingly leaves unqualified supervisors or managers in charge of the company's human resources is nothing less than a dereliction of responsibilities. If a similar scenario occurred with financial management, managers would be defending their positions in court!
- All literature that is meant for the employee group (that is, the employee handbook, bulletin board announcements, letters to the home, newsletters, etc.) should be written in straightforward, clean and uncomplicated language that is "user-friendly." With all due respect to the legal profession, if your lawyer writes the employee handbook, *do not use it*. If your benefits and retirement plan literature is written by an actuary, *do not use it*. Have a business communicator review and edit these documents to make them easy to read and employee-friendly.
- Certain key policies and procedures require special attention to ensure clarity, not only for employees, but for supervisors who use them as the ground rule. These critical policies address the following topics:
    - company values
    - wages, salaries, benefits
    - performance management
    - recognition
    - issues resolution
    - termination.
- Ensure that each of the above policies has a training program attached to it. Each supervisor must understand the "why" and "how" of applying the policies. Leadership behaviors should be included in the supervisors' performance management program. Supervisors who do not adhere to these policies in their leadership of employees should themselves be subject to a performance management program.

▶ If there is no reward for taking the extra effort to be a good leader, supervisors will quickly learn that this is not an important issue.

Communicate — then communicate again

- Make employees aware that the organization sees little or no value in unions and why. The "why" is most important. Emphasize that two-way communication is always better than three-way communication. (Naturally, the organizational values must support this message.) However, we should never lose sight of the reality that joining a union (or not joining) is a Charter or Constitutional right for every employee — the right of free association.
- Consistently support the no-solicitation rule. Don't set a precedent by allowing some solicitation (such as the selling of lottery tickets) and then try to enforce no-solicitation during a union organizing campaign.
- Union organizing activity is not, by law, allowed on private (company) property, but it is on public property (such as sidewalks, public pathways, roads, etc.). Again, do not be compromised. Post signs (for example, in the parking lot) that clearly state: PRIVATE PROPERTY — PRIVATE USE ONLY.
- Impress upon every employee the importance of securing the physical facility. No unescorted people should be allowed on the site or in the building(s). Everyone must sign-in and wear a visitor's badge.
- Employees, particularly those newly hired, are most receptive to messages from the organization. Invest in a *great* orientation program. Make an impact — but be prepared to live up to the "message" in the day-to-day work life. If you use a buddy system to supplement the orientation program, make certain you know what the buddy will say when confronted with questions such as:

  "What do you like about this place?"
  "Do they respect your seniority around here?"
  "Why doesn't this place have a union?"

At the other end of the timeline is the exit interview. This interview is to seek information and advice from those employees who decide to leave the organization. Their reason for leaving may not be relevant. What is relevant are their perceptions of the organization. *Did supervisors/managers behave in accordance with the values? Please give examples. Was this a good company to work for? Why? What went on in your department that your manager really did not understand?* With answers to these and similar questions, a competent interviewer can get a good picture of the company as seen through the eyes of an employee who has voluntarily quit (or who has been terminated by the employer).

Many managers, regardless of their level in the organization, have great difficulty with the concept and practice of leadership. Leadership is about having people follow you because your vision is appealing and it strikes a chord. You cannot build relationships with employees by sitting in the front office and periodically writing memos, letters or a newsletter. Leaders, in order to be leaders, must meet, talk and engage the employees in their workplace. They must show that two-way communication works. You can be sure that the union organizer is going to try to prove that three-way communication works better. If the leader(s) are absent from the workplace and do not have a positive history of engaging the employees, the union organizer can win the argument by default.

An organizing campaign always heightens emotions and frequently brings out the worst in people. To calm the waters, management often begins to send out bulletins, newsletters, special video presentations about the company, etc. Though this may be a good tactic, it is not always a good strategy. Why? Because the union organizer gets the credit for causing all this communication just by his/her presence on the scene. So the message is clear: do not allow a union to give impetus to your communication plans and initiatives. Engage your employees *now* because it's the right thing to do. It's an expression of your values.

▶ **We win union organization campaigns based on our history — the type of track-record we have established with all our employees.**

When it comes to Positive Employee Relations, the effort required to lay the foundation through a pro-active approach will pay lasting dividends. Only then will it be able to withstand the test of time.

EXHIBIT 5.1

SHERBORNE COMPANY

MISSION STATEMENT

1. To ensure our future, we will achieve our goals and objectives by demonstrating an ethical and professional manner in all our relationships with employees, customers, suppliers and the community.

2. To continue to be recognized as a world leader in widget design and manufacturing, we will keep our customers' needs first and foremost.

3. To maintain our enviable employee relations position, we will strive for human resource practices that continually demonstrate our values, including individual employee recognition, job security and workplace safety.

4. To ensure Sherborne's survival and growth, we will strive to earn a consistently fair rate of return while reinvesting earnings.

5. To maintain a growth-oriented posture while expending resources, we will research new and/or additional fields of endeavor within our marketplace.

6. To be socially responsible, we will participate in activities that support our ecology, our community and charities of choice.

EXHIBIT 5.2

SHERBORNE COMPANY
15 BOND ST., WINDRUSH, ONTARIO

Dear (Employee's Name),

Welcome to Sherborne Company. Now that you have joined our organization, I would like to take this opportunity to review some information discussed during your interviews.

At Sherborne we pride ourselves on the quality of our workmanship and the value of our products. While we are in business for economic gain, at the same time we run our business as a team effort; we want you to enjoy working here. *We believe everyone should be treated fairly — you, your fellow employees, our shareholders, our customers, our suppliers and our community.*

We achieve all this by:

- Hiring the best people for all employment opportunities.
- Training all employees so that they are thoroughly empowered to do their jobs effectively and efficiently.
- Providing each employee with reasonable working hours.
- Paying each employee a fair and competitive wage.
- Providing a safe and orderly workplace.
- Ensuring that all employees are fully informed about Sherborne and what is happening with the business.
- Providing opportunities for employees to discuss *any* matter that concerns them.
- Providing each employee with some financial protection in case of sickness, accident or death, and at the time of retirement.
- Encouraging all employees to take pride in the concepts, products and progress of Sherborne.

Because of the size of Sherborne it may take a while for you to know all members of the leadership team. However, if you have a problem or want to discuss any matter, I encourage you to see and talk to any manager, from your team leader to the president. We want to hear from you. We believe that this open communications policy will enable us all to grow.

We look forward to having you grow with us.

Sincerely,

W.H. Burford
General Manager

EXHIBIT 5.3

SHERBORNE COMPANY

GOALS OF OUR
POSITIVE EMPLOYEE RELATIONS PROGRAM

The cornerstone of Sherborne's Positive Employee Relations program has always been *fairness*. In fact, all our guidelines and procedures are designed to promote fairness to everyone associated with our company, including employees, customers and shareholders. The goals of our Positive Employee Relations program are as follows:

1. To ensure that employees are in jobs best suited to their talents and long-term aspirations, Sherborne will continue to hire and promote the best candidate for any position based on that person's qualifications and experience.
2. To promote from within, whenever possible. External candidates will be considered only when internal candidates do not have the qualifications and have been told why.
3. To evaluate positions of equal difficulty and responsibility in the same job category. Salary increases will be based on performance as assessed in performance feedback meetings.
4. To develop salary ranges based on skills, training and work difficulty. Employees are invited to discuss any questions about their individual salary and position within the salary range with their supervisor, their next-level manager, or the human resources director.
5. To provide training to meet the performance standards established for all jobs. Sherborne encourages employees to upgrade their skills, by offering full reimbursement of tuition costs of pre-approved courses.
6. To schedule performance feedback meetings every six (6) months to compare actual performance with performance standards. These are collaborative and developmental discussions in which your manager will be seeking your input.

7. To maintain a healthy, clean and safe workplace in which the legislated health and safety regulations will also be Sherborne's *minimum* standard.
8. To cooperate and aid in the financing of social and recreational activities.
9. To provide employees with the opportunity to discuss their career aspirations, ideas for innovation, and concerns with anyone on the leadership team.
10. To continue building a sense of community at Sherborne and to encourage open and honest relationships, thereby allowing everyone to meet their personal and work aspirations.

EXHIBIT 5.4

SHERBORNE COMPANY

POSITIVE EMPLOYEE RELATIONS POLICY

What we believe

The Positive Employee Relations philosophy at Sherborne Company is to maintain a work environment that recognizes each individual's qualifications, performance, needs, suggestions, concerns and problems. We believe that the interests of each employee and the overall organization are best served through handling employee relations matters on an *individual basis* rather than involving outside third parties who have no real interest in our future.

The open-door policy at Sherborne allows all employees to obtain the answers to their questions directly from their supervisor or *any* member of management. This honest and direct communication solves problems and ensures that concerns are answered quickly and effectively.

The overall effectiveness of Sherborne Company, and each employee's part in it, depends upon an environment of understanding, cooperation and teamwork throughout the organization.

Our human rights policy states: "In employment activities it is the policy of the Sherborne Company to provide equal employment opportunity to individuals in accordance with applicable legislation. This equal employment opportunity policy applies to all aspects of the employment relationship including recruitment, hiring, work assignments, promotion, transfer, termination, wage and salary administration and selection training."

Employee development

It is Sherborne's policy to promote from within whenever possible, thereby creating opportunities for advancement at all levels within the company. These opportunities are based on individual qualifications and performance.

The progress and growth of Sherborne depends upon the development and performance of all of us who work here. We have a long tradition of providing training and development opportunities for employees and encouraging them to take initiative in extending their qualifications.

Everyone here wants you to have every opportunity to develop your capabilities to the full. Your supervisors will keep you apprised of your job performance and progress.

We continually strive to improve our operations and efficiency by using the latest equipment, techniques and processes. This involves changes which create strength and security by ensuring a favorable competitive position in the industry. These changes also generate the growth in which you will have the opportunity to participate. Your contributions will be evaluated and rewarded. You are encouraged to exercise initiative. Every effort is put forth to make all jobs both challenging and rewarding. Our goal is to provide you with the opportunity to develop your potential through personal achievement.

The idea of training and helping employees improve by developing greater proficiency with continued experience is deeply ingrained in our philosophy. It is a natural link to the practice of building careers at Sherborne. As the requirements of your job situation change, you will need to acquire additional or different skills. Our training and development programs cover a wide range of subjects. Although the interests and subjects are varied, these programs are all designed to aid your development and assure the Sherborne Company of an adequate number of trained employees.

Resolving problems

The working relationship with your supervisor is the most important link for maintaining the objectives of our Positive Employee Relations program. Whenever you have needs, questions, suggestions or problems regarding your work or Sherborne policies, they should be openly and frankly discussed with your supervisor. *Questions will not go unanswered; problems will not be left unsolved.*

Misunderstanding can occur in any organization. By maintaining open communications, most matters can be resolved before they cause unnecessary complications. Sherborne is willing to assist in a spirit of mutual support and cooperation. If the situation cannot be resolved immediately you have two avenues open to you.

First, Sherborne's open-door policy allows unresolved problems to be moved up the chain of command — all the way to our president. The issue resolution program allows you to resolve concerns with a panel of your peers and leaders. In either case, you will be treated with respect and provided the confidentiality you request — no issue you raise will ever be used against you.

Two-way communications

To provide you with objective information for assessing and developing your career interests and goals, two-way discussions between you and your supervisor are held on your job performance, progress and potential. Informal discussions on these matters will be an ongoing part of routine job communications. However, formal sessions are periodically scheduled (generally once a year) to provide a systematic format for mutually reviewing and appraising your performance and goals with your supervisor. Such discussions, to be effective, must be two-way in nature and must result in mutual commitment to a program for continued development of your skills, abilities and potential.

Our active and varied communications program will keep you well informed about employee, company and industry developments. Your supervisor, however, is your best source of information. A free flow of information will be encouraged through periodic meetings held in your department to keep you informed on matters of current interest, to answer your questions and to provide you with an opportunity to comment on current operations and problems. Throughout Sherborne are bulletin boards where announcements are posted. Our news-letter is distributed quarterly throughout the company to communicate pertinent news. Information of special interest will be mailed to your home.

At Sherborne, we continually strive to be responsive to each and every person. You are as important to us as our customers.

TAKE ACTION!

1. Anticipate potential trouble spots and work wholeheartedly to prevent their growth.
2. Constantly reassess the organization's underlying philosophy to make sure that it balances economic and human resource goals.
3. Take a hard look at every procedure used in recruiting, selecting, placing, training and compensating employees to ensure that the organization's philosophy is expressed in its actions as well as its words.
4. Articulate the organization's Positive Employee Relations policy.
5. Take these steps to reduce your organization's susceptibility during a union campaign:

   - Create a human resources database and keep it up-to-date.
   - Create a wage and salary database and keep it up-to-date.
   - Market your benefits to your employees.
   - Seek employee feedback.
   - Know the opposition.
   - Ensure that your organization's policies are fair and consistent.
   - Communicate, communicate, communicate.

6
BECOMING AN EMPLOYER OF CHOICE

The best way to avoid unionization is to become an employer of choice. But you cannot *be* an employer of choice if you're not *perceived* as an employer of choice. After you've made the effort to transform your organization into the type of place where people *want* to work, how do you ensure that your people recognize the special qualities your organization has to offer? This chapter focuses on the internal marketing required to be recognized as an employer of choice, as an employer who exemplifies Positive Employee Relations.

EMPLOYER OF CHOICE STATUS: THE OLYMPIC GOLD

Avoiding unionization is by no means the only reason to become known as an employer of choice. No business landscape is complete if it doesn't include *all* the stakeholders: customers, employees and shareholders. The employee group is not an appendage that can be forgotten when all goes well or dealt with when a crisis occurs. *Employees are as important as customers.* Successful businesses invest in the development of a long-term, symbiotic relationship with these two key stakeholders.

▶ To be known as an employer of choice is the highest accolade an employer can receive from its employee group — it's the Olympic gold.

Everything stems from our employees — our products and services, research, preventative maintenance, customer service, financial acumen, etc. Even our management personnel, in many cases, have been promoted from the ranks of the employee group. Our customers are our customers because someone (or some team) was successful at fulfilling their needs and requirements — and probably going the extra mile.

The benefits of achieving employer-of-choice status run the full gamut — from reduced absenteeism to greater innovation. Such organizations tend to attract and retain the best employees, and these employees bring a strong commitment to their jobs: they are more likely to be high-performing, self-motivated, continuous learners who pay great attention to customer care and quality service. (Refer to Chapter 14 for a complete discussion of employee retention.)

QUALITIES OF THE GOOD COMPANY

Good companies share certain elements that are beneficial to both employers and employees:

- clarity of mission and purpose
- responsible, people-skilled leadership
- high degree of job satisfaction
- sense of urgency
- collaboration
- self-managing teams
- vitality, energy, creativity
- open, direct communication
- sense of resilience.

START BY CHECKING YOUR ALIGNMENT

How do we become recognized as an employer of choice? Certainly not by chance. It requires internal marketing that is consistent with our belief system and the way we articulate those beliefs. For example, a manager can allocate resources (money, time, etc.) to have an employee communications program designed. Members of the human resource team can be trained to implement this internal marketing campaign. Each leader *must* understand his/her values — and their expression — in order to see the impact that his/her words have on others. Anything less than a full understanding will drain the spirit away from the employee group.

▶ If the managers' thoughts, values and actions are not re-aligned so that they speak to the integrity, dignity and capability of all employees, then even the best, most expensive internal marketing campaign will fail.

We have all seen examples of where it is easier to "pay your money" than to change what and how you think about employees. Yet how and what we think about our employees is a very good indicator of what we will get back from them. To imagine that this refers to "warm and fuzzy" is to miss the point. "Warm and fuzzy" is a persona that can be put on (or taken off) when the leader wants something special from his employee group. *It's insincere, it's recognized as insincere, it expresses disrespect for the employees and eventually returns as disrespect from the employees.*

All organizations have values that are expressed through the actions of the leadership group. For example, the manner in which employees are recruited and trained is an expression of our values. An organization that does not allow sufficient time for this process, and directs its resources to some other activity, reveals that recruitment is perceived as an activity of lesser value.

Too often, an organization's stated values are out of alignment with its culture. If an organization has published a values statement (which it may alternatively call a credo, guiding behaviors, etc.), but has no feedback mechanism to determine if the front-line and middle management groups are "walking the talk," then there is no assurance that the workplace culture is in harmony with the stated values.

▶ If we do not "inspect what we expect," we will quickly lose touch with our employees' perceptions.

Inconsistency has a detrimental effect on any organization. So if you have published your company's values but are not holding the leadership team accountable for matching its behaviors, actions, policies and procedures with this statement, an internal public relations disaster looms on the horizon.

To understand the seriousness of the problem, consider the effect that such an inconsistency would have if it were applied to your customer/client base. Imagine that your marketing team develops and promotes a particular customer service policy but your sales team makes decisions that bear no relationship to this policy. In the short term, some customers may overlook the inconsistency, but others will complain and eventually most will seek other vendors whose sales practices are consistent with the marketplace image they are projecting. Inconsistency with your values will have the same impact on your employees.

The key to being an employer of choice is to articulate your values and then have *everyone* in the leadership group be just as rigorous about ensuring that their actions are consistent with these values as they would if the values were legislated. For example, in the 1950s few organizations had a policy that addressed non-discrimination (race, religion, color, gender, etc.) in the workplace. Today it is difficult to find a jurisdiction that has not passed human rights legislation. So we have policies, practices and training to assist members of the leadership group in ensuring that their behavior and actions comply with the legislation. Having legislated certain values (for example, all employees, including candidates, are equal regardless of their race, religion, color, gender or sexual orientation), we now find that most workplaces comply and do not discriminate on these grounds. *But why do we, as employers, wait for governments to intervene before we take action?*

Let's follow this line of thinking, but be more pro-active. Assume, for example, that one of your company's values is a "passion for the products/services we provide our customers." The law is not going to intervene here. The employer must become involved if there are going to be policies, practices and training to support this value. Policies will have to be written and carried out with a belief in continuous improvement, doing it right the first time, continual learning and learning from our mistakes; and treating employees as though they are valued internal customers. Leadership personnel will need to be trained in coaching, facilitating and mentoring skills. Employees will also need skills in decision making, problem solving, conflict resolution, etc.

In short, to be an employer who is known by its employees to have a "passion for the products we make" demands behaviors and actions that support this value. Wishes don't count. Planning, training, communicating are the raw ingredients. *The key is to value your employees as much as you value your customers.* And, not surprisingly, this is also one of the cornerstones of Positive Employee Relations.

Understanding employee motivation

We know how to market to our external customers. Most companies contract with marketing firms, advertising agencies, media firms, public relations consultants, etc. to ensure that their message reaches customers and potential customers. We know it is generally less costly to keep existing customer relationships than to turn prospects into customers. Because our employees are our internal customers, it is just as important that we market to them.

In an organization that has a Positive Employee Relations mandate, informing and educating employees on the features and benefits of the company is a natural next step.

▶ If we don't tell our employees about the good things we do — for them, their families and their community — nobody will.

A union certainly won't sing our praises. Its goal is to undermine all of our marketing and communications efforts. Arguably, unions succeed at this every time they win a certification vote.

Internal employee marketing begins with an understanding of employee motivation. Herzberg's Hygiene-Motivation Theory provides a useful starting point. Because it dates back to the 1970s, a wealth of data validates its accuracy. This theory is based on the concept that employees, at least in our Western society, are generally self-motivated and willing to accept personal responsibility when their job is characterized by words such as:

- interesting (versus routine, repetitive).
- challenging (requiring thought and exploration of ideas, skills or techniques).
- developmental (allowing opportunities to seek positions of greater responsibility by increasing their competencies).

However, job motivators (which Herzberg refers to as "intrinsic factors"), do not kick in unless there is an acceptable platform on which they are built. This platform is made up of such factors as working conditions and pay and benefit levels. If these factors are not acceptable to the employees, the consequences are usually low morale, an absence of self-motivation and a general malaise or dissatisfaction. In this state, employees need to be motivated; that is, the supervisor must actually *do* something to cause the employees to want to work. Think of the automobile before the "starter motor" — the driver had to crank the engine until it turned over and then it would operate on its own power.

If employees are dissatisfied with work conditions or their supervisor's relationship-building skills or any other aspect of their working situation, their dissatisfaction will stand in the way of their willingness to be self-motivated. The dissatisfaction, to use a selling term, is the objection; until it is resolved the sale will not be made.

▶ Companies that have a long history as an employer of choice have a "bank balance" of trust and credibility that they can draw upon in cases of emergency.

A company's "deposited" goodwill can overcome the employees' objection. But the bank account is not bottomless and employee patience is not endless.

Before launching any program of internal marketing, you must first resolve the "extrinsic" or hygiene issues; these are factors that are peripheral to the job itself but that nevertheless influence the employee's satisfaction level. Examples include pay, supervisor knowledge and company policies. If the job motivators platform is at an unacceptable level, you can't expect employees to be interested in *any* organizational program, whether it be continuous improvement, zero defects, Kaizen — whatever.

INTERNAL MARKETING — LAYING THE GROUNDWORK

The goal of internal marketing is to create a workplace environment where the employees feel positive and are willing to express and share their positive and negative perceptions with management. Remember that employers are known by how they treat *all* their employees, but particularly those in the most vulnerable positions: entry-level employees; those who work in hazardous environments; those who suffer from workplace illnesses. These cases present the greatest challenges for fair and respectful treatment. And employers often have to wage battle against the company history: it can be uphill work to overcome the effects of poor employee relations of the past.

Becoming known as an employer of choice begins at the grass roots, not at the knee caps. To become known as an employer of choice, follow these ten steps:

1. Articulate your values as they relate to all your stakeholders (shareholders/owners, suppliers, customers, community and employees). If necessary, update the company's vision, mission and values statements.
2. Establish clear, concise guiding behaviors — concrete statements that give direction in how to implement our values.
3. Train all members of the leadership group in why and how they can modify their behaviors and actions to harmonize with the guiding behaviors.
4. Revise all policies, practices, systems and processes to ensure that how the organization works is a reflection of its values and guiding behaviors.
5. Conduct focus group meetings and employee perception surveys to determine employees' current perceptions; compare those to the desired perceptions or guiding behaviors; make changes where necessary.

6. Conduct workshops for *all* employees so they can experience the values and guiding behaviors in action. For example: if respect and dignity are important values, demonstrate *how* this impacts employee-to-employee relationships. Values are *not* intended just for leadership.
7. Include the adherence to the guiding behaviors in the company's performance management program and *reward and recognize* those leaders and employees whose actions have lived up to the values.
8. After six months, repeat steps 1 and 5.
9. Annually thereafter, repeat steps 1 and 5.
10. Remember that training done once is not enough. It is one thing to attend a training program and quite another to put the training into practice by learning how to live the values. *Knowledge that is not transferred to workplace behavior is of little value to the organization.*

By following these steps the culture will change to that described by your values and guiding behaviors. Culture change is a cumulative process — one success builds upon another. It is not a radical, foot-to-the-floor event. It is not even an event. It's a new lifestyle for the organization. This means we have to shed old ways of thinking, behaving and acting — and this does not happen quickly.

INTERNAL MARKETING — TRANSLATING THE GENERAL TO THE SPECIFIC

Conduct employee focus groups

Conduct a survey or series of focus group meetings to determine what employees want to know about the company versus what they currently know. Do employees want more information about insurance-type benefits? Do they want to know more about the various internal job opportunities and career ladders that are available to them? Is the company newsletter useful? If not, how should it be changed? If so, how can the editor make it even better?

Conduct employee perception surveys

Conduct a survey or a series of focus group meetings to determine the employees' level of satisfaction with factors related to their job, versus their level of satisfaction with factors related to the work environment. Using Herzberg's definition we want to assess the level of satisfaction and dissatisfaction for both hygiene and motivational factors. The results will provide an indicator of employee morale.

The feedback on this survey can be used to alter the internal marketing program in order to better explain issues that are currently causing dissatisfaction and to enhance those that are currently viewed favorably.

If, for example, the survey asks employees to assess the quality of leadership demonstrated by their immediate supervisor, this information can be used to:

- implement new training programs.
- revise policies and procedures.
- provide feedback to the leadership group.

The data will also reveal the employees' perceptions about the leadership group. The odds are weighted heavily in favor of employees viewing their direct supervisors as people who lead by authority, not by inspiration. This is important information for internal marketing initiatives. For how can we expect to influence employee perceptions if management thinks its leadership skills and practices are participative, collaborative, and co-operative when those being led view it as authoritative, manipulative or inconsistent with the values?

▶ Our internal marketing efforts must always be seen as trustworthy, honest, fair and credible. When management behaviors and actions do not live up to these high standards, we only have two choices: either upgrade our leadership practices or accept that our internal marketing is flawed and will be seen for what it is — a propaganda tool.

Communicate user-friendly information about your company's benefits, policies, programs and practices

User-friendly does not mean that the pension committee or your actuarial consultants understand the retirement plan and program; it means that the employees and their spouses/partners understand it. If their first language is not English, have the information translated. You would do this for your external customers. In Canada we don't expect to market to customers in Quebec using literature printed only in English; in the United States we don't sell products or services to the Hispanic community using English-only literature; and in Europe we don't assume that one language will cover the Common Market.

▶ Treat your internal customers as you treat your external customers and they will never see a trade union as a beneficial option.

Once you start thinking in a user-friendly manner, opportunities abound. The following ideas will help you get started. First, when informing a newly hired employee about the benefit plans and how to use it, consider having the employee's spouse/partner present. This way the family unit understands what the options are, can make a more informed choice, and will know how to access the programs if needed. Second, package all the information in a binder or packet for easy reference and updating. If you provide separate pages and booklets for each policy or program, some will be inevitably be misfiled or lost. Being user-friendly could also include having your in-house benefits specialist trained in customer service skills, which improves the quality of service provided and, again, demonstrates that the employees are internal customers.

Remember that internal marketing is an ongoing process, not a product

Internal marketing is a strategic move that will have little effect if based on a "tactics-of-the-month" approach. If continuous improvement is one of the company values, apply it as strenuously to internal marketing as you do to product quality or customer service.

Undertaking an internal marketing initiative such as the preparation, for example, of an employee handbook, is just the beginning. In order to be effective the handbook must be updated regularly and it must be perceived as an important communication tool (that is, actually used by supervisors and fellow employees).

If you plan to issue a newsletter, first determine why a newsletter will be beneficial, what you expect to achieve through it and how you will know that it is meeting the desired goals. Once the leadership group has answered these questions, consider who should be the newsletter's "champions." Who determines the content, writing style, who seeks out the information, etc.? If the newsletter is scheduled every three months, then adhere to the schedule — don't make it the "periodic quarterly." Make sure its style is well suited to its intended audience — your employee group. Make sure it takes into account their language skills, demographics, etc., and consider whether a video, or posting your newsletter on your company's website might be more appropriate options.

INTERNAL MARKETING — THE BASICS

Recruitment

Modifying the customer satisfaction paradigm so that we think and behave as though employees are internal customers fits our Positive Employee Relations model perfectly. And internal marketing begins with the recruitment stage. This means that when recruiting new candidates, we must treat them like external customers and conduct employment interviews as though they were important. Be on time. Conduct interviews in a private office. Take a "professional" position rather than a "power" stance. Ask good, open-ended and insightful questions to determine how each candidate thinks, makes decisions and communicates with others. Be an active listener.

The "interview to job offer" ratio is high for a good employer because a good employer works hard to find people who fit the company culture. This is as it should be: being hired by an employer of choice should be a privilege, not a piece of cake; the successful candidate should feel valued by being chosen. By contrast, an employee who lands a job because he's seen as a "warm body" is hardly going to feel privileged to work for the organization.

Orientation and training

You want to assure your newly hired "internal customers" that they made the correct decision in joining your organization. So tell them the benefits of working for you. Too often the word "benefits" is limited to insurance-sponsored benefits. Not so. Benefits coalesce around the job and the responsibility, authority, accountability equation that goes along with it. Newly hired employees want to know that they have been hired because of their competencies, their experience, their ability to think clearly and make good decisions. No one wants to be just another payroll number on the time sheet.

Communication

The most effective way to communicate is face-to-face. All other communication methods are of secondary value when compared to the opportunities for clarity, listening, intuition, etc. that are available in one-on-one communication. Though the most effective, it is also the most time-consuming, and therefore the most costly. For this reason, and because most front-line supervisors are not adequately trained as communicators, the face-to-face approach is left for a few critical events — employment, performance feedback, discipline and termination interviews.

The least effective way of communicating with employees is in writing. Some employees don't read well, some read very selectively, and others complain that the writing style lacks clarity, or enthusiasm, or is just too wordy. Whatever the reason, just watch how many pay envelope/packet inserts get thrown into the trash in the mad rush to see the amount of the paycheck.

So what is the right way to communicate? Unfortunately, there is no simple answer. It depends on the sender and the receiver. For example, in an advanced technology workplace (where the average education level is likely to be college or university graduate), a computer-driven overhead presentation might work well. In a multi-branch/site organization, electronic communications may achieve the results, whereas in a factory located in a multi-cultural metropolitan city, translators may be needed because of an illiteracy factor and because English may not be the first language of many employees.

The correct communication method may also depend on the topic being communicated. Promotion about the company picnic is very different from that of an individual's retirement plans and options. When the topic is simple and straightforward (for example, the date and location of a company golf tournament) and the employees' comprehension level is high, then a complex communications strategy is not required. However, if the organization wishes to communicate information about its Positive Employee Relations program and the benefits to employees of the one-to-one relationship it has with the leadership group, a simple poster or short article in the newsletter will *not* do. Considerable time is needed to plan such a campaign — clearly understanding the employees' perception about the job satisfaction-dissatisfaction platform and knowing which features and benefits to highlight.

INTERNAL MARKETING — WHAT IS AT STAKE?

With the guidelines outlined in the previous pages, I'm recommending a high standard. It's part of a long-term solution, not a quick fix. But look at how much is at stake:

- your reputation as an employer of choice.
- your ability to hire and retain good (and perhaps even the best) employees.
- the organization's ability to deliver outstanding products and/or outstanding customer service.
- your success in convincing your employees that you — not a trade union — have their best interests at heart.
- your ability to build a track record of Positive Employee Relations that is the only winning factor in the event of a union campaign.

THE ROLE OF RECOGNITION

Most people, regardless of job responsibilities, work for two fundamental reasons. First, to earn the financial resources to ensure that their basic physical, psychological and, to some degree, social needs are satisfied and secure. Second, people work to achieve their higher-level needs of self-esteem (or self-worth) and self-actualization (or the creativity at the core of their being). It is too often the case that people cannot satisfy these needs in the workplace because their job has little inherent depth or substance. So they seek to satisfy these needs outside the workplace and we, as employers, miss a significant opportunity. Just think about all the creative talent that leaves the workplace at the end of the day: craftspeople, writers, computer wizards, artists, volunteers, musicians, politicians, Olympic-class athletes — the list goes on.

In pragmatic terms there are two ways to remedy this brain-drain. First, put decision-making back into people's jobs. Ask employees to work smarter, not harder.

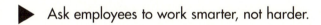

▶ Ask employees to work smarter, not harder.

People who experience their supervisor as one who challenges their thinking, innovation and creativity are more likely to build a quality/professional relationship than those who see their leader as a task master.

Second, recognize and reward the results and the efforts of employees who put their brains to work for the organization. Nothing does more to satisfy employees' self-esteem and self-actualization needs than genuine and deserved recognition for the thought and creativity they put into their work.

Countless human resource research projects have confirmed that one of the most frequent employee complaints is that their efforts are not recognized by their employer. Although supervisors/managers often say that their most valuable resources are their human resources, they don't always behave in ways that make employees feel truly appreciated. Unfortunately, it is quite common to criticize employees when things go wrong, and far less common to acknowledge their successes in a formal way. *Only you, as the employer, have the power to recognize employee achievement — don't let this opportunity slip by.*

PRINCIPLES OF RECOGNITION

An effective recognition program will reward employees for behavior and performance that are consistent with the organization's values and goals.

▶ Leadership and employees know that if something is not formally rewarded, it is not a priority.

Companies whose recognition programs consist entirely of long-term service awards are sending a clear message that seniority is the greatest achievement an employee can attain. Surely there are better ways to maximize employee contribution without using a union tactic. A core value in the union movement is seniority, which is why the trade unions handle seniority-related recognition better than most employers.

Employees who believe that their efforts lead to rewards become productive and stay productive because the rewards meet their expectations for self-esteem. Organizations then develop the capacity to attract, retain and encourage a motivated work force. Recognition encourages people to become excited about their workplace and the work they do.

RECOGNITION PROGRAM GUIDELINES

When customizing your own recognition program, the following ten guidelines may provide a useful starting point.

Rewards must be clearly tied to values and goals

Often leaders assume that employees intuitively know what is expected of them. But specific behaviors must be encouraged by positive consequences. We must work at increasing the behaviors that will help us achieve core organizational values and goals.

Goals and rewards must be well understood and publicized

All employees need to know exactly what they must do to earn a particular reward. Goals should be as specific and measurable as possible. Providing information to employees on how well they are progressing towards goals keeps motivation and enthusiasm high. If employees know how much farther they have to go to achieve a goal, they will be much more likely to get there. *A recognition program will only be as important to the employees as it is to the leaders who sponsor it.* If supervisors/managers are lax in promotion and enthusiasm, the employees will care less too.

Rewards must be perceived as fair

If employees believe that only those personally favored by the leadership group will be rewarded, the recognition program will have a *negative impact* on morale. Steps to reducing charges of favoritism may include setting measurable objectives or performance goals and seeking peer input into nominations for recognition.

Goals must be realistic

Competition between individuals or departments can lead to a reduction of team spirit and even sabotage of one another's efforts. An organization's beliefs and goals should not become the victims of competition. Co-operation and collaboration, rather than competition, are Positive Employee Relations values. It is preferable to structure rewards so that the criteria is based on reaching a measurable, objective target rather than merely being better than others. In this way all strong contributors will be rewarded rather than one best performance.

The cost of the award is less important than the prestige associated with winning it

The recognition program is in place to address the employee's self-esteem needs — whereas the pay check is there to take care of the monetary needs. Public acknowledgment is very powerful; it makes people feel good about themselves. An article and/or picture in the organization's newsletter or the community newspaper lets employees bask in the glow of the spotlight — something they may not experience very often. Similarly, a plaque or gift is a symbolic representation that serves as an ongoing reminder of things done right. Team clothing, watches or mugs can be displayed with pride to improve feelings of belonging. Lunches or dinners can make the employees feel special and important. Giving cash is nice, but the effect usually lasts only as long as the money does.

Just as with food, presentation makes a difference

Management creates the symbolic worth of a reward through the manner in which it is presented. By carefully structuring who presents the reward and when and how it is presented, leaders invest the award with many times its financial value. It is essential that the presenter cite the accomplishment clearly and sincerely express appreciation. And the higher the status of the presenter, the more impressive the presentation. Thus, senior executives will often present the most significant rewards. Whenever possible, award presentations should be made in the presence of all the employees. The symbolic significance is greatly enhanced by the presence of others, and the effects on employee attitudes are much more profound as a result.

Rewards should be customized when possible

What works for one organization or one department may not work for another. While it is certainly easier to have a standard list of rewards to be distributed when necessary, it doesn't take a lot of extra time to match the rewards to the people receiving them. For example, one group may wish to have team hats emblazoned with the company logo while another group may greatly prefer t-shirts or coffee mugs. One person may wish to have an extra vacation day, while the next might prefer lunch with his/her partner. Making a contribution to an employee's favorite charity is another option.

Give rewards as soon as possible after the goal is reached

One reason why wages make a poor primary reinforcer is because it is so difficult to connect the money to the actual effort given. A paycheck doesn't increase proportionately from one week to the next if the employee has gone that extra mile in effort. Some recognition programs fail because by the time the rewards are given out, people can barely remember the work that earned it. It is like telling a student to do an onerous homework assignment because it will really pay off one day when they apply to college or university. As a rule, we humans have a hard time stretching ourselves today for a benefit that seems far in the future. Therefore, distributing rewards on an annual basis will almost certainly ensure failure. Of course, circumstances may make it impossible to give rewards immediately in some cases, but the sooner they are given the more influential they will be.

Recognition programs will need periodic adjustments

It is reasonable to expect goals to change as circumstances do. Reviewing the program every six months to a year allows leaders to keep goals challenging yet realistic. If too few or too many employees are hitting goals, change is in order. Also, some components may have to be re-addressed or dropped if they are not working as well as planned, while new components may be integrated depending on employee feedback. Periodic evaluations keep any program fresh and exciting to employees.

Employee input on the design and maintenance of the program is essential

Recognition is for the employees — so who better to help make it work? Management can never be truly confident about what employees find rewarding unless they ask. Additionally, employee involvement will make the entire employee population much more tolerant of the inevitable glitches in the system.

INTERNAL MARKETING GUIDELINES

When preparing for an internal marketing or internal public relations program, apply the same standards that you would if your organization were communicating with external customers or shareholders. Selling, marketing and public relations skills, both visual and verbal, are unfortunately not skills that all human resource professionals possess. So, if required, make contact with an employee communications specialist to plan and implement your program. However, part of his/her mandate should be to train an in-house resource person.

The following is a brief list of guidelines:

- We all are bombarded with media messages every day from television, radio, the Internet, newspapers, magazines and books. Your messages and the media used to convey them should appeal to your specific employee audience and treat them as adults by not talking up or down to them.
- Professionalism is needed at all times. You, as an employer, *are* your message. What you say, the positions you take, and how you package the message, talks to and about your organization's values.
- Always assume that others will know about your internal marketing programs. That could reasonably include the employees' family and friends, the community press, a union wishing to organize your employees, etc.
- Touch the employee's life. Encouraging and supporting the employee's desire for a better lifestyle (career, self-development, special volunteer opportunities, etc.) is frequently more meaningful than financial data about the company's performance.

The nature of business is survival and growth. These goals are achieved through good fiscal management of profit. However, profit is the end result of having sound business systems and practices. All business systems and practices have been and will continue to be developed, maintained and up-dated by your leadership and employee groups. Never lose sight of their value and importance to the organization. Your internal marketing program will live or die on the success of reinforcing the message.

INTERNAL MARKETING OPPORTUNITIES

Consider adapting any of the following ideas to create internal marketing opportunities that support your organization's unique values and guiding behaviors. Concentrate on finding opportunities to make employees aware of how the benefits of working for your company affect them personally. One of the goals of marketing is to make the invisible visible.

What is your job worth?

You can create a document demonstrating the actual value of an employee's job, using your payroll system or payroll supplier. It should show the value of the employee's salary when the cost of benefits has been included. For example, a salary of $10 per hour is likely to show up as $13 per hour if the organization is paying for benefits at the rate of 30 percent on each payroll dollar. Benefits, in this context, include those provided by insurance premiums, vacation plans, recreational and social activities, education assistance, subsidized cafeteria, etc. The cost of benefits is the direct cost to the employer shown as a percentage of payroll dollars.

Benefits can include the following:

- Regular earnings
- Overtime earnings
- Accident/illness benefits
- Shift premiums
- Allowances (e.g. call-in pay)
- Jury duty leave
- Bereavement paid leave
- Grief counseling

- Vacation pay
- Service awards
- Suggestion awards
- Holiday pay
- Automobile lease or allowance
- Recognition program
- Club memberships
- Relocation expenses
- Profit sharing, stock or cash bonuses
- Lunch and coffee breaks
- Employee assistance programs
- Health/fitness programs
- Scholarships for employees' children
- Social and recreational programs
- Paid parking
- Food services
- Medical facilities
- Pension plan or RRSP contribution
- Matching donations to major colleges and universities
- Medical insurance
- Dental insurance
- Stock purchase or savings plans
- Social insurance tax on wages and salaries
- Cost of premium on Workers' Compensation
- Cost of tuition refund program
- Cost of safety equipment

Benefit payout

Available from your employee benefits provider is the cost of benefits paid over any period you select. This information is normally not shared with employees, which is a missed opportunity to educate and inform employees about the "benefits of the benefit." For example, if the long-term disability and weekly indemnity payout amount to a significant number, you can communicate this type of job security (or job protection) and the value of the payout as another example of your Positive Employee Relations program. This link between premiums and paid-out benefits can apply to any type of benefit program (for example, dental or medical). Keep in mind that this information should be communicated without singling out or naming the recipients of the benefits; an employee newsletter is an appropriate medium to convey the information.

Life-long learning

A similar idea to the previous example is to market the benefits of the company's educational assistance program. For example, if the organization co-sponsors employees who further their skills, competencies or general level of academic education, this can be expressed as the number of educational hours or credits earned by the employees, and the number of dollars spent by the employees and the company. If the organization supports 100 percent of further education, the message is even stronger. This also applies to scholarship programs for the children of employees.

Offering courses in life management skills can be an immense bonus to employees. A colleague of mine has created a life management skills workshop that is, in my opinion, well worth integrating into your Positive Employee Relations program. Please refer to Appendix F for an overview of the workshop.

Volunteerism

Another internal marketing idea is to discuss the volunteer contributions supported by the organization. This might include the financial support to local charities and the number of company-paid "work hours" employees have spent in charitable and civic events. Another variation on this message is the number of retired or disadvantaged individuals the organization has provided employment opportunities for or the amount of support given to these individuals who, in turn, give time back to the community.

Social and recreational activities

The communications about specific activities (for example, the annual picnic, children's Christmas party, etc.) are frequently the employer's responsibility. However, the marketing of these events is generally lackluster. Why not recognize the individuals who devoted hours to plan and organize these events? The organization likely spends more on the Christmas party than on all other social events within the year. If we do not share with our employees the financial support the organization provides, no one will. This approach to internal marketing can apply to all recreational and social events.

TAKE ACTION!

1. Follow the ten-step "alignment check" detailed in the section entitled "Internal Marketing—Laying the Groundwork."
2. Conduct employee focus groups to determine what employees want to know about the company versus what they currently know.
3. Conduct an employee perception survey to assess employee morale.
4. Plan an internal marketing campaign that begins with recruitment and extends to all facets of employee life. Make sure that it involves an on-going process that includes opportunities for recognition of exemplary behavior.
5. Communicate information about your company's benefits, policies, programs and practices.

7
SELECTING SUPERVISORS

In maintaining an organization's union-free status, commitment at the senior level must be accompanied by a *commitment to action at the first level of supervision*. Though senior management must determine the policy and subsequent strategies for remaining union-free, the front-line supervisors will be responsible for carrying out these strategies and ensuring that the organization's Positive Employee Relations program meets its objectives.

Each supervisor must be trained in the art and skills of effective supervision, human relations and communications in order to understand the concepts and practices underlying Positive Employee Relations. Once trained, supervisors will require regular practice and reinforcement in order to apply their new skills successfully. However, before training begins, supervisors must be carefully selected and hired by a senior management team that is sensitive to the needs and requirements of the Positive Employee Relations program.

▶ Selecting the right supervisor is critical; the supervisor will be the most influential link in your Positive Employee Relations program.

SUPERVISORS ARE PEOPLE MANAGERS

An effective supervisor must have superior leadership qualities as well as the ability to understand and communicate management's viewpoint. Yet supervisors are not always chosen with regard to these skills. Often, the employee who produces the most widgets becomes the supervisor of the widget production line. Unfortunately, the very qualities that make someone the best widget maker in the industry may in fact be a hindrance in the new role as supervisor. For example, new supervisors are often intolerant of employees who are now performing the supervisor's former job. Also, new supervisors are now expected (by themselves as well as by management) to be the best in a new role that has little to do with widget making.

We must change our approach. To avoid falling into the traditional traps, we should begin by determining the tasks for which the new supervisor will be responsible. In addition to the normal technology-related responsibilities, we should account for the human resource side of the supervisor's job. We must consider the supervisor's capacity for understanding and carrying out Positive Employee Relations activities.

While no single conceptual model is accurate for all industries and all companies, Figure 7.1 shows a typical relationship between technical, human and conceptual skills, and their importance at each level of the organization. Unfortunately, most of our job descriptions for supervisory and management positions do not reflect the real importance of human resource management and leadership skills.

FIGURE 7.1 — Skills Needed at Different Levels of Management

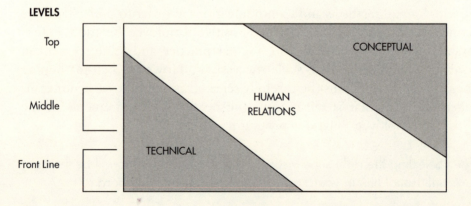

DEVELOPING PEOPLE-MANAGEMENT SKILLS

Keep in mind that supervisors, like most other employees, will, under normal circumstances, carry out the tasks assigned to them. The word "assigned" presumes that both supervisor and next-level manager understand the tasks (what they mean, how they are to be carried out, how they will be measured).

When it comes to technology-oriented (as opposed to people-oriented) tasks there is usually little difficulty in determining how and why a job should be done. But when talk turns to a supervisor's responsibility for the human resource side of the job, the lack of understanding and decisiveness is astonishing. I have met very few supervisors who comprehend the nature and scope of their people-oriented responsibilities. They do not know how to interview and/or counsel fellow employees, conduct performance interviews, give positive recognition, handle problem employees, etc. There are many reasons for this and chief among them are the following:

- Middle managers (who should be leading by example) do not know what to expect from their supervisors, particularly when it comes to human resource management.
- Managers do not reinforce and recognize supervisors who handle human resources effectively.

Supervisors, like other employees, learn by observing their managers. Even if their manager is incompetent or unsure of how to deal with people, most supervisors will likely assume the behavior they see is acceptable. To develop human resources skills in supervisory staff:

- Outline the tasks to be performed. Clearly indicate job responsibilities, accountabilities and level of authority.
- Explain the standards of performance.
- Let the supervisor know, in detail, what is expected regarding people-oriented duties.
- Review the values and guiding behaviors that support Positive Employee Relations.
- Behave as you expect supervisors to behave in dealing with their employees.

- Give positive reinforcement, recognition and praise when you notice the supervisor handling people situations correctly.
- Set high standards for your supervisor and expect them to be met.

▶ Be a positive role model for your staff. Mediocre performance on the part of the manager begets mediocrity.

FINDING NEW SUPERVISORS

Prior to selecting a new supervisor, establish a realistic, detailed and all-encompassing job description. Then list the competencies and behaviors required to handle and fulfill expectations outlined in the job description. For example, if the supervisor is to manage an organizational unit making widgets, then presumably the candidate should have widget-making skills. The job description should also indicate that the individual will require the skills to communicate effectively with other employees, to handle problems and grievances fairly, to cope constructively with conflict and so on.

When considering these skills in addition to the widget-making skills, you may see that the best widget maker is not the logical candidate for a supervisory position after all. Instead, you may select a candidate whose technical skills are either good or average and whose human resource management skills are above-average or excellent.

How do you identify human resource management skills in people who have never held supervisory positions? In large organizations, the human resources department may provide assistance and/or establish a center to assess people who have the potential to move into supervision and later into management. Candidates are engaged in a series of role-playing exercises while skilled assessors judge how well they meet pre-determined behavioral criteria.

Usually this selection technique is carried out in an assessment center. Because of its high cost and the need for skilled assessors, the process may not be available to smaller organizations. During the past few years, however, there has been a marked increase in the use of other assessment instruments designed to place people in situations where they will have a high likelihood of success. Research, both current and past, indicates that the key determinants of success in a role go far beyond the traditional "how-to" factors of knowledge and thinking skills. While these factors will

SELECTING SUPERVISORS

be criteria for a supervisory position, other factors play a more significant role in determining success.

CRITICAL "FIT" FACTORS

One thing we know for sure is that people succeed in their job responsibilities for exactly the same reason people fail in jobs — fit! But fit to what? A good fit comes when knowledge, ability and desire exist in equal measure (see Figure 7.2). The key factors, listed below, become increasingly important in positions of greater responsibility and leadership, accounting for over 75 percent of the elements for success in a position. Research also validates the fact that people are most successful and contented when they do what comes most naturally to them. So, in addition to the appropriate knowledge, skills and experience which are fairly straightforward to discern, the critical "fit" factors are:

- alignment of the candidate's natural behaviors with the behavioral demands of the supervisory role.
- alignment of the candidate's expectations of the position with the demands of the position.
- alignment of the candidate's values and principles with the culture of the organization. Motivation and performance will be maximized when all of these factors are in harmony.

FIGURE 7.2 — Role Suitability

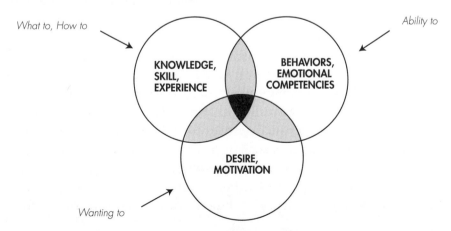

When selecting leaders, the objective is to create "win-win-win" situations. That is, a high likelihood of performance and career success for the supervisor, improved outcomes for his/her team, overall performance results for the organization, and enhancement of the Positive Employee Relations culture. Selection processes with these goals in mind are in the best interests of everyone.

Establishing a benchmark

While various assessment tools are available, assessments have meaning only when examined in relation to a benchmark. We need assessment instruments that can measure the culture of your organization as well as the behavioral demands of the supervisor role you have developed. These assessments need to be converted in a database against which the candidate can also be assessed. With our consulting clients, we use the Activity Vector Analysis (AVA) system developed by Walter V. Clarke Associates, Inc. Please refer to Appendix C for more information about the AVA process as it applies to selection and development of leaders.

Using the AVA involves a two-stage process. First, working with your organization, we determine its culture (desired, perceived and actual). Second, working with management and successful supervisor(s)/incumbent(s), we assist in developing the outcomes and expectations for the role of supervisor. This leads to identification of the behaviors necessary for success in the role. From this data, a benchmark profile is developed which includes energy demands, behavioral demands and values appropriate to the desired culture of the organization and the role.

The benchmark establishes the behavioral profile that will have the highest likelihood of success in the role. Once the benchmark is established, any candidate can be assessed in relation to the benchmark. The process measures five basic drives found in all individuals in varying degrees: assertiveness, sociability, work pace, structure and principles. The combination of these drives results in hundreds of different personality styles; identifying those personality styles provides unique insight into an individual's attributes in areas such as leadership, motivation, communication, decision making and conflict resolution. The assessment results can be utilized not only to assess fit but also to develop strategies for reinforcing change in the supervisor's job performance and career direction.

Because the process allows for more informed hiring decisions, it also has a great impact on employee retention. Terminations, whether voluntary or involuntary, are based largely on the employee's expectations.

▶ Research suggests that upwards of 80 percent of all employment "dislocations" are the result of a gap in expectations — either from the perspective of the employer or the supervisor.

The AVA process also provides feedback as to the suitability of the candidate (strengths and weaknesses relative to the demands of the role), an explanation of the consequences of the particular "gaps" from the benchmark, training suggestions and coaching tips for managing the candidate. We have found no process where the return on investment is higher.

▶ Putting the right people in the right position is one of the most important aspects of your Positive Employee Relations program; it also improves organizational effectiveness.

Good selection decisions can be made using the AVA assessment techniques only in conjunction with your own observations of the potential supervisor. Look for signals that indicate a candidate's aptitude for working with people, solving people problems and working enthusiastically toward personal, departmental and organizational goals. Then make a balanced hiring decision by weighing all the issues raised by your observations, the assessment results and the requirements outlined in the job description and performance standards.

Consider the internal labor pool

In recruiting supervisors, consider first the existing labor pool. That is, promote from within your employee group. The benefits to your organization include the following:

- Employees see management demonstrating a policy of internal promotion. This adds significantly to management's credibility.

The company will be perceived as responding to normal and legitimate employee concerns for job advancement and career growth.
- You will interview and consider people who have established a track record with the company. "Better the devil you know than the one you don't" is an adage worth remembering. The advantages of hiring a new employee for a supervisory position dwindle in importance when you consider that no employee is really new. Other employers have put the employee through orientation, supervisory and technical training programs and reinforced behavioral traits particular to their organizations.
- By promoting from within, you obtain a supervisor who already knows the product or service, the organization's policies and procedures, the environment and the people with whom he/she will be working.

Keep in mind, however, that *hiring supervisors from within demands a commitment to training*. Good employees don't always make an easy or successful transition to supervisory roles.

INTERVIEWING SUPERVISORY CANDIDATES

When interviewing potential candidates for a supervisory position the process should be as extensive and lengthy as is practical for your organization. If you've set aside no more than an hour for this process, you're likely way off the mark. It is difficult to measure the candidate's values and intentions in any number of interview hours but the fewer hours devoted to this task, the greater the risk of making a very costly error.

What questions do you ask a supervisory candidate? How do you know he/she will be a suitable supervisor? You need to know what to ask and how to interpret the responses. The latter, from my experience, is the more difficult task. Why? Because the interviewer must be able to tune in to the intent of the response as well as the actual words spoken by the candidate. By misinterpreting or not hearing the intent behind the candidate's answers, the interview, at best, is an exchange of factual information with limited depth or understanding.

If the hiring manager or the interviewing team have before them the best questions to ask, but don't know how to interpret the responses, then even the best questions become meaningless. Knowing how to interpret requires the following abilities:

- To know the difference between what is said by a candidate and what is meant. Sometimes the candidate doesn't even know there is a difference.
- To be grounded in your organization's value system; to know what "fairness," "equity" and "respect" mean in your organization. To appreciate that these concepts are meaningless without knowing the behaviors that back them up.
- To know that the answers to general, non-specific responses are just that — general and non-specific. We begin to scratch the surface when we ask for examples and how the examples were carried out. We come closer to the intent when we ask how the experience "felt" or how it "affected" the candidate in dealing with others.
- To know that there is a cost to asking questions. As a guideline, the interviewer should spend 30 percent or less of the total interview time either talking or asking questions. And the questions should be open-ended, beginning with phrases such as:
    "What do you mean by..."
    "How did you feel about..."
    "What was your intention..."
    "How did your manager behave..."

Only by listening to the candidate's answers and *making connections with what the candidate said previously* can the hiring manager begin to understand the candidate's interests, drives, motivations, passions and values.

▶ It is at the "feelings" level that we begin to understand the candidates we are interviewing.

If you agree that employee pro-union sentiments are grounded in dissatisfaction and that the supervisor is the company in the employee's eyes, then the supervisor *is* the key to the success of your Positive

Employee Relations program. Any step (including rationalizations and excuses) that devalues the integrity of the interview process is a perfect example of short-term gain for long-term pain.

Knowing what to ask is the second ingredient for a successful interview. If we apply the 30/70 rule, then each segment of the candidate's experiences will include many "why" questions. For example, imagine that you are considering a candidate whose resume indicates that he graduated from a technical college two years ago. You will need to discuss what courses he took and what he liked and did best in at college. His answers will constitute the factual data, or information. To better understand the candidate's motivations and values, ask some of the following questions:

- Why college and not university?
- Why technology as opposed to business, etc?
- Why this particular college?

The fact that the candidate has successfully completed a three-year course in mechanical technology is already on the resume or application form. You want to know why the candidate chose mechanical versus architectural versus electrical. Answering these open-ended questions gives the candidate an opportunity to talk about his interests, motivations and intentions. The answers are still "coded." By listening 70 percent of the time, and being well grounded in your company's value system, you can break the "code" to see patterns emerge that will reveal, for example, the degree of:

- assertiveness versus aggressiveness.
- high risk taking versus low risk taking.
- shyness versus sociability.
- competitiveness versus collaborativeness.
- orientation to detail versus an ability to see the big picture.

Until you have a picture of the candidate against parameters such as the above, you will be unlikely to know enough to make a good "hire/no hire" decision. Please remember that *unionization is the result of the attitudes and practices of supervisors and managers.*

See the next chapter to learn how to conduct a thorough interview process for supervisory and other vacancies.

TAKE ACTION!

1. Identify human resources management skills in people who have the potential to move into supervisory positions.
2. Determine tasks for which the new supervisor will be responsible and develop a detailed job description.
3. List competencies and behaviors required to meet expectations outlined in the job description, paying attention to human resource requirements as well as technical requirements.
4. Develop a benchmark behavioral profile that details the behavioral demands of the supervisory role.
5. Make an effort to fill the position through your company's internal labor pool.
6. Have each candidate complete a behavioral assessment to determine their "fit" with company's values.
7. Conduct in-depth interviews with a view to understanding candidates' interests, drives, motivations, passions and values as well as competencies.

8
RECRUITING AND SELECTING EMPLOYEES

In a Positive Employee Relations program, each employee is viewed as an integral part of the organization. To use a sports analogy, no team wins the gold with second-rate players. Similarly, no company can achieve its potential with employees who are poorly matched to the organization's vision and goals. Moreover, while an employee's value to the organization far exceeds the value of his or her vote during a union certification vote, it is worth keeping in mind that each employee can vote "for" or "against" the company. And it takes just one vote to win.

▶ Every hire decision is an important decision. Ideally, the most difficult experience a candidate should ever have is getting hired!

THE RECRUITMENT PROCESS

A rigorous recruitment process demonstrates right from the start that the organization values top-quality employees and that hiring decisions are not trivial, not to be taken lightly by either party. How valued would you feel if you were hired by a company who determined that you were the right candidate for the job only after a thorough investigation to ensure that your qualifications, your experience, your abilities and your values were a good fit with the company? By contrast, how valued would you feel if you were hired by a company whose selection process was loose and sloppy? To suspect that the employer managed the process by default, that any warm body would have done, would not be flattering.

Employee selection is where the rubber meets the road. Too often we find that all the talk about visions, culture and teamwork is forgotten when an urgent production schedule must be met. The human resource department receives a frantic request from someone in production or distribution to hire 5, 10, 20 or 30 new employees by tomorrow. Or — if they've got some lead time — the day after tomorrow.

> Without a good selection process, a pro-union supporter could easily be recruited, look good during the probation period, and be put on full-time employment without management being any the wiser. And, in most companies, the hiring manager would never have to face the consequences of his or her poor decision-making skills.

Managers rationalize their demand for instant employees by saying that they are busy and have no choice. But management does have a choice and too often it makes the most expedient choice rather than the best choice. This can be traced to a set of assumptions that includes a propensity to:

- see quantity over quality.
- see a planning cycle only one day at a time.
- view the probation period as an alternative for a sound interview process.

Managers who demand this type of hiring practice send a clear message regarding the low esteem in which they hold the entire human resource function, as well as how little they value the individual worth of employees.

Consider a company that has secured a "quality standard" for both its administrative practices and the product/service it provides — for example, the ISO 9000 series. If this means more than just another banner decorating the reception area, then it suggests the importance of quality processes and outcomes. What could be more important to a union-free employer than to ensure that the values the organization holds important (for example, quality, continuous improvement, doing it right the first time, etc.) are matched to similar values held by the employee? How can the hiring process be disconnected from the principles of continuous improvement? Arguably, the idea of congruence will not allow such disparities, but it happens all the time in virtually every organization and results in a widespread epidemic of corporate cognitive dissonance. Briefly, cognitive dissonance is a psychological term that describes what happens when we hold two incompatible beliefs or attitudes. We seek to eliminate the dissonance. In the case of a discrepancy between attitudes and behavior, we are more likely to change our *attitude* to accommodate our *behavior* than the other way around.

▶ Managers who find that their values are in conflict with their actions are more likely to change their values than their behavior.

IS OUTSOURCING THE HIRING FUNCTION THE ANSWER?

Many organizations turn to employment agencies for a supply of instant employees. While this can be helpful, it must be managed as carefully as any other resource or service that has been subcontracted. If we rely on an agency to make our hiring decisions, we place our business at some degree of risk. We are, after all, just one of many customers. Arguably, the only resource that does any work in your business is the human resource, so why let an employment agency make such a critical decision on your behalf? Especially when the agency's accountability is limited to replacing an employee who doesn't work out with another employee selected through the same process.

Managers tend to rationalize the employment agency fee on the basis that the agency: (1) makes new employees available quickly, (2) tests the candidates, (3) allows for a probationary period, which is preferable to an extensive interview, and (4) keeps the human resource staff to a minimum. To imagine that a three-month temporary contract constitutes a probationary period is a mistake. Seeing a temporary employee doing the job does not replace the need for an interview. Such managers argue that if the employee doesn't work out, their contract simply won't be renewed. But this rationale is antithetical to any Positive Employee Relations effort because it undermines the goal of developing individual one-on-one relations with employees. Keep in mind:

New employees are never new

Each individual brings a wealth of experiences, perceptions and attitudes to your workplace. During the three-month contract, they will show you what they *think* you want to hear and see. They will be selling themselves. You are unlikely to get to know them until they are on your payroll.

Employees are not an expense

From a Positive Employee Relations perspective, employees are an asset, an investment. What message does the employer send when contract employees know that they are receiving only 50 to 60 percent of the agency fee? How do they feel about doing the same job as a full-time employee without any of the benefits? How does this align with the organization's values?

In a values-centered employee relation environment, there are no second-class employees

Permanent employees are fully aware of the injustices inherent in an employment strategy that requires contract employees to work side-by-side with full-time people. The only conclusion is that the organization's stated values are not to be taken seriously.

The goal of any Positive Employee Relations program must be to ensure that all employees are treated with fairness, equity, respect and dignity. In return, we expect them to produce top-quality widgets and deliver first-class customer service. And it all begins with the selection process, which must integrate our desire to be a good employer with our values and, most importantly, our practices. The position being filled and even the candidate being interviewed have less effect on the success of the outcome than does the process itself. If the logic behind the process is understood, then it can be applied to any vacant position and any interview situation.

A detailed guide to the selection process is presented below. Keep in mind that this is, above all, a decision-making process. The interview process is meant to collect the information needed to make an informed decision. All decisions, however, involve risk. A good interviewer will be aware of the risks and capable of making a decision within the parameters of those risks.

▶ A good hire decision will enhance the company's goals, objectives and values. A poor hire decision will undermine them. It's worth the effort.

JOB ANALYSIS

The first step in the recruitment process is to collect background information about the vacant position. If you have only a vague notion of the skills, capabilities and attitudes this position requires, you're going in blind. If you wait until the position is filled to determine this information, it's too late! The information collected during the job analysis will be used to produce a job description that will be of enormous value not only during the recruitment process, but after the employee has been hired as well.

Let's look at the example of a production expediter. One of the critical components of this position is that the incumbent advises his/her manager of anticipated production shortfalls as soon as possible. But in order to translate this specific job responsibility into terms that will be useful when recruiting and interviewing candidates, we must operationalize it. To develop an effective job analysis we need to know the answers to questions such as the following:

- Must the employee keep up-to-date schedules of work-in-progress or is this someone else's responsibility?
- If another person is responsible for the schedule, what kind of relationship is required to permit information to be exchanged smoothly between these two employees?
- Is the employee responsible for ensuring that the schedule is reliable and accurate if it is kept by someone else?
- Does the employee's ability to accurately predict anticipated shortfalls require experience with this particular production item and its peculiarities? Or is it possible to make the necessary predictions by studying a current schedule?
- Will the employee be expected to make decisions based on impression, intuition or facts?
- What kind of facts will be required? How will the employee obtain them and what skills will be needed to gather, organize and evaluate them?

Clearly, a wide variety of knowledge, skills and attitudes are required for a single job responsibility. It may seem daunting to gather the information required for a job analysis. But if you skip this step, you are likely to hire a candidate who lacks the necessary skills.

The job analysis focuses on what the employee must *input* to the job — whatever knowledge, skills and attitudes are required to handle the job effectively.

For example, the *knowledge* needed to do the job may include:

- knowing how to operate particular equipment.
- knowledge of and facility with technical terminology.
- specialized technical knowledge.
- knowledge of company procedures.

The *skills* required to do the job may include:

- communication skills.
- analytical skills.
- human relations skills.
- physical skills (e.g. co-ordination, vision, hearing).
- learning skills.

Similarly, the *attitudes* necessary to handle the job may include:

- readiness to relate to and communicate with supervisor and co-workers.
- self-confidence.
- self-respect.
- acceptance of one's role.
- stability and maturity.
- willingness to meet high standards of performance.

The information that is used in a job analysis may be gained through the following three methods, either alone or in combination:

Direct observation

A job analyst observes the actual work-in-progress, recording notes or questions regarding the specific knowledge, skills and attitudes necessary to perform the job.

Interviews

The analyst raises questions with current and past job holders, direct supervisors, managers and internal customers to evaluate their observations and compare the perceptions of everyone intimately involved in the success of the position.

Worksheets

The job holders complete a job analysis worksheet in which they record and analyze their own work over a pre-determined time frame.

This information must be interpreted by the job analyst to determine the correct performance standards and criteria for the effective performance of the position. Since these will by no means remain static, it is wise to review the appropriateness of the performance standards on an annual basis. An ideal time would be when the annual performance review is completed. Effective performance usually requires a balance between tasks and people, so standards should address these three aspects of achievement:

- Tasks: Specific performance standards.
- Team: Productive relationships within the work group, with internal vendors and customers as well as with external groups.
- Incumbent: Personal development goals, performance standards and contributions to the cohesiveness of the team.

Please refer to Exhibit 8.1 for a job analysis worksheet.

JOB DESCRIPTION

The analysis stage produces the raw material with which to produce a relevant job description. If you find yourself responding skeptically to the value of a job description, you're not alone. More job descriptions are produced than ever used. Why? Because if they are not the outcome of a job analysis, they will be irrelevant to the day-to-day management of your department. We need to take a fresh look at the necessary components of a useful job description. These would include:

- name of job holder
- title of the position
- objectives (or rationale for why the job exists)
- tasks/responsibilities to be performed
- performance standards (the level of excellence required)
- experience required (to perform at entry level)
- education required (to perform at entry level)
- compensation: salary grade and range.

Please refer to Exhibit 8.2 for a sample job description for the position of technologist. Notice that it is written to assist the candidate in his/her decision about working for your company. It spells out the key responsibilities rather than bureaucratic minutiae. The candidate will go into the interview with a clear knowledge of what is expected should he/she accept the position. The candidate will be able to engage the interviewer in useful dialog about how any previous experience might be applied to the key tasks and performance standards of the new job.

This job description format can be used as a guide in the employee orientation process. Similarly, on-the-job training can be tailored to the performance expectations/standards for this position. Finally, the job description can be used at every performance review or planning discussion. By linking the performance expectations to each key task, the discussion about performance successes and/or failures will be more relevant and professional and less likely to inspire negative reactions from personal failings. If the newly hired employee is to be part of a probationary review, the job description provides an ideal platform to address why he/she successfully passes through the gate — or why not.

FINDING GOOD CANDIDATES

Although the pool of qualified candidates is not always overflowing, the sources of candidates may be broader than you think. Consider the following avenues:

- newspapers: (a) national (b) local (c) campus
- radio and/or television: (a) national (b) local (daily) (c) local (weekly) (d) college and/or university stations
- job fairs: (a) single employer initiated event (b) multi-employer initiated event (c) industry association initiated event (d) third party agency initiated event
- internet: (a) employer's website (b) agency website (c) government agency website
- private employment agencies: (a) contingency (percentage of salary) (b) fee-based (fixed fee for time required)
- government and local support groups: (a) government-sponsored employment services (b) youth opportunity centers
- educational institutions: placement office: (a) high school (b) college (both public and private) (c) university graduates and

alumni (d) private technical schools/colleges (e) private business schools/colleges
- current employee populations: (a) job posting (internal advancement) (b) promotions (c) friends and/or relatives of employees.

No single source is likely to satisfy any employer's complete needs. Different positions call for different levels of experience and drive different recruiting strategies. Frequently, entry-level positions will be filled within your local community. As the complexity of the positions increase, so will the geographic boundaries of your search.

Regardless of your recruiting method, build a bridge to those resources. Like many events in the business world, relationships frequently make the difference between failure and success. If you plan to use an agency (government-sponsored or private), invite the consultant to visit your facility and present him or her with a thorough overview of your culture (including values, behavior, etc.), profiles of "good employees," and policies and procedures.

PREPARING FOR THE INTERVIEW

Planning for the interview is an important step that is often overlooked. The fast pace of business activities and the short lead time available to find candidates makes it tempting to prepare for the interview by trying to dig up an old job description from a dusty file. However, skipping this step in the process usually leads to problems down the road when a candidate is selected who:

- does not have the necessary skills to perform the job.
- has not shared all the relevant information about his/her background.
- will become a quick turnover statistic.
- may have a hidden agenda (and may, for example, agitate, spread discontent, embark on a personal "power trip," etc.)
- fits the interviewer's unconscious bias, leading to a poor hire decision.

Create a "picture" of the ideal candidate

Begin by reviewing the job description, which was designed to focus on the key responsibilities of the position. These responsibilities are not merely the preferred requirements of the job — they *are* the essential requirements. Building on the job analysis, the job description will identify the specific *knowledge*, *skills* and *attitudes* the candidates must have in order to be considered beyond the initial screening interview. Use the ideal candidate worksheet included as Exhibit 8.3.

THE INTERVIEW

A job interview is a time-consuming exercise, but one that can be valuable to both the candidate and the organization if conducted properly. It presents an opportunity for an exchange of information that will determine whether the candidate is suited to the job and whether the job is suited to the candidate.

▶ Time invested in a thorough interview will pay significant dividends in terms of public relations, reduced staff turnover, and a smoother transition on the part of the employee to the new position.

The structure for the interview process is outlined in the following eight steps. You will find sample questions and wordings in the detailed interviewing guide, included as Exhibit 8.4. The questions are designed to elicit thoughtful and candid responses to these sensitive questions, rather than brief yes/no answers.

- Greet candidate.
- Ask preliminary questions.
- Describe the organization, its culture and the position.
- Ask in-depth questions.
- Provide further information.
- Invite candidate to ask questions.
- Ask final questions.
- Wrap up.

Greet candidate

This sets a friendly, respectful tone for the interview. Begin by expressing appreciation that the candidate has attended the interview. Explain that the purpose of the interview is to exchange information so that both parties can make an informed decision about employment opportunities. Stress that the organization is looking for a mutual fit — that the candidate has to fit with the organization's culture and the organization has to fit with the candidate's needs. Briefly describe the interview format and point out that you will be taking notes.

Ask preliminary questions

Ask detailed and open-ended questions regarding the candidate's work history, skills, education/training, career goals and personal work style.

Work history
Ask the candidate to identify key responsibilities, and most and least enjoyable aspects of each job, beginning with the most recent or current position. Find out why the candidate wants to leave the position and whether the current employer is aware of this desire. Ask whether the decision to leave originated with the employer, the candidate, or whether it was mutual.

In reviewing the responses to these questions, the interviewer should watch for and ask the candidate to explain any:
- inconsistencies with resume.
- unexplained gaps in employment.
- inconsistencies in answers. (For example, if the candidate says she left one job for "more responsibility" and her subsequent job doesn't appear to have more responsibility, then ask her to explain the discrepancy.)

Job-specific skills
These questions are designed to determine whether the candidate's job-related skills match those that have been identified (through the job analysis and job description) as required to successfully perform the job.

Education/training
The candidate's resume will outline his/her education and training. The questions, therefore, should focus on determining the candidate's inclination to work hard for what he/she wants.

Career goals
These questions are intended to provide the interviewer with some insight into the candidate's degree of satisfaction with his or her career choice. For example, asking what responsibilities the candidate would like to have in his/her next job and why, affords an opportunity to compare what the candidate *wants* with what the organization has to *offer*. Be leery of pursuing a candidate who wants responsibilities that are quite different to those required by the position. For example, a candidate who expresses a desire for supervisory responsibilities would not be a good long-term hire for a job in which there are none.

Personal work style
The answers to these questions will provide some insight into the fit between the candidate's personal style and the culture of the organization. Questions concerning relationships with co-workers, supervisors and team members will be revealing, as will questions regarding the candidate's response to criticism, frustrations and various management styles.

Describe the organization, its culture and the position

Offer information to the candidate regarding the history of the organization, its culture and the position.

▶ Hiring mistakes are as likely to result from candidates accepting the wrong position as they are from employers choosing the wrong candidate.

Use this opportunity to sell the organization and the position to the candidate, but don't oversell. Be candid; just as candidates have downsides, so do opportunities — mentioning these up front demonstrates your sincerity and may avoid an inappropriate hiring.

Some interviewers offer information to the candidate at the beginning of the interview. They believe it can save time in cases where the candidate learns of information that makes the job unattractive and therefore withdraws from consideration. But with proper screening, that situation should rarely occur. There are two benefits to waiting for the candidate to answer the main interview questions before providing the candidate with information about the job. First, it prevents the candidate from deliberately tailoring answers to match the job requirements. And secondly, if the candidate is highly desirable, it allows you to stress those specific job benefits that you know to be important to the candidate.

Ask in-depth questions

Now that considerable information exchange has taken place, it is time to get down to specifics. Ask the candidate questions regarding the position and the company to give you an idea as to how well the candidate listened to what you had to say. Assess whether the answers make sense, given the information that has already been exchanged. Decide whether the candidate understands the job requirements and has a realistic sense of how easily he/she could perform the job. Find out whether the candidate is aware of any differences in culture between your organization and the candidate's former workplace. Decide how well you think the candidate will adapt to your organization's culture.

Ask the candidate specific questions regarding his/her current compensation package and expectations. Generally, it is wise to avoid hiring someone whose previous compensation package was more than 10 to 15 percent greater than what you plan to offer. Often such candidates, if they do accept the position, will be less than satisfied with the compensation and will ultimately look elsewhere for employment, making them a short-term solution to the hiring problem.

Provide further information for the candidate

Provide information to the candidate regarding the compensation program for the position, and explain the organization's probationary period.

Invite candidate to ask questions

Now it is the candidate's turn to ask you questions. Answer these to the best of your ability. Be open and forthright. If you cannot answer a question, say so.

Take note of the questions that the candidate asks. Are they good questions? Do they show an interest in the job? Do they demonstrate that the candidate was listening while you spoke? Do they show that the candidate can *think*?

Ask final questions

Ask the candidate about the people listed as references. These questions are designed to allow the candidate to share with you and explain the circumstances surrounding any potentially negative comments that might be forthcoming. It is also a good opportunity to back-check the candidate's earlier answers. Be alert to any inconsistencies between the information provided in answer to these questions and that provided earlier in the interview.

Next, ask the candidate some questions about his/her job search. These questions are designed to give you an idea of the urgency of the search from the candidate's perspective, as well as the legitimacy of the search.

Finally, ask whether the candidate is still interested in being considered for the position. The answers to the three final questions in Exhibit 8.4 will provide a good reality check. They will also serve to highlight what the candidate thinks is really important.

Wrap up

Indicate that the interview is over. Let the candidate know what to expect in terms of the next step. Tell the candidate whom to contact if he/she needs additional questions answered. And thank the candidate for his/her time and interest.

TIPS FOR AWKWARD SITUATIONS

If the screening process is less than adequate, you may find yourself interviewing a candidate who proves to be missing one or more required skills for the position. Should you "go through the motions" and complete the remaining steps of the interview when you are certain the decision will be negative? Generally, I suggest that in such cases you curtail the interview. If the candidate is a potential fit for another position that is (or is expected to become) open, you could make a statement such as the following:

> "At this point, I would normally ask for your questions about the job. But with your interests in mind, I don't see that as a productive use of our time today. The job definitely requires a candidate with proven skills in vector drives and as we have just confirmed, your background has not yet provided you with an opportunity to acquire those skills. It seems, however, that you might well be qualified for [another job title]. Would you be interested in being considered for that type of position?" If the answer is yes, arrange a referral to another department.
> If no, thank candidate for time and interest.

If, however, it is clear that the candidate has little potential fit for other jobs in your organization, then it is best to curtail the interview in the following manner:

> "At this point, I would normally ask for your questions about the job. But with your interests in mind, I don't see that as a productive use of our time today. The job definitely requires a candidate with proven skills in vector drives and as we have just confirmed, your background has not yet provided you with an opportunity to acquire those skills. I want to thank you for your time and interest. I've enjoyed talking with you today and regret that our screening process did not highlight the situation before now. However, I would be less than honest if I completed our interview and led you to believe that you might be offered this position."

Allow the candidate an opportunity to respond. If he/she expresses anger, apologize once again for any inconvenience and empathize with any disappointment.

You or your organization may choose to complete all interviews as a matter of policy. While there may be some legitimate reasons for doing so, you may also be giving your candidates false hopes. You must decide on the procedure that will provide you with the most benefits from a public relations and legal perspective.

There is one situation in which it is advisable to complete the interview, despite obvious limitations on the part of the candidate. That is when the candidate is being sponsored by some influential person. For example, you are interviewing the vice-president's nephew. Unless you know for certain that your judgment about his qualifications will be the sole factor in the hiring decision, it is best to continue with the remainder of the interview and seek advice on how to handle this situation after the nephew has left your worksite.

POST-INTERVIEW TASK LIST

Immediately following each interview, complete the following tasks:

- Review your interview notes. Make sure they are complete. Finish any incomplete sentences or ideas.
- Outline the candidate's highlights — those attributes that make him/her a desirable candidate.
- Outline any concerns you may have and indicate how you would address them.
- Compare to other candidates and assign rankings.
- Draw a conclusion as to whether the candidate is worth pursuing to the next step.

Making and communicating the decision

Once you have completed all your interviews, compare each candidate with your definition of the "ideal candidate." By comparing each candidate's qualifications with your pre-established requirements you will be less likely to be distracted by personal biases or other factors. Next, check your post-interview notes to see how you ranked this candidate in relation to the others interviewed for this position. Chances are good that this process will have narrowed down your choice of candidates to two or three. Decide whether to recommend a job offer to the candidates on your short list or whether to put them on hold, pending other developments.

In some organizations, the selection process deteriorates after the interview stage. Poor follow-up and untimely or inappropriate post-interview communications can result in a poor start to an otherwise positive employee experience. The following guidelines will help ensure that the last part of the selection process is as professional as the first part.

- In all post-interview communications, specify positive things about each candidate. Even the weakest candidate is certain to have strengths. Emphasize these, even when informing the candidate that no offer will be extended.
- In cases where candidates are "on hold," keep them informed of their status. Waiting is stressful for the candidate, and many organizations lose good candidates who accept jobs elsewhere because they assume the worst when they hear nothing following their interview.
- State the decision clearly in written communications. Some organizations cushion the news in such confusing language that candidates find it difficult to determine whether or not they are being offered a job.
- Once your decision is made, communicate with all candidates quickly so that they hear the results from you first.
- Coordinate communications with other departments to ensure that appropriate follow-up takes place on schedule.
- As a courtesy to your candidates, take steps to ensure that they are not left hanging, even when follow-up is officially the responsibility of someone else. A candidate who's told that someone else "dropped the ball" will find that of little consolation if he or she has been waiting by the phone or the mailbox for word of a decision.

EXHIBIT 8.1

JOB ANALYSIS WORKSHEET

A. Date: _____
   Interviewer: _____
   Person interviewed: _____

B. Present job title: _____
   Suggested job title: _____
   Name of manager: _____
   Job title of manager: _____
   Department: _____
   Job location: _____
   Number of employees on this job: _____

C. Describe the PRIMARY duties that the employee or employees on this job perform daily. If important duties are performed at less frequent intervals, describe and state the frequency of performance.

   _____
   _____
   _____
   _____
   _____
   _____

   Describe the SECONDARY duties that the employee on this job performs at periodic intervals, such as weekly, monthly, quarterly, etc., and state frequency of performance.

   _____
   _____
   _____
   _____
   _____
   _____

Describe any other duties that an employee on this job may perform.

_____
_____
_____
_____
_____

D. List the computer and office equipment used.

_____
_____
_____
_____
_____

List the production machines and equipment used.

_____
_____
_____
_____
_____

E. Describe the working conditions. Refer to all legislated, industry and company requirements.

_____
_____
_____
_____
_____

F. Describe the formal education or its equivalent required for satisfactory performance of this job.

_____
_____
_____
_____
_____

Specify the special training or education necessary before an employee is assigned to this job or the training necessary immediately after assignment.

_____
_____
_____
_____
_____

Describe any job experience required and indicate the time needed to obtain such experience and state whether the experience may take place in this organization or elsewhere.

_____
_____
_____
_____
_____

G. Describe the proximity, extent and closeness of supervision required by an employee on this job. To what degree does the immediate supervisor outline methods to be followed, results to be accomplished, check work progress, handle exceptional cases, check job performance?

_____
_____
_____
_____
_____

Describe the kind of supervision the employee or employees on this job give to the other employees. What degree of accountability exists for results in terms of methods, work accomplished and personnel?

_____
_____
_____
_____
_____

How many employees are supervised directly? Indirectly?

_____
_____
_____
_____
_____

In a team-based environment, describe the role and authority of team leaders and team members.

_____
_____
_____
_____
_____

H. Describe the responsibility for accuracy. What is the seriousness of error on this job? Who would discover it? State whether errors affect the work of the employee making the mistake, others in the same department, people in other departments, and/or persons outside the organization.

_____
_____
_____
_____
_____

I. Describe the responsibility for confidential data. State the type of confidential data handled (personnel, salaries, policies, business secrets, etc.)

_____
_____
_____
_____
_____

J. Describe the kind of personal contacts made by an employee as he/she performs this job. Specify whether these contacts involve people in the department, in other departments, and/or outside the organization. Describe the importance of these contacts to the organization.

_____
_____
_____
_____
_____

K. Describe the complexity of the job. What degree of independent action is permitted the employee? What decisions is the employee permitted to make?

_____
_____
_____
_____
_____

L. List any unusual physical requirements of this job, such as vision, strength, etc.

_____
_____
_____
_____
_____

EXHIBIT 8.2

SAMPLE JOB DESCRIPTION

TECHNOLOGIST POSITION

Name of job holder:
Current date:
Position title: Technologist
Objectives: To provide repairs and maintenance to electronic equipment.

1. Tasks/responsibilities
- Develop schedule for routine and preventative maintenance for equipment within your control, including:
    - Variable frequency drive, vector drives, server drives and DC drives
    - Level, motion pressure and temperature sensors
    - Transducers and signal converters
    - Load cells and integrators on weigh scales
    - A/B intelligent motion controllers and Siemens PLCs
- Perform routine and preventative maintenance in accordance with schedule.
- Repair equipment as required.
- Analyze and solve problems encountered in operations of machines.

2. Performance standards
- No downtime resulting from non-performance of routine or preventative maintenance.
- Repairs conducted in timely and cost-efficient manner.
- Documentation is complete.

3. Experience required
- 5 years' experience in industrial electronics.

4. Education required
- Electronics Technologist certificate, computer literacy, knowledge of instrumentation.

5. Compensation
- This is a Grade 10 position in our job evaluation program that equates to a hiring range of $35,000 +/- 3 percent and a performance-based salary band of $35,000 – $50,000 – $65,000.

    All company benefit plans are applicable, including ten statutory holidays and three weeks' vacation during the first five years of continuous employment.

EXHIBIT 8.3

IDEAL CANDIDATE WORKSHEET

TECHNOLOGIST POSITION

Job title: Technologist
Date:
Prepared by:

Core Responsibilities

1)
2)
3)

To be able to perform the above responsibilities to the level established in the Performance Standards, the "ideal" candidate MUST have the following:

    Knowledge:
    1)
    2)
    3)

    Skills:
    1)
    2)
    3)

    Attitudes:
    1)
    2)
    3)

EXHIBIT 8.4

DETAILED INTERVIEWING GUIDE

TECHNOLOGIST POSITION

Candidate name:
Date:
Interviewer name:

1. Greet candidate
- Express appreciation for attending interview.
- Ice-breaker (weather, ease of finding the place, etc.).
- Explain purpose of interview.
  Note that the interview will involve an exchange of information: "We want to learn more about you and we want you to learn more about us so that we may both make an informed decision about employment opportunities."
- Discuss success factors at organization:
  - Job-related skills
  - "Fit" with organization culture (noting that fit is a two-way street)
- State that the interview format will allow you, the interviewer, to ask a series of questions which will give the candidate an opportunity to provide information about himself and his work. Let the candidate know that he/she will have the opportunity to ask questions.
- Mention that you will be taking notes.

2. Ask preliminary questions
A: Work History, current (or most recent) position
- What are your key responsibilities?
- For which accomplishment would you most like to be remembered?
- What did you most enjoy about the job you did? Can you explain why?
- What did you least enjoy about the job you did? Why was that?

- Why do you want to leave this position? (Or why did you leave this position?) Is your employer aware of your desire to leave? (If yes) Did the decision to leave originate with you or with your employer, or was it mutual? (If no) Will your employer be surprised? Do you think your employer will try to stop you from leaving? How? What could they do that would entice you to stay?

Repeat these questions for all jobs in the past eight years or (if the candidate has had only one job for the past eight years) for at least three positions. Be sure to clarify start and end dates for each position.

B. Job-Specific Skills
- Confirm certification as electrical and electronics technologist (place of certification).
- What computer programs have you regularly used in your past job? Give me an example of how you used them.
- Tell me about a particularly difficult repair problem that you had to solve. How did you go about it?
- What kind of maintenance would you recommend performing on a variable frequency drive? Why?
- What safety precautions do you follow when you perform repair work on temperature sensors? Why?
- Tell me about a challenging project that was assigned to you. How did you tackle it?
- In the context of your technical skills, what do you consider to be your strongest assets? Why? Give me an example of when you have used these assets recently.
- Again, in the context of your technical skills, in what areas would you like to enhance your skills? Why? How would this have helped you in your current (last) job?

C. Education/Training
- Tell me a bit about your educational background — what did you study? How were your grades?
- How did you get your training for your skills as a technologist? (On the job/through an institution?)

- What do you do now to stay current in your trade?
- What do you do now to develop yourself?

D. Career Goals
- Why did you decide to become a technologist?
- Looking back, do you believe you made the right choice? Why?
- If you were to go back and start over again, would you still become a technologist? Why? (Why not? If not, what would you rather be doing?)
- Describe the responsibilities you would like to have in your next job. Why would you like to do these things?
- Do you have a longer-term career goal? If so, what is it? What steps are you taking to achieve it?

E. Personal Work Style
- Of the various positions that you have held, which job did you enjoy the most? Why?
- Which did you enjoy the least? Why?
- Of the different managers/supervisors for whom you have worked, which one enabled you to do your best work? Describe that manager's supervisory style.
- Describe a management style that would make it difficult for you to do your job. Has this ever happened to you? If so, how did you deal with it?
- Tell me about a time when you were frustrated in your job. Why was this frustrating? How did the frustration manifest itself? What did you do about it?
- Tell me about a time when your work has been criticized. How did you respond to the criticism?
- Tell me about a time when you have had to work as part of a team. Did you enjoy it? What role did you play on the team? (Leader, participant?) Were you able to influence others on the team? How? Which do you prefer, working as part of a team or working on your own? Why?
- When did you last have a performance review? What areas did your supervisor highlight as your having done particularly well? What suggestions did your supervisor make to help you improve your performance? Do you think these were valid suggestions? Why? Why not?

- If I were to ask your co-workers about you, what do you think they might say? Why?
- Describe what you would consider to be the ideal company to work for. Why are these characteristics important to you?

Describe the organization, its culture and the position

A. History of the Company
- When it was started
- Ownership
- Nature of the business
- Historical growth
- Future plans

B. Culture of the Company
- Teamwork
- Hardworking
- Very busy
- (etc.)

C. The Position
- Describe the key responsibilities.
- Describe how performance will be measured.
- Explain why the position exists (replacement, new, etc.)
- Explain the training that will be provided to a new employee.
- Describe the management style of the supervisor.

Ask in-depth questions

A. The Position
- Now that I have described the position, does it interest you? (If yes) Why? (If no, probe for the reason and unless it can be turned around, thank the candidate for his/her time and terminate the interview.)
  What do you think would be your biggest challenge in performing this job? Why? How would you overcome it?
- From your past experience, what do you think would help you the most in performing this job? How?
- What additional skills do you think you would need to learn to be able to do this job well? How would you develop those skills?

- How long do you think it would take you to become familiar with this job?
- (If the candidate has previously expressed a longer-term career goal...) How would this job fit in with your longer-term career goal that we spoke about earlier?

B. The Company
- Is this a company that you would like to work for?
- How does the culture here compare with what you're used to? What do you see as some of the major similarities? Major differences?
- What difficulties do you think you might have in adjusting to our culture? How would you overcome them?

C. Compensation
- What is (was) your current (most recent) salary?
- When did you last have a salary change?
- How much of an increase did you get at that time?
- When do you anticipate your next salary increase will be? (Assuming candidate is employed.)
- What kind of a benefit package do you have? (Get details.)
- Is it company-paid or do you contribute to the cost?
- How much vacation are you entitled to?
- Do you participate in a bonus plan or an incentive plan? (If yes) How much did you earn under the plan last year?
- Is there a pension plan? Is it contributory? When does it vest?
- Are there any other significant components to your compensation package? If so, what?

Provide further information
A. Compensation
- Provide information about the compensation program for the position, including:
    Salary range
    Benefit package details and cost (provide brochure, if possible)
    Vacation
    Other elements
    First review

- Explain the company's probationary period to the candidate.

Invite candidate to ask questions
Allow the candidate to ask questions about the position and the company. If the candidate asks a question that you cannot answer, an appropriate response might be, "That's a good question, but one that I can't answer at this time. It might be more appropriate at a second interview." Or, "Let's pursue that if we go forward with an offer."

Ask final questions
Just a few more questions…

A. References
- Who would you provide as references? (Take note of their names and relationship to the candidate.)
- What do you expect your references will say about you?

B. Job Search
- Tell me how you're going about your job search.
- How long have you been looking?
- Have you had any offers? (If yes) Why haven't you accepted it/them?
- Do you have anything that is quite active now?
- If you were offered a position here, when would you be available to start?

C. This Job
- After all that we've discussed, are you still interested in being considered for this position? What most attracts you? Do you see any disadvantages to it? What?
- What additional information or activities would you like to see before you would be able to make a decision, if this position were offered to you?
- If you wanted me to remember three things about you, what would they be?

Wrap up

Let the candidate know that the interview is over by saying, "Well, that concludes our interview."

If you are exceedingly interested in this candidate, you might sum up how fine an opportunity this position is for the candidate. Point out the synergies between the position, the company and the candidate's goals. Otherwise, just proceed as follows.

Explain the next steps in the process and the time frame for each step. Indicate when the candidate can reasonably expect to hear from you. Be realistic in your assessment of when you will get back to the candidate. Don't promise a time commitment you know you can't meet. Allow for the unexpected to delay your process!

Indicate whether you will be contacting the candidate's references, and allow the candidate an opportunity to alert references before your call.

Tell the candidate whom to contact if he/she needs additional questions answered.

Thank candidate for his/her time and interest — warmly. Don't worry that your warmth will be interpreted as a job offer! A lack of warmth, especially after a thorough interview, will be interpreted as bad public relations. You could say, "It's been a pleasure talking with you today. We are (I am) pleased that you were interested enough in our position to spend this much time with us (me) today. Thank you."

TAKE ACTION!

1. Commit to making the best choice when it comes to employee selection, not necessarily the most expedient choice.
2. Collect background information about the vacant position through a thorough job analysis.
3. Use the data collected in the job analysis to create a relevant job description (without focusing on minutiae) and determine what information is needed from the candidate.
4. Explore all avenues for a broad source of candidates.
5. Prepare for the interview by creating a "picture" of the ideal candidate.
6. Conduct the interview, allowing for an *exchange* of information.
7. Review interview notes; outline candidate's highlights, note any concerns, rank candidate and decide whether this candidate is worth pursuing to the next step.
8. Evaluate the data and make a decision about the candidate's qualifications.
9. Advise candidate either that 1) a job offer will follow, or 2) he or she was not the most qualified candidate.
10. Coordinate communications with other departments to make sure that the appropriate follow-up takes place on schedule.

9
TRAINING AND MANAGING SUPERVISORS

Communication is the key to remaining union-free and front-line supervisors are the "guardians of the key." As can be seen from Table 9.1, the supervisor is the prime element in communicating up, down and laterally throughout the organization. It lists both *upward* communication techniques — how employees can get through to management — and *downward* communication techniques — how managers can reach employees.

These represent both formal (such as suggestion boxes) and informal (the "grapevine") communication channels, and senior management must heed the messages coming from both. When implementing a Positive Employee Relations program, we must make very sure that supervisors are well-equipped to communicate the proper message. Have the front-line supervisors (and the employees they lead, for that matter) been told of management's feelings concerning unionization? Have we explained to our front-line supervisors that the company's policy is to nurture an atmosphere of *individual* employee recognition in which unionization is not considered by employees as either a need or a benefit? Have we emphasized the supervisor's role in identifying trouble-spots and alerting management to the need for positive corrective action (as opposed to reaction)? Have we trained the supervisors to treat employees as though they were our customers?

TABLE 9.1 — Employee Communication Techniques

Upward Communication Techniques	Downward Communication Techniques
• performance appraisal • grievance or complaint procedures • informal inquiries or focus group discussions with employees • front-line supervisor • the "grapevine" • counseling • formal meetings • suggestion system • perception surveys • question-and-answer column in company magazine or newsletter • gripe boxes • telephone hotline • "Let's Talk©" program (see Appendix D) • lunch with the plant/office manager • job postings (to which employees apply)) • job interviews • exit interviews	• front-line supervisor • department or company-wide meetings • employee publications • bulletin boards • pay envelope inserts • letters to employees • posters • multimedia presentations • annual reports • public address messages • news stories in local press, television or radio • job postings (management's willingness to share job openings with employees and offering them opportunities for growth) • email, internet, intranet • town hall meetings

TRAINING IS ESSENTIAL TO WINNING SUPERVISORY COMMITMENT

But why should front-line supervisors be committed to the cause of union-free management? Frequently required to make difficult people-related decisions, they are often attracted to the certainties of a union/collective agreement. On the surface, it appears to afford a base from which to make easy decisions on day-to-day issues. Furthermore, many supervisors retain feelings of loyalty toward the group or team they have recently left. This problem of confused identity seriously detracts from the front-line supervisor's commitment and subsequent ability to carry out the organization's Positive Employee Relations program.

So now we are back where we started. Before senior management can ensure that front-line supervisors will carry out the organization's Positive Employee Relations program, the approval — both intellectual and emotional — of the front-line supervisory group must be obtained. The following strategies can help:

Involve supervisors in the process

Invite front-line supervisors to participate in the decision-making process leading to the development and implementation of your organization's Positive Employee Relations program.

Ensure that senior management will lead

Ensure that senior management fully appreciates the social and psychological implications of the Positive Employee Relations program that they are asking the supervisory group to implement. Once understood, the senior leadership team must demonstrate behaviors in their relationships and dealings with the supervisory group that reinforce what they wish the supervisors to do. If supervisors are to be leaders of employees, they must demonstrate qualities that inspire followers, show patience in listening to an employee's ideas or concerns, be prudent in their decision-making capabilities, and so forth. The supervisors' next-level managers must not only have these same qualities but the ability to bring them out of the supervisors and reinforce the very good examples of leadership.

Ensure adequate supervisory skills

By using a training needs analysis and/or a supervisory needs inventory (refer to Exhibit 9.1), determine the existing supervisory skill level and immediately reinforce with an ongoing training program. Under no circumstances assume that the supervisory group has skills to meet the union-free objective, even if you have the group's avowed commitment to that objective.

Ensure broad-based training for supervisors

Ensure that supervisory training encompasses a broad range of information and skill development. As a bare minimum, the program should spell out the company's policies and procedures as they relate to employee relations, human rights, problem solving, discipline, counseling, interviewing, listening and so forth. (Refer to Exhibit 9.2 for an outline of a supervisory training program that addresses Positive Employee Relations.)

Keeping an organization union-free requires an extensive plan, usually in the form of the organization's policies and procedures. And, for human resource policies, a training program should be attached to each one. Do not expect a supervisor to know how to conduct a corrective action interview just because the organization has a policy on performance management.

▶ Every human resource policy should have a training program attached to it.

In training supervisors, it is important that the training be relevant to actual day-to-day situations. Trainers are often hired to conduct "packaged" supervisory skills seminars, but this approach is more often than not counter-productive. The learning content should be specific to your organization. Training should be continual — one work day a month, on company time — and take place in an environment conducive to learning.

▶ All training, whether managerial or supervisory, should be designed to change behavior and/or upgrade skills.

However, the responsibility for becoming an effective supervisor or manager rests with the individual and not with the training department. Newly hired employees and employees in entry-level jobs can legitimately expect supervisors and facilitators to train them. But when people become supervisors and managers, they take on the responsibility of development — for themselves and their work group. The organization, of course, can help by providing courses and resources.

One approach I have used when called in by management to train supervisors is to distribute a training and development needs analysis prior to the training session (see Exhibit 9.1). Another approach, which is less subjective and hence attracts a higher credibility rating, is to use a behavioral assessment of supervisory and management proficiency. This process and the benefits of competency-based training are explained in Exhibit 9.3.

Some management groups prefer to select a packaged training program despite drawbacks such as limited relevancy and transferability. There are many suitable programs available through universities, training associations and local colleges. If the training program is to deal with fundamental concepts and principles, the packaged course is probably a good initial approach. If, however, you wish to change behaviors and reinforce this behavioral change in the workplace, you will need more than packaged training.

COMMUNICATION IS PARAMOUNT

In recent studies of several union-free companies, the quality of front-line supervisors' communications skills was found to be the most important consideration in their Positive Employee Relations program. The following are some of the specific measures taken by various companies to improve and/or support their supervisors' skills:

- Procedures were established to distribute all announcements to the supervisors before general release to the employee population. This ensured that supervisors were aware of the communication before it was circulated to their staff, and allowed time for the message to be clarified.
- A vice-president established a continual series of letters to supervisors. These letters covered various aspects of management, including how to manage the company's resources: people, facilities, money, material and time. Special emphasis was placed on the need to maintain respect for the individual and to encourage an environment of trust in the workplace.
- Communications professionals advocated weekly 15-minute informal meetings on work-related topics for the supervisor and his/her group. These sessions were informal and allowed both supervisors and employees to discuss any work-related topic they wanted.
- Human resource policy and benefit booklets were distributed and discussed personally with each employee by their supervisor. This reinforced each employee's right to approach the supervisor about anything that affected the employee's duties, security or future.

But supervisors are not clones. In the companies studied, it was recognized that a variety of techniques was needed to keep the many supervisory messages accurate and on target. These included company publications and intranet, bulletin boards, handbooks, video tapes and other media. These also had the effect of reinforcing and supporting the supervisor's role in communications.

LINKING COMMUNICATIONS TO SUPERVISORY TRAINING

One way to link communications to supervisory training is to create a 12-month communications schedule. Decide on 12 issues — such as Positive

Employee Relations, employee counseling, benefit programs, grievance procedures — then focus on one each month (see Table 9.2). Let that topic be the theme for bulletin board materials, letters to the employees (mailed or included in pay envelopes), the intranet "link-of-the-month" and in-house magazines. Give it full coverage for that month.

TABLE 9.2 — Training and Communications Schedule

Month	Supervisory Training Topic Conduct *first* Monday of the month	Employee Communication Topic Implement *third* Monday of the month
January	Maintaining our union-free environment through Positive Employee Relations.	Employee Charter of Rights.
February	Performance appraisal: guidelines for evaluating employee performace.	Employee performance reviews and self-development plans.
March	Dynamics of face-to-face communications.	"Sherborne employees are #1 with us!"
April	Problem solving and issue resolution.	"It's easy for you (employee) to air your concerns."
May	Training and coaching: steps to improve performance.	How on-the-job training ensures job knowledge and skills, and provides employees with opportunities for advancement at Sherborne.
June	Conducting effective meetings and conferences.	Department meetings and how they benefit both employees and Sherborne.

Month	Supervisory Training Topic Conduct *first* Monday of the month	Employee Communication Topic Implement *third* Monday of the month
July	Wage and salary administration.	How the Sherborne wage/salary scales are developed (job evaluation, surveys, internal equity) and this year's salary structure
August	Benefit plans: their design and administration.	What the Sherborne benefit plan means to you and your family in case of illness, accident, retirement or disability.
September	Conducting employee salary/merit reviews.	The new salary structure has now been approved by the Sherborne management committee. This month, your supervisor will discuss your individual salary program.
October	Conduct annual employee perception survey.	Provide your feedback on how successful Sherborne has been as an employer.
November	Product training: how we make our products, new processes, new applications and new customers for next year.	The "widget" and how you have made it world famous.
December	Annual company-wide review. What we did well, where and how we need to improve, etc.	Annual re-orientation program and holiday greetings for all employees, spouses, partners.

To involve, inform and educate supervisors, send a summary (similar to a press release) to all of them so that they will be prepared to talk about that month's topic with their employees. This summary becomes the basis for a supervisory meeting at the beginning of each month. Supervisors are asked to prepare questions on the topic. At this meeting, the supervisors' input is combined with that of more senior management. The result is a newsletter distributed to all employees two weeks later. It reinforces the original training material and incorporates the supervisors' opinions (opinions that supervisors are gratified to know are valued). Management will then be making intelligent use of its most-often overlooked resource: *its supervisors*.

An extension of this communications technique is now being used by a manufacturing company with 65 supervisors and 800 employees. It was developed in response to a request by supervisors who were required to conduct performance reviews every six months. The supervisors wanted ice-breakers. "How do you start a discussion when the employee knows the real agenda is job performance?" they asked. The answer was a one-page summary of the combined news releases, which was sent to the supervisors every six months with the employee appraisal forms. It provided a script for opening up discussions that more professionally set the stage for either salary reviews and/or individual performance.

▶ The traditional organization, which has not yet developed a planned communications program for supervisors, could begin by discussing various topics in the employee handbook or human resource policy manual.

It is critical to get involvement from the supervisors, and this is best done with supervisors at a roundtable discussion talking about their needs and the needs of the group. The resolution of these needs/concerns becomes the basis for co-ordinated supervisory communications throughout the organization.

Having set the precedent...

In some jurisdictions the beginning of a union organizing campaign puts a freeze on management's ability to freely manage its "people systems." The presence of the union drive causes management to limit itself to long-standing practices or precedents. By following the schedule outlined in Table 9.2 when the company is non-union, management can ensure that communications events occur on a regular basis — for example, every quarter. Then, each of those communications events (such as wage and salary administration, employee perception survey, and so on) can be conducted during the union campaign because they have already been established as practices for your company.

SUPERVISORY RESPONSE TO AN ORGANIZING DRIVE

The prospect of unionization may be attractive to some employees because they do not know management's opinion (and management has not established a credible pro-people philosophy). This is another instance in which the supervisor's role as *key communicator* is vital. The supervisor can make sure employees are aware of these six facts:

1. That union fines for infractions of union rules (as outlined in the union's constitution) may cut into their paychecks.
2. That union insistence on promotion by seniority may be a disadvantage to employees who are young or recently hired, highly motivated and/or highly skilled, as well as candidates from minority groups.
3. That in a "union shop" all employees become union members whether they wish to or not.
4. When using the Ontario model, that signing a union card does not constitute a vote for unionization; but that if it comes to a vote, *failure to vote is a vote for unionization*. In other jurisdictions, this may be reversed, and signing a card is a *de facto* vote.
5. That unions tend to protect and encourage mediocrity.
6. That group interests transcend individual interests, and that the employee loses the freedom to be an individual.

Yet unions appeal to employees' needs for job security; for someone to listen and attend to their grievances; for reasonable remuneration, benefits and regular wage increases. *These are needs that responsible leadership should satisfy as a matter of course, if only to gain the highest yield from its investment in human resources.*

▶ To maintain a union-free environment, concerned managers will need to adopt the organizer's pro-people approach, and train front-line supervisors to make this approach work for them. Treat employees like internal customers.

Union organizers looking for a weak spot may woo the supervisor in an attempt to scuttle the company's Positive Employee Relations program. If the supervisor has been trained to lead people as well as manage production, and if the supervisor has been genuinely accepted into the ranks of leadership and not left to flounder in that limbo between workforce and management, then all may be well. But if the supervisor decides that managing unionized workers would simplify a job that he/she really has no clear notion of how to perform, then the supervisor will be an asset to the union cause, even if the supervisor's stance is neutral!

Managers in a union-free environment often avoid training supervisors in labor relations, which is quite unfair to both the supervisor and the organization. All supervisors should be familiar with the applicable labor legislation in their jurisdiction. They should know what they can and cannot say to employees during an organizing campaign, and what should have been said and done before relations between management and employees deteriorated.

Organizing campaign training exercise

In customized supervisory training programs I have used a unique "war games" exercise designed to encourage supervisors to think about potential employee relations problems and the probable strategies a union would use in response to these problems. Using information gathered during this exercise, the supervisors develop a tailored approach to maintaining their union-free status.

On the last day of a three-day leadership development program, newly appointed supervisors are divided into three teams and sent into separate training rooms. Group A takes the role of the company's senior management team, Group B becomes a union organizing team and Group C an employee team. Their assignments are summarized in Exhibit 9.4.

The war game takes two to three hours to complete. Separately, each team records their strategies, observations and comments. When they reassemble as a total training group, each team is given the opportunity — through their spokesperson — to present its findings to the entire group.

Typically, the strategy of the management team members (Group A) is to give a rundown of all the normal housekeeping issues that it had introduced. They address hygiene issues, such as the newly paved parking lot, the up-to-date employee handbook and recreation activities (for example, the Christmas party). And when all is said and done, they reject the premise of the whole exercise by stating that they don't really think there is a union drive anyway and that "things are pretty good around here." Does that sound familiar?

Meanwhile, the employees' team (Group C) has made a long list of grievances and the union team (Group B) has come up with a ten-page strategy for capitalizing on this dissatisfaction. After a lunch break, we take each issue raised during the morning's war game and talk it through. As a group, the supervisors develop strategies for eliminating the reasons why employees might support a union. It is the beginning of a Positive Employee Relations program.

Do not accept poor performance — from anyone!

But what if, despite all attempts to prepare the supervisor to become an effective key to communicating your pro-people philosophy, the supervisor is still using the "I'll show them who is boss and to hell with the soft approach." What can management do? This poses a very serious problem. If the supervisor has not responded to his/her manager's advice, counsel and appraisal, the next-level manager may be faced with an issue of termination. However, this should not be considered until every reasonable attempt has been made to redirect the supervisor's behavior. Please note that transferring the problem to another department is just relocating, not resolving, the situation. From my experience, the likelihood of demotion working is very limited. It is not a strategy I would recommend without knowing the supervisor's frame of mind.

COMPETENCY-BASED MANAGEMENT DEVELOPMENT

Training is a process, not a product. Its success is measured by improved performance in the workplace, not by the acquisition of new concepts and procedures in a workshop.

In technical courses and programs that teach specific "how-to" skills and procedures, trainers can observe and measure the transfer of training (improved performance) from workshop to workplace. Moreover, there are established performance standards, and the facilitator, trainee and trainee's supervisor have a common stake in seeing that these standards and expectations are met.

When we enter the area of supervisory training and management development, we face a number of challenges and seemingly impossible tasks relating to course design and delivery. However, these deserve a high priority. When it comes to successfully implementing a Positive Employee Relations program, there is no position of greater impact than that of the front-line supervisor.

▶ Front-line supervisors are the "living values" of the organization as seen by the employees. They are accountable to instill and develop the desired corporate culture within their team.

Developing employees is intended to achieve better results for the organization and individuals in order to improve the return-on-investment (time and/or dollars) for each. But despite countless continuous improvement programs, many organizations still greatly under-utilize their human resources. Performing tasks may be synonymous with achieving results in certain roles, such as that of a production machine-operator. However, at the level of a supervisor, performing tasks does not necessarily produce the desired results. The difference between employee and supervisory skills can be characterized as the difference between "doing the work yourself" and "getting the work done through others." Technical know-how may be the selection criteria for the supervisor's role, but it is not the main determinant of success. Therein lies the challenge for designing a training program. We are not starting with a clean slate. "One size fits all" does not apply because both our supervisors and employees are at different starting positions. They think differently, they likely learn in different ways and at different speeds. Compounding this is the tremendous acceleration in the rate of change now affecting organizations, not just in the area of technological change (how-to-do) but particularly in the area of changing expectations regarding the desired outcomes (what-to-do).

▶ Not only is the target moving at an ever faster pace, but the skills required to hit the target are also changing.

Assessment — to determine needs

When supervisors are asked to attend training sessions, they do so at a tremendous cost to the organization. There's the financial cost: estimates run up to hundreds of dollars per participant per hour of instruction. And there's the lost productivity: managerial time is one of the most precious resources an organization has. Thus, every hour or module of training must be targeted to meet organizational and individual needs. Several observations are relevant here:

- Although a number of organizations conduct needs analyses, these usually reveal wants rather then needs. Supervisors often do not know what they need. See Exhibit 9.3 for a different approach.
- Supervisors show up at classes they've been invited to attend without knowing why or what outcomes are expected of them. Training is still something the instructor does for you. The buy-in and commitment of participants is often low.
- Management development programs are frequently a patchwork quilt of topics that are the organization's attempt to provide for the needs of all supervisors and managers — one size fits all. This is increasingly impossible.

The purpose of assessment is to pinpoint specific needs, establish a benchmark of performance, plan individual programs of training and development, measure improvement over time and make sure that training takes place at the right time (based on the needs and priorities of the supervisors).

Thus, every supervisor and manager should have a plan for personal growth and development. This plan requires a solid database that may include:

- past performance appraisal data — strengths and weaknesses.
- objective measures of performance (i.e., feedback from next level manager(s).
- opinions of stakeholder groups (i.e., 360° feedback).
- awareness of all available personal development options.
- the behavior profile (as described in Exhibit 9.3).

This plan lists all the developmental activities a supervisor intends to undertake during the next 6 to 12 months, along with a time frame and expected results for each activity. By sharing this plan with key stakeholders (next-level managers, peers, team members), a supervisor widens the support base and deepens the commitment to implement the plan. These plans, in the aggregate, become valuable input to the training department as a guide to know what courses (competencies, modules, etc.) to offer.

A two-stage process

Improving the organization's return-on-investment means improving bottom-line results. Results are a product of the intentions and actions of people. Actions are driven by people's beliefs and behaviors. The leadership role is to align the actions with the desired results by promoting, demonstrating, communicating and inspiring the appropriate beliefs and behaviors. This then becomes the focus of a competency-based development program. The desired result is to continuously improve our return-on-investment, which, not surprisingly, is achieved by the same steps needed to implement and maintain a Positive Employee Relations program.

We recommend a two-stage workshop process for developing supervisory personnel. As detailed in Exhibit 9.3, the first stage involves working directly with the management and supervisory group to establish a consensus as to where the organization is at present and where it needs to be in the future to achieve the desired results as related to culture. The second stage involves the development and implementation strategy for changing the culture throughout the organization in order to drive the desired results.

DEVELOPING EFFECTIVE SUPERVISORS AND MANAGERS

There are many avenues other than training that a supervisor might take as part of a personal development plan: coaching by a manager, mentoring by an expert, serving on a task group (committee, project team), participating in professional associations, attending a national business conference and so on. Indeed, some of these are more effective than training programs will ever be in shaping certain kinds of managerial behavior. However, training workshops will still be the mainstay of supervisory and management development programs because of the many benefits that they offer:

- impact on the organization's culture across the board.
- team building (networking, sharing, strengthening the informal organization chart).
- cost effectiveness (one facilitator and course design can reach hundreds).
- critical mass (leverage) of participants in groups (versus learning as individuals).
- participants becoming resources to each other, sharing experiences, serving as examples, etc.

The trend in management development is toward modular (one- or two-day) workshops that address specific competencies, and away from five-day off-site programs that scatter a lot of buckshot in an attempt to hit everyone with something. Targeting instruction means that participants attend because they want to and need to, and the behavioral outcomes are known and subscribed to in advance.

Although participants and their managers should select the courses (content) based on their needs, the trainers should specify the course design (process) that produces maximum transfer of training from workshop to workplace. These design factors should include:

- an executive briefing for the managers of participants prior to launching a management development program.
- the use of self-inventories, planning sheets, checklists and other tools to be taken back and used in the workplace.
- the use of action plans that each participant prepares during the workshop and shares with the manager following each training session.
- an alumni day (three or six months after the training program) at which participants report the results of applying what they learned.

Exhibit 9.2 outlines a ten-session (generic) supervisory training program developed to train supervisors in how to lead effectively in an environment of Positive Employee Relations.

From training to practice

To what degree has performance improved as a result of training? What opportunities exist for further development? How does the cost of the program compare with the benefits? What is the return-on-investment? Where does the training program or the performance maintenance system need strengthening?

By reassessing participants at an appropriate interval after the course (usually three or six months), we can answer these questions. Given the cost of training and development today, organizations are no longer content to evaluate courses solely on the basis of the end-of-course reactions of participants. By measuring performance against the same standards used to assess needs *prior* to the course, we can obtain clean data on the gain attributable to training.

To be sure, many factors operate in the work environment that will both help and hinder participants as they translate their new learning into improved performance. However, one purpose of the action plans and the partnerships between participants and their managers is to prepare "graduates" to take advantage of the reinforcers and to overcome the constraints. Training programs are designed to prepare participants for performance *at work*, not merely in workshops. Thus, reassessment must take place after the intervening reinforcers and constraints have had time to operate. Immediate post-testing merely measures what was learned; senior management is interested in performance improvement in the workplace.

EXHIBIT 9.1

SUPERVISORY NEEDS INVENTORY

Listed below are statements describing the needs of supervisors and/or managers. In the brackets preceding each, place the number 3, 2 or 1, to indicate the degree to which they apply to you (or your supervisor, if you've been asked to evaluate his/her training needs).

3 = Extremely important (supervisor requires training on this issue)
2 = Fairly important
1 = Not important (has necessary skills or topic not relevant to supervisor's job)

( ) ability to transfer company values into day-to-day interactions with employee.
( ) ability to set realistic goals and standards, define performance requirements and develop action plans for achieving and for tracking performance.
( ) ability to communicate effectively in face-to-face situations with employees, peers, managers, customers, etc.
( ) ability to conduct selection interviews in a way that produces the information needed to make sound hiring decisions consistent with company policy and legislation.
( ) ability to balance daily activities between the demands of the task (production-oriented side) and of the employees (people-oriented side).
( ) ability to challenge and motivate employees, thereby increasing their job satisfaction and developing a team of enthusiastic employees.
( ) ability to give on-the-job training and counseling relating to behavior at work.
( ) ability to appraise performance objectively and to conduct regular, constructive performance reviews that are two-way dialogs.
( ) ability to write letters, memos and reports that are clear, concise, complete and compelling.

( ) ability to manage time (of self and others) effectively by prioritizing, controlling interruptions, measuring cost-effectiveness, investing rather than spending time, etc.
( ) ability to cut costs through methods improvement, work simplification or reallocation, flow charting, analysis of procedures, etc.
( ) ability to hold meetings, briefings, conferences that are well organized, crisp and results-oriented.
( ) ability to negotiate and resolve interpersonal conflict.
( ) ability to listen in-depth, drawing out what is and isn't said, summarizing and clarifying and organizing the speaker's message so that it can be acted upon.
( ) ability to identify problems, separate causes from symptoms, evaluate evidence, weigh alternatives and select and implement appropriate solutions.
( ) ability to apply management by objectives at the department level (preparing action plans, performance documents, etc.).
( ) ability to make effective presentations and sell ideas in a persuasive, well-documented manner to management, employees and customers.

Comments:
_____
_____
_____
_____
_____
_____

Survey completed by: _____
Date: _____

EXHIBIT 9.2

GENERIC MODEL OF A SUPERVISORY TRAINING PROGRAM

Session 1 — The Management Process
- The universality of the process we call management.
- The difference between managing and leading.
- Developing an understanding of "What is management?" and "What are supervisors supposed to do?"
- Understanding the similarities and differences between managing at the first level and managing at higher levels.

Session 2 — The Supervisor's Role as a Leader
- Guidelines for making the transition from employee to supervisor.
- The difficulty of being a first-level manager.
- The functions of leadership.
- The role and responsibilities of a first-level supervisor as part of the management team.
- Translating the company values into guiding behaviors for supervisors.
- Common mistakes made by new supervisors and how to avoid them.

Session 3 — Law and the Workplace
- Understanding supervisory responsibilities included in occupational health and safety, employment standards and human rights legislation.
- The supervisor's legal role and responsibility in maintaining our (privileged) union-free status and his/her responsibilities under the law.
- Understanding employee "rights."
- Knowing how far, in "words and deeds," a supervisor can exercise his/her authority.

Sessions 4 and 5 — Establishing and Maintaining Effective Working Relationships
- Understanding people's needs and their behavior.
- What factors, events, conditions and situations affect people's behavior.

- Understanding how and why people's needs and behavior change over time.
- "Why do people work?" and "What affects people's conscious and subconscious efforts to cooperate?"
- Understanding the uniqueness and similarities of the people you supervise.
- The value of work as a means to other ends or as an end in itself.
- Understanding the values and attitudes of people.
- Approaches and techniques for effectively motivating employees to maintain or improve their job performance.
- Understanding and managing small group behavior.
- The role of the informal group leader and how he/she influences the behavior of others.

Session 6 — Managing Change in the Workplace
- The process of change.
- Understanding why people and organizations on occasion resist change.
- Approaches and techniques for overcoming resistance to change.
- Making positive changes that lead to quality and customer satisfaction.

Session 7 — Managing Performance
- Identifying and understanding the reasons why performance situations occur.
- Understanding employees' needs for fairness and justice.
- The importance of taking corrective action when the need arises.
- Why management so often fails to manage employees constructively.
- The tests for just cause under company policy.
- Conducting a fair and impartial investigation.
- The necessity for maintaining up-to-date and accurate records about the positive and negative aspects of employees' behavior.
- Managing the difficult employee during an interview.

- Approaches and techniques to manage employees constructively.
- How to be consistent yet flexible when determining the appropriate action.

Session 8 — Effective Employee Counseling
- How to identify potential employee behavior problems.
- Recognizing when an employee needs professional assistance and how to get the employee to see it.
- How to conduct a counseling interview.
- Helping the employee to be better able to control his/her own life.
- Learning how to give advice constructively.

Session 9 — Conducting Performance Appraisals
- Techniques for obtaining employee involvement.
- How to manage differences in the perception of job performance.
- How to create action plans for follow-up.

Session 10 — Interviewing and Selection
- How to plan for the interview by establishing job requirements and applicant requirements.
- Using strategies to establish trust and rapport with applicants.
- Reviewing and summarizing information received during the interview.
- Giving appropriate information to the candidate.
- Concluding the interview.

EXHIBIT 9.3

COMPETENCY-BASED TRAINING AND DEVELOPMENT

The following process is designed to maximize the potential of your supervisory personnel. The first stage identifies the gap that exists between your organization's present culture and its desired culture. The second stage involves the development and implementation strategy for changing the culture throughout the organization in order to achieve the desired results. For a model of the Activity Vector Analysis (AVA) process, please see Appendix C.

Stage 1: Four phases, including assessment, interpretation, feedback and training

Phase 1: Assessment
The Activity Vector Analysis (AVA) process allows this phase to be easily administered. Use the diagnostic instruments to assess:

1. The desired culture (what it should be) and the perceived current culture of the organization.
2. The specific job analysis of the supervisor's role — the outcomes desired, and the actions necessary for success (as determined by management and successful incumbents).
3. The individual behavioral profiles of each individual supervisor.

Phase 2: Interpretation
The interpretation of the three assessments identifies any gaps that exist between the ideal and the reality. These gaps relate to how the culture and the behaviors required in the supervisory role need to change.

First, supervisors need to have a correct understanding of what is expected in the way of behaviors. Despite their best intentions and effort, if their expectations are not appropriate, then frustration is inevitable. Identifying any gaps will allow training initiatives to bring supervisors' perceptions and beliefs into alignment with the reality of what is expected of them. By shifting their paradigm, supervisors can focus on attaining the appropriate behaviors for their responsibilities. This is a very dynamic process because it first establishes a consensus for the desired culture (for example, Positive Employee Relations) as well as the actions, beliefs and behaviors required to be successful in moving towards this culture.

Phase 3: Feedback

The feedback workshop is powerful in terms of getting to the core of what is organizationally needed and where individual supervisors are at before commencing the training.

At this point we have a behavioral profile from each supervisor (and therefore for the overall supervisory group) which describes the key behavioral dynamics of:

- the desired culture, the currently perceived culture, and the actual culture (as it is today).
- a consensus of benchmarked behavior for each supervisor's position.
- the specific demands of each supervisory position, according to the perceptions of each supervisor.

The feedback now takes the following form:

1. Discuss the consensus outcomes of the group.
2. Provide each individual with the results they generated.
3. Share the individual outcomes with the group.

This workshop takes on relevance to each of the supervisors by focusing on their individual needs. As Socrates said, "Above all else, know thyself." It establishes their training and development needs relative to others on the team. Further, it establishes consensus as to desired outcomes of the training initiatives. It is a powerful team building process, as participants better understand the behavioral drives of other supervisors and relate it to recent at-work experiences.

This workshop starts the process of alignment. It assists and supports supervisors as they align their paradigms to be consistent with the organization's values and vision. This is at the core of making substantive change in how supervisors interact with the employees in their team.

Phase 4: Training
This phase reviews the beliefs and behaviors required for success and illustrates the gaps that exist within the group in relation to the benchmark (consensus).

Recognition of these behavioral gaps is a major step in changing the supervisors' paradigms and gaining acceptance for the behavioral changes required. The nature of the gaps will vary between groups and the training initiatives should be designed to meet specific situations of each.

The training relates to the behaviors needed in leadership roles. For example, the types of gaps identified may indicate that coaching is required to teach supervisors how to:

- increase their level of assertiveness — taking charge, decisiveness, holding others accountable, being results-oriented.
- improve people skills — engaging, inspiring, communicating, delegating, motivating, commanding respect, empathy, consistency, etc.
- alter work style — become less reactive, perhaps more proactive, improve listening skills, increase sense of urgency, etc.
- become less dependent or process-driven, more self-reliant, resisting the temptation to micro-manage others, overcoming fear of failure.
- focus more on the big picture rather than the details, better at developing others.

A competency-based development program such as this is less about building supervisors' "how-to" skills and more about developing their competencies in handling themselves and relating to others. When supervisors share beliefs that are aligned with the desired culture, then the process of achieving these results accelerates dramatically.

Stage 2: Implementation
Much of the success of this stage depends on the leadership requirements learned in Stage 1. Leadership is the key element in successfully implementing cultural change in order to achieve desired organizational results (implementing the values that support Positive Employee Relations).

Since results are driven by the actions of people, we focus in the second stage on teaching supervisors how to recognize the workplace actions necessary to achieve the desired results. Actions that produce desired results will need to be sustained or expanded. Actions that do not produce the desired results will need to be stopped. And some actions may have to be initiated as new behaviors.

In a culture of self-responsibility, the role of the supervisor is to transfer and reinforce those beliefs and behaviors that will create a positive climate. The supervisory training then should revolve around how to create experiences and provide workplace feedback that will foster the appropriate beliefs and reinforce appropriate behavior consistent with the desired culture.

Managing the culture is the key to living Positive Employee Relations. Training aligns supervisors, and those they lead, with a Positive Employee Relations culture. By managing beliefs and behaviors consistent with the company vision, your organization can retain its union-free position.

EXHIBIT 9.4

WAR GAMES EXERCISE

This exhibit includes the three separate workshop assignments that are distributed during the "war games" exercise. The participants are divided into three teams: management, union and employees. Each team receives the appropriate workshop assignment, is sent to a separate "breakout" room and is given two to three hours to complete its project.

When the assignments are completed, the three teams reconvene in the main training room and present their findings to the entire group. Usually I ask the management team to make its presentation first, followed by the union and employee teams. The presentations are quite lively with a mixture of humor and critical self-analysis. By the end of the exercise, the participants have *demonstrated to themselves*:

- how quickly employee concerns can be identified
- how union organizing strategy can take advantage of these concerns, and
- how unprepared management is when viewed from a proactive point of view.

WORKSHOP ASSIGNMENT A: MANAGEMENT TEAM

Assume you are all senior managers at the Sherborne plant, involved directly with the widget production (i.e., manufacturing, maintenance, quality departments). You have just received information (which you believe is very reliable) about a pending union campaign. It appears the drive will be launched by the IBWW (International Brotherhood of Widget Workers) with backing from the IBWW local representing the Sherborne "Magic Widget" Division in Toronto.

You need to **develop a strategy to fend off the pending campaign**. In preparation, analyze Sherborne's strengths and weaknesses as you see them and as you think the union might see them. With this data, outline, in detail, your union-free (Positive Employee Relations) campaign.

N.B. You have just received a call from the corporate offices indicating that the chairman of the board is most anxious to keep the Sherborne plant union-free. You were left with the impression that thwarting the union drive would be very favorably viewed (and probably rewarded).

WORKSHOP ASSIGNMENT B: UNION TEAM

Assume you are all members of a union organizing team from the IBWW (International Brotherhood of Widget Workers). You have been asked by the international representative to **develop an organizing strategy** for an upcoming drive (campaign) against the Sherborne Company.

Be detailed and specific in your strategy.

In preparing your strategy, you will need to consider the strengths and weaknesses of the total Sherborne plant so that your plans will accentuate the weaknesses and downplay the strengths.

The campaign will cost the union a lot of "seed" money and your careers, as union organizers, will no doubt be influenced by the success of your organizing strategy and subsequent campaign.

N.B. A phone call last night indicated that the IBWW local president, representing the Sherborne Toronto plant, will arrive today to help in your planning.

WORKSHOP ASSIGNMENT C: EMPLOYEE TEAM

Assume you are a group of non-supervisory production employees at the Sherborne plant. You have been approached informally by a union representative who has offered to help organize the plant employees.

You are all in agreement that the threat of a union drive would scare management into being more liberal with wages, benefits and working conditions. Some of you even feel that being represented by the IBWW would be very beneficial.

Prepare a list of all employee grievances, complaints and management's broken promises relating to both the Sherborne working environment and the plant jobs that would help the union organizer in his/her campaign strategy. Tell the organizer everything you can to help him/her organize the Sherborne plant.

N.B. You have just received a call from the IBWW organizer offering a $500 bonus to each of you if you can: (a) provide a list of plant employees, their addresses and phone numbers. Can you get such a list? If so, how? (b) place IBWW website on the company's intranet so employees can sign up on-line. Can you do this? If so, how?

TAKE ACTION!

1. Enlist the buy-in of front-line supervisors:
   - Invite them to participate in the development and implementation of the Positive Employee Relations program.
   - Ensure that senior management fully appreciates the psychological and social implications of the Positive Employee Relations program.
   - Make sure that senior management demonstrates the appropriate behavior for your supervisors to model.

2. Link communication skills to supervisory training by creating a 12-month communication and training schedule.

3. Make supervisors aware of the six key facts about unions, so that they can make employees aware of the disadvantages and dangers.

4. Conduct "war games" training exercise for supervisors.

5. Conduct a training needs analysis and/or supervisory needs inventory to determine the existing supervisory skill level.

6. Conduct competency-based training and development for supervisors and make sure that training encompasses a broad range of skill development.

7. Treat employees—including supervisors—like internal customers.

8. Do not accept poor performance from anyone—especially leaders.

10
COMMUNICATING YOUR MESSAGE

Effective communication is the lynch pin around which a successful organization is based. A good idea expressed well is a thousand times more valuable than a great idea expressed poorly. Weak communications can be held responsible for over half the problems faced in the workplace on any given day.

Employees in today's workforce are no longer satisfied with being treated as "alive equipment." Employees are recruited to be active participants in helping us succeed; they are partners in our success. They expect and deserve to be able to achieve a sense of worth, self-confidence, a sense of contributing, status, appreciation, respect and an expectation of improvement. Communications that bypass or assail any of these create resistance and resentment.

Strategies that provide opportunities for input from employees are based on the premise that no one can understand a job as intimately as the person actually doing it.

▶ Leaders at all levels can learn critical information from employees that will directly impact quality, customer service and other key success factors.

Organizations that don't take the time and effort to listen to their employees lose the opportunity to be alerted to potential problems, to be offered workable solutions, and to otherwise make use of employees' workplace ideas. Spotting problems before they erupt and being proactive about solving them is infinitely more effective. It is another example of the Positive Employee Relations program going live.

EMPLOYEE EXPECTATIONS AND NEEDS

The toughest part of good communications is being able to see things from the employee's point of view. Too often we are so involved in the "busy-ness" of our jobs that we do not think about how our words and our non-verbal messages impact the employee(s). By not slowing down and taking the time to determine how to send our communications effectively we have a 50/50 chance of being off the mark. In the case of leaders who have a history of ineffective communications, the ratio in favor of being on target can drop to as low as 0/100 — employees have become so accustomed to poor communications that they become deaf to their supervisors' attempts to get through.

Employee expectations from the company

The following list highlights what employees, as legitimate stakeholders in your organization, expect from their employment relationship. Many studies have been made to determine what employees *want* from their jobs. My research and experience indicates that the following list represents the ten most important *needs* of employees.

1. To receive fair treatment when raising concerns or complaints.
2. To know that management will go out of its way to provide for job security.
3. To be known for their skills and accomplishments.
4. To receive praise and credit for their contributions.
5. To have any disciplinary matters handled constructively, confidentially and in an "adult" manner.
6. To see that compensation is based on good performance and not favoritism.
7. To trust that promotions will be based on qualifications.
8. To have clear evidence that management expects only reasonable amounts of work.
9. To know that salary and benefit plans are at least equal to the going rate in the community/industry.
10. To receive reasonable credit for length of service.

Surprisingly, research has shown that such bread-and-butter items as pay and benefits rank relatively low in importance. This suggests that in our current socioeconomic climate employees are more influenced by sophisticated needs (Maslow's upper-level needs) that focus on the quality of employee-management relationship. And, as has been pointed out in previous chapters, the front-line supervisor *is* management in the eyes of the employee.

Employee needs from their leaders

How are the top ten employee needs expressed in terms of their working relationship with their supervisors? Survey after survey shows that employees want their supervisors to:

1. Know how to perform their supervisory job well.
2. Provide timely, honest, clear feedback.
3. Deal respectfully and fairly with everyone.
4. Take action on employees' complaints and problems.
5. Provide the information employees need to do their job well.

6. Listen to what employees have to say.
7. Give recognition for work well done.
8. Support employees when convinced they are right.
9. Encourage suggestions for improvement.
10. Know what to do when things go wrong.

An effective program for ensuring Positive Employee Relations will satisfy employee needs, whatever they may be. Employee needs vary from company to company. Each company has the responsibility of determining the needs of its own employees. What those needs may be is less important than that they be assessed accurately and then addressed promptly.

When reviewing a list of employee needs, some managers may raise the concern that employees do not really care about the organization and the products/services it provides. This is not necessarily accurate. The more the organization encourages and allows employees to apply their brains to the job (through decision-making, creativity, etc.) the more the employees will align themselves with the product/services being delivered. The reverse is also true. If the job activities can best be described as routine or repetitive (that is, decision-making has been taken out of the job), how can employers align or commit themselves to the product/service? This situation reveals a gap between the objectives of employees and those of management, which creates a dilemma for management.

▶ Achieving management's goals depends on employee effectiveness and yet the work of employees becomes effective only when their individual goals are met.

The successful organization ensures, first, that employee goals can be met on the job, and second, that employees are made aware of the economic realities of a free enterprise society.

MANAGEMENT MUST TAKE THE FIRST STEP

Internal communications play a key role in aligning employee needs with organizational goals. Employees want to know, participate, understand and contribute. *However, their opinions and feelings surface only when the level of trust, openness and understanding in an organization is high*. This is the essence of the Positive Employee Relations program. If these latent desires are to be satisfied, management must ensure that employees are consistently and accurately informed about plans and results. Also, all levels of management must be acutely aware of the needs and feelings of employees.

My experience tells me that if management expects to maintain a union-free environment, it must commit itself to spending about 5 percent of the gross payroll annually, not on additional salaries and benefits, but on communications and employee and leadership education, to ensure that employees are involved in their jobs, their careers and their company.

▶ The reality of human resource management today is that employers must take the first (and probably the second) step in opening up the lines of communication.

However, this requires more than spending money, which — as in signing a check requisition — is an entirely impersonal act. It requires a long-term strategy to shift management and employee attitudes. Stereotyped values and beliefs must change. And the initiator of this change must be leadership — as individual managers and as a team. Openness, trust and understanding must be clearly demonstrated and reinforced by management before employees will feel secure enough to speak their minds, face issues squarely and participate as business partners in the achievement of organizational goals.

A COMMUNICATIONS PROGRAM — THE BASICS

If management is to take the initiative to open up communications, which of the many available doors should it open? To be effective, an employee communications program should begin with a plan based on the premise that communications must *engage, inform, persuade and respond*. Though some aspects of the communications plan should be in writing (such as the employee handbook), the best employee communications are verbal and held in a person-to-person setting.

Creating an effective communications program can be achieved only after auditing your current communications practices (such as newsletters, meetings, bulletin boards, etc.) and determining your employees' communications needs. Such an audit is beyond the scope of this book; however, the following generic communications plan can be adapted to the needs of your company.

▶ **The best employee communications are verbal and held in a person-to-person setting.**

It is based on the premise that your employees are stakeholders in the success of your company and should be treated accordingly. The following are the components of this basic communications plan:

- recruitment
- orientation
- newsletter
- department meetings
- company meetings
- Let's Talk© program
- employee handbook.

Recruitment

Communications begin when you place an employment advertisement and the candidate responds by phone, letter, email or fax. Your handling of a job interview will reflect how you feel about the candidate as an individual and as a potential employee. (Refer to Chapter 8 for more on recruitment and selection.)

Orientation

The candidate has now been hired and, probably for the first time, will hear about the company's history, objectives, plans, the marketplace, the job expectations, benefits and available communications programs. What is said and how it is said will go a long way toward reinforcing that the employee has made the correct decision to join your company.

Newsletter

Though one of the most commonly used employee communication tools, the company newsletter frequently misses the mark. To be effective, a newsletter must have senior management's commitment. That is, the resources to write, edit and reproduce the publication, the budget to produce a respectable publication, and the determination to see that it is published and distributed on schedule.

The newsletter should not be devoted to company history; old news just doesn't have much appeal. It should focus on human interest stories, the goals and plans of the company and feedback from the marketplace. Each edition of the newsletter should also include a section that markets the "benefits" of being employed by this "employer of choice" (see Chapter 6). Be sure to include lots of pictures, especially of employees at work and enjoying their leisure time. Training employees to write some, or all, of the copy or to provide illustrations or graphics will reinforce the employees' ownership of the newsletter.

The newsletter need not be produced monthly. Every two or three months is acceptable as long as the publishing schedule is adhered to. I recommend that the newsletter be sent to the employees at home. This will assist in making the employee's family more aware of the company. The goal is to produce a newsletter that management can be proud of and that employees look forward to receiving.

Department meetings

Meetings are an important part of the communications plan. Unfortunately, as we know from experience, meetings can be a big waste of time. Meetings should be planned around either information-giving or problem-solving topics and should follow the principles of good meeting management. Refer to Exhibit 10.1 for a meeting planner and checklist.

A monthly meeting, lasting 45-60 minutes, can focus on resolving a number of the department's operational problems. This is an ideal setting in which the supervisor can demonstrate concern for achieving high standards of excellence, openness to employees' requests for information and responsiveness to suggestions.

An interesting variation on the department meeting format is to have the supervisor appear at every fourth or fifth meeting *without* an agenda. Allow the first ten minutes for *the employees to set the agenda without the supervisor present*. This will bring forward the employees' high-priority issues. It also encourages those employees who need the security of their fellow employees around them in order to speak up. While employees prepare the agenda, the supervisor should excuse him/herself for about ten minutes, coming back to the meeting when the agenda has been set. The meeting then follows the same practices as other department meetings: each agenda item is discussed fully, alternate solutions are proposed, answers or decisions are reached and outstanding items are tabled to be resolved by the next meeting.

Company meetings

Another component of the communications plans is the all-employee meeting. Naturally, this option is open only to companies with an employee population that will permit such a gathering. Special arrangements will be required to accommodate multiple shift operations. Every effort should be made to hold these meetings during regular business hours — for example, the last one or two hours of the business day.

This all-employee meeting (held off-site, if necessary) is an ideal opportunity for senior management to discuss company plans, accomplishments and proposed changes that will affect the whole organization. This is also a good time for service and performance awards to be distributed. The meeting should last no longer than 45 minutes, with the presentation handled in a professional manner (for example, a multimedia presentation that treats employees as stakeholders in the business). This allows management to demonstrate that it believes that its most valuable resource is its human resource.

After the formal presentation, coffee and sandwiches should be made available to all. The remaining portion of the meeting should be devoted to social time. All managers and supervisors must be requested to mingle with the employees and to respond to their inquiries, suggestions and concerns. Remember, you are demonstrating a Positive Employee Relations climate. Managers should not stay with their own employee groups but should talk with as many employees as possible, making themselves available to any individual employee who wishes to talk.

To gain the fullest possible value from this type of meeting, managers must be prepared in advance to present their information in a professional manner and to speak knowledgeably to questions from the floor. Afterwards, debriefing is very important. The morning after the all-employee meeting, the management group should confer and summarize the questions they were asked. Look for patterns, trends and oddities. Assess the morale or climate of the employee group.

Let's Talk© program

The next aspect of the communications plan, and one that I recommend wholeheartedly, goes right to the heart of the Positive Employee Relations philosophy. The Let's Talk© program focuses squarely on the relationship between employee and supervisor. The beauty of this program is both its simplicity and the depth of information that it generates. Managers frequently ask their supervisory staff to go and "talk with your employees." It makes sense, but it never seems to take place. Not enough time is set aside for it, supervisors are not recognized for doing it and often there is no training or support program established to ensure that supervisors actually do talk with their employees.

The Let's Talk© program is designed to encourage each employee to meet with his/her supervisor at least once every three months to discuss *anything* the employee would like. To make it as easy as possible for the employee, there is a Let's Talk© agenda or checklist on which the employee indicates the specific areas for discussion. The employee gives a copy of the completed agenda to the supervisor two days in advance of the meeting so the supervisor can prepare. At the conclusion of the Let's Talk© meeting (normal duration is 30 minutes), either or both parties complete an action planner that outlines those items that require follow-up. Copies of the action planner are distributed to the employee, supervisor, department manager and human resources.

A sample employee's guide to the Let's Talk© program is shown in Appendix C. The Let's Talk© program, though uncomplicated in its design and methodology, does require senior management's commitment. This commitment includes:

- a willingness to invest time and money to train managers and supervisors in interpersonal communication skills, conflict resolution, problem-solving and decision-making.
- a willingness to conduct the Let's Talk© meetings with all the managers and supervisors, thereby demonstrating good role model behavior.
- a willingness to allow each employee to spend 30 minutes, every three months, in a very important Positive Employee Relations activity.

Employee handbook

An employee handbook is the primary written component of the communications plan. Regardless of how well a handbook is produced, it will not succeed in conveying its message if every management letter, memo or booklet is greeted with distrust and/or skepticism.

▶ No employee handbook should be a unilateral declaration by management.

The first stage in preparing a handbook is to consider the employee population and their needs. These will influence and largely determine the handbook's content, form and style. Though handbooks may be useful during major recruiting campaigns, they are primarily intended for current employees who usually have well-established views on what they need to know. If employees are expected to use the handbook, they should be involved in deciding its content, form and style. Communications are undoubtedly improved when the parties concerned meet to discuss the purpose, meaning and implications of the message.

Employee committees can be of great benefit in a number of areas (such as drafting the employee handbook). These committees should be made up of volunteers who work on specific projects with limited time frames. When the project is completed the committee should be recognized and then disbanded.

The employee handbook should aim to present useful information in a clear and readable style. The popular press has developed the art of making reading easy. Attention-getting headlines, short sentences using basic English, brief paragraphs and illustrations all stress the human angle and appeal to our emotions. Writers of handbooks should not be ashamed to use these techniques to convey their undoubtedly serious messages.

The language will, of course, vary according to the reading level of the recipients. However, handbooks must always be written in a straightforward style — particularly if there are readers whose mother tongue is not English — and, where appropriate, translated. People cannot be expected to carry out instructions that they do not understand. Even a statement such as "Drinking is strictly forbidden on the company's premises" could lead to dehydrated employees if applied literally.

The style of writing is bound to reflect, to some extent, the attitude of the organization and of those submitting ideas and information. It will become quite impersonal unless one person, preferably someone with some skill as a writer, produces the final document. Advice, suggestions, information and criticism should be welcomed from many sources. Existing committees should participate in assembling material for various sections, but organizing the final product is better done by an individual than a committee. This individual need not be someone closely concerned with the content. For example, the expertise of the public relations department might be used for both the writing and layout.

Appendix E shows a sample table of contents for an employee handbook as well as a sample introductory chapter.

MANAGING COMMUNICATIONS

A well-managed communications program creates a climate that will allow a company to reach its quality and production goals as well as its Positive Employee Relations objectives. Shaping the climate through managed communications eventually results in a culture that is truly communicative. It is a culture in which clear direction, open communications, innovation and high productivity are a way of life.

Exhibit 10.2 presents a model of an effective departmental communications program. It is applicable to most working relationships, from management and the employee group to the individual supervisor and his/her employees. The model outlines a communications pattern that is integrated with the company's major organizational sub-systems: social, operational and administrative. Also, the model is progressive — each stage in the communication process is a building block for the subsequent stage.

This model outlines a manageable communications approach. Its success depends directly upon a commitment to manage communications, including taking responsibility for fair and prompt responses to all inquiries.

CRITICAL COMMUNICATION SKILLS

The toughest part of a good communications program is being able to see things from another point of view.

▶ It doesn't matter how well the leader thinks the conversation went, all that really counts is how the employee feels about what he/she heard.

Seldom will a listener interpret the message exactly the way it was intended. Many meanings may be applied to the spoken/written word. Interpretation depends on the past experiences of the listeners and their current attitudes and mental state. Additionally, nonverbal behavior — eye contact, posture, gestures, body movements, and the use of space — may actually contradict a verbal message. Obvious body gestures include shaking of the head, a smile, a shrug, a smirk, turning away and crossed arms.

Communications involve both what you intended to convey and what someone thought you meant. The goal is to bring these into alignment so that they communicate one message.

Even when the message is perceived correctly, the average person remembers about half of a message immediately after receiving it; only a quarter after two weeks. Repetition and reminders are necessary to ensure that employees recall important information.

The leadership team must also ensure that the messages sent to employees are consistent across supervisors and over time. And, of course, actions must support the messages sent. Employees will believe actions long after the words are forgotten.

When an employee has a concern or offers input, it is essential that the supervisor respond in a timely manner. Inform the employee if it is going to take some time to provide an answer. A general rule is that most requests should receive a response within two days. When listening to an employee, the supervisor should act as though he/she is talking to the organization's most senior executive. There is no one who is more important at that moment.

Encouraging an upward flow of information

An upward flow of information is more likely to occur when employees have:

- **Access** to all leadership personnel;
- **Input** into decision-making (too often they are asked for an opinion after the decision has already been made);
- An **understanding** of the business in order to feel comfortable enough to ask questions;
- **Feedback** on in impact of their input;
- Enough **trust** in management to know reprisals won't come down upon the bearer of bad news. This is the only way to ensure that information will not merely be that which the manager wants to hear.

Occasionally, some information cannot be provided. When that is the case, employees should be told when they can expect a more thorough explanation. They should also be told why they could not be told earlier. There will be some information that is not appropriately shared with the employee population at large, and this is understandable, as long as it is possible to give employees a plausible reason why.

Critical communication skills

- Know the employee's perceptions.
- Listen actively.
- Be aware of body language.
- Repeat key messages in different ways.
- Be consistent over time.
- Be consistent with what others are saying.
- Give a timely response to employee communications.
- Care about what the other is feeling.

TEN COMMUNICATION DO'S

1. Speak as one adult to another (the way you would like your manager to talk to you).
2. Overdo it. Communicate more than you have to or need to. Make it your top priority.
3. Find something positive. No matter what the message is, find a way to include something positive.
4. Be clear and concise. Be as specific as possible in the words you use.
5. Care. If you are ambivalent about your message or audience, the communication will reflect that.
6. Double check. Probe to check that you understand and that the other person understands you.
7. Be honest. It's the only way people will believe what you say.
8. Encourage input. Always solicit employee ideas, suggestions and reactions.
9. Follow through. Always. No exceptions.
10. Be helpful. Recognize that the job of the manager is to remove roadblocks, irritants and frustrations, not put them there.

TEN COMMUNICATION DON'TS

1. Command. Ordering people around tends to produce resentment and anger. Do your best to avoid statements beginning with "You must," "You have to," or "You ought to."
2. Threaten. Statements such as, "If you don't," or "You had better" encourage rebellion and attempts to beat the system.
3. Give unsolicited advice. The only advice that is valued is advice that is requested.
4. Use vague language. Saying "We need to come up with a better system" produces confusion. What exactly are you asking the listener to do?
5. Withhold information. If employees can't hear certain information, make sure there is a good reason for holding back and tell them that reason.

6. Call names. Confronting employees by saying "You are careless" or "You're getting lazy" only produces defensiveness. These statements do not provide any direction on how an employee can improve.
7. Patronize. No one likes to be talked down to. Every employee is important or else he/she would not have been hired in the first place. A supervisor is 100 percent dependent on his/her employees for success.
8. Generalize. Although it's easier to categorize things as black or white, it's rarely the reality. Saying "You never do anything I ask you to" is probably untrue. Every low performing employee does some things right, and every star employee messes up sometimes.
9. Ignore the other person. Delivering the message is only half the communications picture. How is the employee taking it? Is it understood the way you intended?
10. Rush. If you don't have enough time for back-and-forth dialog, then wait until you do have time. The only time this rule does not apply is in case of fire!

EXHIBIT 10.1

MEETING PLANNER AND CHECKLIST

Listed under each of the following four headings are critical issues that should be considered when arranging a meeting.

Planning
- Establish a need for the meeting.
- Define the problem(s).
- Research the facts.
- Establish meeting objectives (usually in the form of a preliminary agenda).
- Determine the most suitable type of meeting.
- Determine, in broad terms, what you expect to achieve or accomplish.
- Consider the appropriate leadership strategies.
- Decide who should attend and why. Ask potential participants to indicate whether or not they will attend.
- Determine the pre-meeting information needed by each participant and the data the participants are required to bring to the meeting.
- Schedule time to prepare for the meeting.

Organizing
- Prepare a more formalized agenda including who is responsible for each topic or item.
- Prepare (as chairperson) your subject material.
- Determine the format of the minutes, including a feedback system regarding action taken.
- Consider a dry run and, if necessary, make appropriate changes.
- Determine the criteria for agreement on issues.
- Consider the contributions required from the participants, particularly the key or influential members.
- Check for convenient time and location and confirm with participants.
- Become familiar with actual meeting place and surroundings.

- Prepare meeting materials (multimedia or audio-visual aids, reports and handouts, coffee).
- Determine who will be recorder and secretary, define the role(s) and obtain agreement as to expectations and timing.

Facilitating
- Introduce the participants and their respective roles.
- Discuss the style of the meeting and the chairperson's role.
- State the problems and criteria for agreement (agenda).
- Develop guidelines for solutions and agreement.
- Ensure that all possible solutions are reviewed.
- Keep on target, periodically restate the meeting objectives and consider the time frame.
- Summarize problems and agreements.
- Encourage intra-group communications.
- Resolve conflict.

Guiding
- Restate objectives and conclusions; obtain agreement.
- Resolve problems and/or conflicts not adequately handled.
- Decide on a course of action, that is, implementation of conclusions or decisions.
- Expedite this plan and follow through to conclusion.
- Establish a distribution pattern for the minutes. If possible, distribute minutes within three days.

EXHIBIT 10.2

COMMUNICATIONS MODEL

Step 1 — The goals of the department
Communicate:
- Department goals.
- Department objectives and targets.
- Department accomplishments.
- Employee's questions and suggestions on goals/progress.

Step 2 — Individual job responsibility and standards
Communicate:
- Employee's job responsibilities.
- Employee's job performance standards (or expectations).
- Answers to employee's questions about the job.
- Policies and procedures affecting the job.

Step 3 — Individual performance feedback
Communicate:
- Performance feedback fully and on time.
- Personal appreciation for effective performance.
- Areas for performance improvement as needed.
- With employee, action needed to improve performance.
- Employee's value to the department.

Step 4 — Individual's needs and concerns
Communicate:
- Willingness to listen to personal concerns and employee relations problems.
- Willingness to assist employees in resolving their job-related conflicts.
- Timely feedback to all job-related concerns, questions and suggestions.
- Career opportunities.
- Your need for feedback on your managerial performance.

Step 5 — Information, suggestions, proposals to be made upwards
Communicate:
- Successes and failures of department in meeting objectives.
- Problems or obstacles to achieving objectives.
- Suggestions for actions and policy changes by senior management.
- Proposals to address opportunities, efficiencies.

Step 6 — Department's place in the company
Communicate:
- How department's goals affect the company.
- Major business issues affecting the department.
- Basic business strategy of the department.
- Role of other departments, as needed.
- All business action affecting work unit.

TAKE ACTION!

1. Commit to spending approximately 5 percent of the gross payroll annually on communications, employee education and leadership development to ensure that employees are involved in their jobs, their careers and their company.
2. Conduct an audit of your company's current communications practices and determine your employees' communication needs.
3. Create an employee communications plan based on the premise that communications must engage, inform, persuade and be responsive. Consider including the following components:

   - recruitment
   - orientation
   - newsletter
   - department meetings
   - company meetings
   - Let's Talk© program
   - employee handbook.

4. Create a communications plan for each department according to the six steps detailed in Exhibit 10.2.

11
APPRAISING EMPLOYEE PERFORMANCE

Probably one of the most difficult tasks for managers and supervisors is to conduct regular and worthwhile assessments of individual employee performance. This difficulty stems partly from human nature: people shy away from making *critical* judgments of other people. Why? For two reasons:

1. The way managers and supervisors (early in their work career) were treated during their first performance appraisal reviews: *I went in raw and came out bleeding!*
2. Managers' and supervisors' lack of understanding and training in this area.

And precisely because of this lack of understanding, supervisors frequently pull away from conducting performance appraisals. Positive Employee Relations means many things. *But one aspect that is critical is feedback to employees on job performance.*

WHY AN APPRAISAL IS IMPORTANT

- It lets the employee know where he/she stands.
- It identifies the employee's performance strengths and areas that need improvement so that the supervisor-employee team can then work together to improve job-related performance and behavior.
- It provides information for making salary decisions, since salary is normally related to performance.
- It provides manpower planning information by identifying the organization's talented performers, and by identifying training and development requirements.

A performance appraisal is not merely a tool for motivating employees. Like many management practices, it has evolved over the last 30 years from an evaluative tool to an aid in *employee self-development and learning*, which leads to improved performance (see Table 11.1). This is the developmental component of performance reviews. It is used by supervisors and managers as an aid in making decisions regarding promotions and transfers. It should never be used as a disciplinary tool. See Chapter 12 for more on managing employee performance.

TABLE 11.1 — Evolution of Performance Appraisals

	Evaluative Role	Developmental Role
Focus	Past performance.	Improvement in future.
Objective	Improve performance.	Improve performance through self-learning and growth.
Method	Variety of rating and ranking procedures.	Series of development steps (e.g. standards of performance and behavioral indicators).
Role of Manager	To judge and evaluate.	To counsel, mentor or guide.
Role of employee	Passive or reactive, frequently to defend oneself.	Active involvement in learning and decision making.

MOTIVATIONAL FACTORS

On-the-job performance is determined primarily by the employee's ability and motivation. These, in turn, are influenced by workplace environmental factors, including the activities supervisors undertake to improve employee performance. When supervisors know the needs and goals of employees, then they can influence motivation.

But first, let's clarify the distinction between needs and goals. Needs may be defined as unsatisfied desires.

▶ People are motivated to act by a lack of satisfaction with their current state of existence.

People are *pushed* into some form of behavior because of some felt deficiencies. Goals, on the other hand, *pull* the individual towards a desired object. When the drivers are achieved (either goals or deficiencies), the individual is satisfied.

Abraham Maslow's hierarchy of needs provides a useful starting point when viewing motivation, especially in the context of Positive Employee Relations. According to Maslow's theory regarding the nature of human needs, people have five broad classes of needs:

1. self-actualization, or the need to excel by reaching one's potential.
2. self-esteem.
3. belonging, or love.
4. safety, both physiological and psychological.
5. primary needs such as air, food, water, shelter, clothing.

The theory holds that individuals are primarily concerned with the lowest-order (primary or physiological) needs until these needs are satisfied. Then concern for second-level needs dominates.

▶ As each level of need is satisfied, the individual's attention is focused upwards.

But if workplace environmental factors prevent the fulfillment of lower needs, the move upward is halted. The union movement has traditionally viewed unsatisfied lower-level needs as fertile ground.

Another important consideration is that once a need has been satisfied, a person is no longer motivated *by that particular need*. For example, employees who have adequate social relationships with friends and family will probably not be motivated to form additional ties at work.

The relationship between outcomes and motivation was stressed by industrial psychologist Frederick Herzberg. He identified several factors, which he divided into *intrinsic* and *extrinsic* outcomes that reinforce employee behavior.

TABLE 11.2 — Outcomes that Reinforce Employee Behavior

Intrinsic (Motivators)	Extrinsic (Hygiene)
Work itself	Salary
Responsibility	Relationships
Achievement	Technical supervision
Growth	Policy and administration
Satisfaction	Working conditions
Recognition and pride	Job security

Extrinsic factors (such as hygiene and workplace environmental issues) are primarily responsible for determining the amount of dissatisfaction experienced on the job. More important for our purposes is the belief that intrinsic factors (those related to job content and personal growth) are important for motivating higher performance, while extrinsic factors are not.

▶ The real rewards from a job are not monetary, assuming that wage levels are established competitively within your industry and labor market geography.

Motivating employees depends on linking their efforts to improved performance and, in turn, making employees realize that improved performance will lead to outcomes they value. These outcomes are primarily intrinsic — satisfaction, challenge, advancement, knowledge and self-esteem.

Moreover, if the hygiene factors do not meet the employees' perceived standard of acceptability, the gap this causes will lead directly to workplace dissatisfaction. This presents opportunities for union organizers to make their case about employer insensitivity, unfairness, etc.

This dissatisfaction also becomes a roadblock to the employees' ability to experience and appreciate the benefits of the motivational factors. When people are concerned about low wages or a reduced benefits program, it is difficult to give their commitment to the learning opportunities inherent in the scope and breadth of their job.

Of great surprise to many managers is the apparent lack of appreciation for rectifying the causes of dissatisfaction. For example, if the organization determines its wages are below the community standard and then they make an upwards adjustment, employees will not flock to their door in gratitude for correcting what employees knew all along was a problem.

CREATING A CLIMATE FOR CHANGE

▶ No performance appraisal system can be effective unless management has established a climate that is conducive to change.

A climate that is conducive to change depends on a workplace that encourages, enables and rewards performance. In this environment, typified by Positive Employee Relations, an enlightened perspective on the part of management counts for more than any book of rules. This perspective should be grounded in the following basic conditions:

Employee appraisal and development involves the senior executives of the organization

This does not mean that the president administers the program; rather, senior management wholeheartedly endorses the effort, not only through words but through actions. The most powerful stimulus to appraisal and development comes from the president, who talks supportively about performance appraisal with all leaders and participates in appraising the performance of his/her direct reports.

Supervisors must understand human behavior

An appraisal program fights an uphill battle when supervisors fail to see employee development as the key to organizational development, or when they cannot understand how behavior can be changed or modified. In developing more effective performance, the objective is a change in behavior, not personality. The supervisor works with employees in such areas as interpersonal skills, styles of communication, quality of judgment and use of authority. There should be no attempt to change underlying personality traits.

The supervisor-employee relationship is recognized as critical

There can be no substitute for an employee's own supervisor when making assessments about performance. Real development takes place on the job and the supervisor plays a vital role in this process.

Motive and attitude are recognized as more important than technique and skill in the appraisal process

Training films, books and discussions stress the form and technique of performance appraisals. However, mastery of technique does not guarantee effective appraisal. The most important factor is the supervisor's genuine desire to understand, assess and help the employee to develop. With this desire, supervisors will find their own best way of getting the job done.

A motivating force (or dynamism) is created that lends vitality to the appraisal program

The way people feel about their jobs, about each other and about their company depends upon the quality of leadership. Dynamism is the sum of many things: a management philosophy to make the company's existence meaningful, an attitude of *joie-de-vivre* and an inherent expectation and enjoyment of change.

ADULT-TO-ADULT FEEDBACK

Traditional performance appraisals tend to focus on after-the-fact subjective evaluation. The focus in these appraisals is best seen in their documents, which take the form of check-lists and call for judgments about an employee's performance regarding factors such as dependability, flexibility, adaptability, etc. A predetermined rating scale is included so that each factor is measured on a scale of five or ten.

But what does an employee really know, at the end of a year's work, when his/her supervisor indicates a 6 out of 10 on flexibility? What is the context of this evaluation? What development plans can be established from this information? How can this lead to an atmosphere of mutual respect?

A number of progressive organizations, however, have developed appraisal systems that emphasize *adult-to-adult feedback through problem solving*. This is consistent with Positive Employee Relations. Employees and supervisors first seek a clear mutual understanding of the specific results to be accomplished, deadlines and costs. As soon as possible after completing a set of tasks, employees and supervisors discuss the results, including the reasons for satisfactory and exceptional results as well as any problems encountered. They agree on what needs to be done to overcome difficulties, who will do it and by when it must be done.

Three basic assumptions underlie this process:

Employees need to know what is expected of them

Performance improves when employees know, in advance, the results expected, how results will be measured, what resources are available and which tasks take precedence. Performance also improves when employees can influence these factors.

Employees need to know how they are progressing

People learn more effectively when accurate, specific and immediate feedback of interim and final results is provided regularly. Work planning develops specific, measurable objectives for this purpose. Progress reviews then allow employees and supervisors to measure results against these objectives.

Employees need to be able to obtain resources and assistance

Employees must be encouraged to ask questions and request help when necessary. If they feel their requests will be ignored or that they will be ridiculed or criticized for asking, they won't ask.

In an enlightened performance appraisal system, an organization can foster employee cooperation leading to improved performance. Rather than building on mistakes to justify salary decisions or storing up a paper trail of employee errors and omissions, supervisors and employees search together for ways to solve problems and capitalize on opportunities. Subjective opinions and "constructive" criticism give way to work-oriented analysis of hard facts about what really has been accomplished and what still needs to be done.

▶ The focus is on performance and not on personality.

ESTABLISHING PERFORMANCE STANDARDS

An effective system for reviewing performance must be based on clearly understood criteria. When these standards are specific, it is easier for employees to judge their own performance and to set appropriate improvement goals.

▶ Performance standards are useful only if they are attainable, specific and a valid measure of the task.

When establishing performance standards, the following guidelines will prove useful:

Be specific

Ambiguous terms accomplish little in communicating what management expects of the employee.

Avoid words such as:
acceptable
adequately
approximate
maximum
as soon as possible
carefully
reasonable
courteously
desirable.

Use self-defining terms:
with no more than 4 percent rejects
within one day after receipt
by Tuesday twelve noon/no later than the 15th day of the month
according to instructions in our procedural manual.

Standards should always be viewed within a normal range or, statistically, a bell curve. Some people will exceed the standards, most will meet the standards and some will fall short.

If a standard is unachievable, employees will tend to give up and perhaps perform less satisfactorily than if no standard had been set. If a standard is too easily achieved, employees will not expend extra effort and the standard will eventually have a negative effect on performance.

As well as being specific and attainable, a standard must differentiate between *activity* and *accomplishment*, focusing on the latter. It must also take into consideration those conditions that the employee cannot control.

Set valid goals

To expect an employee to make 75 telephone calls a day is not a valid standard because it addresses the activity only. It is better to expect the employee to make ten sales a day (the accomplishment) as a result of the telephone calls (the activity). Do not stipulate that an employee attend two seminars a year; rather, expect the employee to *acquire and use specific skills* related to current projects. Don't make the employee responsible for identifying cost-related problem areas. Instead, stipulate that the employee should *hold costs down* to three percent of the budget.

Authority levels

In its aim to sweep away the gray areas, management should make sure that levels of authority are clearly understood. A common cause of misunderstanding between an employee and supervisor is a lack of agreement about the employee's authority. An employee who seems to lack initiative or who, alternatively, oversteps bounds may be confused as to the degree of authority he/she possesses. Authority levels should be clearly expressed. For example, employees with:

- complete authority are expected to take action to carry out a key responsibility without consulting or reporting to the supervisor.

- normal authority are expected to take action but to report the action to the supervisor.
- limited authority are expected to present their recommendations, although action will not be taken until a decision is reached by management.

Level of authority is an important but not universal issue. Each key area of responsibility should be examined to establish its importance. For instance, if performance is less than satisfactory, the supervisor should check to see if a misunderstanding concerning the employee's level of authority has been a contributing factor. Similarly, it may be prudent to lower the degree of authority where performance is concerned, thereby encouraging more frequent discussions with the employee.

THE PERFORMANCE APPRAISAL DISCUSSION

Your discussion with the employee will likely be the most critical step in the appraisal and development process.

Goals of the meeting

- Clarify the employee's role in meeting the goals of the organization.
- Set the tone for an ongoing relationship.
- Act as a major motivational event.
- Provide an opportunity to indicate, by your behavior, the nature and depth of your concern for the employee.

Preparing for the meeting

Thoughtful preparation for the appraisal discussion will ensure a more successful and productive outcome. Paying attention to the following issues has proven helpful to many supervisors and managers:

- *The meeting should be private, taking place where there will be neither distractions nor interruptions.* This tells the employee you consider this to be an important meeting, worthy of your undivided attention. If your office is not satisfactory, look for a conference room.
- *Timing is important.* Make sure the employee has enough time to review your data on his/her performance and prepare for the discussion. This emphasizes that the discussion is not a lecture, and is evidence of your desire to be fair and reasonable as well as open and collaborative. It clearly demonstrates that you "walk the talk" regarding adult-to-adult relationships.
- *The discussion should be unhurried.* The length of time required for an appraisal discussion will depend on the employee, the location of the job in the company hierarchy and the anticipated depth of the appraisal interview. Allow sufficient time, frequently an hour, so the employee does not feel that this matter is a chore you have sandwiched between appointments that you have given higher priority.
- *Be up-to-date.* Make sure your assessment of the employee's performance is based on current and adequate information, preferably learned through first-hand observation. Make sure you have sufficient information on the day-to-day problems faced by the employee.
- *Remember that you are a role model.* Ask yourself if you would like to see your own behavior modeled in the employee. Do not assume the employee knows which behaviors are important. You may find that you have a simple misunderstanding to deal with rather than conscious resistance.
- *Try to anticipate the employee's response.* It may be cooperative, defensive, submissive or hostile. The employee may see no need for change and therefore be unwilling to commit to improving performance. Or the employee may not believe you really understand his/her position. Keep these points in mind when preparing for the interview and plan ways to deal effectively with these issues.
- *The aim of the appraisal is to assess the individual's total performance.* Consider performance in relation to all the specific

responsibilities of the job, taking into account their relative importance. Don't zero in on one responsibility only. And don't focus on one or two incidents that happen to stand out in your memory. Try to consider performance in all areas of the job over a significant period of time. The "halo effect," a major detrimental dynamic in a performance discussion, occurs when the appraiser holds very positive, or very negative, views about the employee's performance in the recent past. For example, satisfying a customer last week overshadows many months of mediocre or lackluster customer satisfaction levels.

- *Performance assessment is made in relation to the individual's accomplishments in the job.* Subjective factors — such as your like or dislike of the employee or your knowledge of his/her private affairs — have absolutely no place in an assessment interview.
- *The interview is not the place to make decisions concerning difficult salary problems.* This is a separate step and requires the consideration of factors that go beyond the performance assessment. Do not let your knowledge of existing salary problems affect your objective assessment of performance. (Some of the factors you may wish to take into consideration at salary review time are the accuracy of the job evaluation, the employee's past performance, future organizational plans and comparison of this employee's salary with that of others in the organization.)

Appraisal discussion pitfalls

- Be aware that if you once had personal experience in a particular job, it could influence your assessment of how the incumbent is handling it. The nature of the job may have changed since your association with it, so concentrate on the job as it is presently structured.
- Try not to be influenced by your knowledge of how others have performed in that job, or by your anticipation of how it will be performed in the future. Assess performance as it stands now, based on your observations during day-to-day contact.
- Beware of letting your assessment of the employee's performance be swayed by personal feeling of whether or not the job

is vital. Consider performance in relation to the job description/performance standards and assess performance of the specific responsibilities cited.
- Resist the subconscious tendency to rate more highly the performance of a person in a higher position. Remember that the higher the level, the greater the requirements of the job against which performance must be measured.
- Do not lose sight of the connection between results and standards. Your assessment should agree closely with the overall results achieved in the job by the incumbent.
- Consult your manager or the human resource department if there are problems in assessing performance. In making the assessment, you may also want to ask the opinion of those senior to you in the organization who are closely acquainted with the individual's work.

CONDUCTING THE APPRAISAL

The organization appraises employee performance for two reasons: to assess performance and to counsel the employee. The ultimate goal is to inspire the employee to reach his/her potential. Exhibit 11.1 outlines a nine-step approach to conducting a performance appraisal.

▶ The ultimate goal is to inspire the employee to reach his/her potential.

Ideally, appraisal procedures are geared to the employee's level of performance. They may focus on developing a promising employee, maintaining current satisfactory performance, or remedying substandard performance. To be successful, the appraisal procedure must be clearly understood by the employee and the supervisor. The goal of the appraisal must be attainable and the appraisal must be a valid measure of the employee's effectiveness, taking into account his/her level of authority.

Refer to exhibits 11.2 and 11.3 for detailed performance appraisal documents that can be adapted for use by your organization's employees and leadership personnel. You'll see that in the final summary section, an overall review of performance is required. This is based on a balanced, objective analysis that reflects the preceding comments on performance. The employees should be encouraged to make comments on the form. These need not be a rebuttal (although this is possible). Ideally, they will address suggestions, career expectations, etc. Both supervisor and employee should sign and date the completed performance review. The employee's signature is a confirmation only of the discussion.

Should a disagreement arise between employee and supervisor about the performance review assessment and/or development plan, both parties should make a concerted effort to reassess the data and seek an agreement. Subsequent meeting(s) may need to be scheduled. If required, time should be used constructively (and not as a point of pressure). When reviewing the performance data, other resource people such as the next-level manager and/or the human resource manager may need to assist.

EXHIBIT 11.1

CONDUCTING A PERFORMANCE APPRAISAL

Conducting an effective performance appraisal is not a "sit down, shut up and listen while I tell you your strengths and weaknesses" presentation. In fact, the most effective appraisal interviews are just that — interviews. They are two-way discussions that involve preparation and participation by both the supervisor and the employee. The following is a nine-step approach for conducting an effective performance appraisal:

1. Prepare.
Plan the appointment two to three weeks in advance, and at that time give the employee a blank copy of the form that will be used in the interview. Ask the employee to fill it out in advance of the meeting. This encourages the employee to think through his/her own job performance. Before the meeting, the supervisor should list the employee's key strengths and areas that need improvement.

2. Greet the employee.
Greet the employee warmly, getting out from behind your desk to reduce the "I'm the boss" image that can easily inhibit communication. Say something like, "During this interview, I'd like to offer any assistance I can give and answer any questions you may have. It's your interview and I'm here to help in whatever way you wish me to."

3. Determine the topic(s) the employee wants to discuss first.
This can be achieved by having you and the employee exchange the draft performance review form you have just completed. There is a strong likelihood that the two of you will have independently reached agreement on many of the factors. Beginning with a topic or factor that the employee is prepared to discuss can reduce tension. It may also increase the employee's acceptance of changes that you suggest be made later in the interview.

4. Discuss concerns not mentioned by the employee.
Ask the employee to describe why he/she chose that particular

self-rating. Probe into the rationale with open-ended, non-judgmental questions. Seek out facts, reference points and previous performance reviews to better understand the employee's perspective. Keep the discussion on objective issues (that is, performance versus personality).

Then, as the leader, explain why you chose your particular rating for the factor. Again, deal with objective data (not your "gut feeling" or hearsay). At this point there is usually enough new information or clarification about old information on the table, so that one or both parties can see themselves logically revising their assessment on the factor. In this way both parties demonstrate their willingness to listen, learn and change position based on new inputs.

This type of problem-solving discussion will repeat itself until all factors have been covered.

5. Develop a written action plan for carrying out key solutions in a specific time period.

6. Give specific feedback to the employee on positive performance that has not already been discussed.
- Describe the employee's positive behavior in specific terms and give examples.
- Tell the employee why his/her positive performance is important to you, your organization and to the employee.
- Spell out your future expectations of the employee.
- Express your appreciation.
- Develop action plans for utilizing the employee's strengths, if appropriate.

7. Summarize the interview and discuss ratings.
The supervisor should communicate the ratings now rather than earlier in the interview. This helps the employee to accept the ratings since critical job performance areas have already been discussed in detail.

8. Set follow-up dates.

9. Thank the employee.

EXHIBIT 11.2

PERFORMANCE APPRAISAL
For Employees

Name:
Date:
Department:
Position:
Manager:

Our approach

Sherborne Company has a deeply ingrained Positive Employee Relations philosophy that says, in effect: "make our employees winners," "let them stand out," and "treat employees as individuals." We believe that the real difference between success and failure at Sherborne can very often be traced to the question of how well we bring out the energy and talent of our employees. And that is what this performance review is all about. Further, the task of every Sherborne leader is to get his/her employees from where they are to where they have not been. For the Sherborne culture and management system to work, it is necessary to inspire employees at every level of the organization.

Sincerely,

W.H. Burford
General Manager

GUIDELINES FOR CONDUCTING A PERFORMANCE REVIEW

Introduction

Day-to-day coaching of employees is a vital responsibility of every leader. However, daily discussions are likely to be concerned with immediate problems. The six-month performance review cycle will help both parties focus on the critical issues. The purpose of the Sherborne performance review program is to provide an opportunity for a comprehensive discussion of overall performance.

A carefully thought out semi-annual review of performance, with the development of improvement plans, provides each employee with the knowledge of where he/she stands. A jointly prepared and implemented performance review, with sound improvement plans, motivates individuals to make the most of their abilities. Such a working climate is a clear demonstration to all Sherborne employees that our "values" are at work.

The leader and the employee should separately review the data necessary to prepare the performance review. Independently, each party should review the job description, performance standards, current development plans, and any tasks or objectives that were established for the preceding six months. This will result in two "draft" performance review documents being completed — one by the leader, and one by the employee.

The leader should receive the approval of his/her next-level manager before the performance discussion takes place. The goal here is to ensure that the leader has the buy-in of his/her manager before decisions, commitments, etc. are made to the leader. However, caution is needed. The employee should not be put in a position of supporting his/her draft against a "done deal" completed by the leader and the next-level manager.

Using the "draft" performance reviews, the leader and the employee will work towards a clear understanding of the employee's accomplishments, areas needing improvement, and training needs. The leader will complete, during the latter part of the discussion, a new and final performance review that summarizes the discussion and the improvement plans to which both have agreed.

The factors contained in the performance review document address the employee's behavior and performance. For each factor there is a scale that runs from unsatisfactory to meets standards to outstanding. For each of these ratings you are asked to record incidents, situations, issues, etc., that support the assessment.

GUIDELINES

This performance review includes seven performance areas. More topics can be added if needed; however, this should be done in conjunction with the employee. There is a further area entitled "Additional Comments" which encourages comment on performance not specifically addressed in the previous areas.

It is anticipated that an assessment will be made in each area which is appropriate to the performance being reviewed. The "Examples/Supporting Information" section must be used in each case.

In the section called "Development Plans/Target Dates," it is the leader's responsibility to initiate the discussion relative to training and development plans. It is in this section that the leader can truly perform his/her human resource management responsibilities by counseling, guiding and coaching the employee to improve job performance and/or broaden career aspirations.

In the final section, "Summary," an overall review of performance is required. It should logically reflect the performance levels indicated above on the form, but it should not be the result of a simple mathematical formula.

The following is an example of how to interpret the assessment factors:

(12) **Outstanding** — Performance, results and contributions are above expected levels to meet position requirements. All areas of job responsibility are being exceeded in terms of results and productivity.

(10) **Exceeds Performance Standards** — Performance, results and contributions are above expected levels to meet position requirements. All areas of responsibility have been met in the most achievable manner.

(8) Meets Performance Standards — Overall performance, results and contributions are fully satisfactory when measured against overall standards for the position. While actual results of performance may vary above or below standards for different job responsibilities, the overall contribution is meeting job requirements.

(4) Needs Performance Improvement — Overall performance, results and contributions are below expected levels for the position responsibilities. Partial job requirements and standards are being met. Specific plans to ensure progression must be developed by the employee and the supervisor/manager.

(1–3) Unsatisfactory Performance Level — Current performance, results and contributions are inadequate for the position responsibilities. Without significant improvement in performance, retention of the employee in the position is unacceptable. Specific plans for improvement and a timeframe for measuring results must be developed by the employee and the leader.

Both leader and employee should sign and date the completed performance appraisal. The employee's signature confirms the discussion only.

PERFORMANCE AREAS

1. Applying job skills

This factor addresses the employee's ability to quickly aquire and effectively apply job knowledge and job skills. Good performance is measured by the successful accomplishment of job responsibilities and performance standards using skills appropriate to the Sherborne business practices in his/her department.

Examples/Supporting Information
_____
_____

Development Plans/Target Dates
_____
_____

2. Being productive
Works independently or in a team, where appropriate, to produce agreed upon results (performance standards, key success factors, etc.) Rarely requires reminders of job-related process/practices and overall objective and (missing text)

Examples/Supporting Information
_____
_____

Development Plans/Target Dates
_____
_____

3. Applying Sherborne knowledge
This factor measures the application of Sherborne culture, values and goals for the resolution of issues, concerns or problems brought forward by external or internal customers/vendors. The employee demonstrates a passion to continually improve the business process and systems in his/her department in order to satisfy the work needs of others.

Examples/Supporting Information
_____
_____

Development Plans/Target Dates
_____
_____

4. Being a team player
This factor assesses the extent to which this employee is a team player — that is, willingly and in concert with peers, works to achieve department goals, including any unexpected problems or concerns that arise. Works collaboratively with next-level supervisors/managers in offering constructive feedback and suggestions.

Examples/Supporting Information

_____

_____

Development Plans/Target Dates

_____

_____

5. Using change constructively

Consider the employee's active participation in the change process. He/she demonstrates that change is both natural and positive in a customer-/market-driven organization. Examples of this behavior will include working productively when priorities change; taking initiatives; within the scope of his/her job, to change/improve processes and activities that hinder/prompt response to changing external/internal customer/vendor requirements.

Examples/Supporting Information

_____

_____

Development Plans/Target Dates

_____

_____

6. Resolving problems

This factor assesses the employee's skills at identification and resolution of problems that reflect the needs of the department (including internal and external customers). The employee is not seen to procrastinate when decisions are needed. Makes more acceptable decisions than unacceptable ones. Demonstrates a willingness to put his/her initiative, judgment and problem-solving skills on the line.

Examples/Supporting Information

_____

_____

Development Plans/Target Dates

_____

_____

7. Taking ownership

This factor reviews the employee's behavior in accepting ownership for tasks and completing them in a timely manner. Regularly sets priorities and plans work effectively. Meets deadlines with most problems solved. Knows the status of current job tasks and projects when asked.

Examples/Supporting Information
_____
_____

Development Plans/Target Dates
_____
_____

Employee's comments (on both the performance review and the development plans):
_____
_____
_____
_____

I have read this review. it has been discussed with me and I have a personal copy.

Employee's signature:

Date:

EXHIBIT 11.3

PERFORMANCE APPRAISAL
For Leadership Personnel

Name:
Date:
Department:
Title:
Manager:

Introduction

This performance appraisal is a continuous and systematic process in which you and your manager discuss your achievements over the past year and plan for the next year. This is a collaborative process. Your manager participatively works with you to:

- Identify and agree to the responsibilities and performance standards that are essential to your job.
- Determine and agree to specific job objectives for you that relate to the goals of Sherborne and/or your unit.
- Coach, guide and counsel you on a consistent basis for more effective performance and career development.
- Identify any application of knowledge or skills that are affecting your overall job performance and develop an action plan.
- Discuss and assess your overall performance in this appraisal.
- Develop a career development plan that will help you achieve your aspirations.

GUIDELINES

This performance appraisal has been divided into three sections. The first deals with twelve critical areas of managerial performance arranged around three topics:

(i) You the Technical Manager
(ii) You the Business Manager
(iii) You the Human Resources Manager.

There is a further area entitled "Additional Comments" which encourages comment on performance not specifically addressed in the previous twelve areas.

It is anticipated that an assessment will be made in each area that is appropriate to the performance being reviewed. The comments section must be used in each case. The majority of the comments concerning the twelve areas should deal with specific information relative to where improvement is needed or performance is better than acceptable. Each area should be reviewed separately to minimize the possibility of the "halo effect."

In the section entitled "Action Plans," it is the manager's responsibility to initiate the discussion relative to training and action plans. It is in this section that the manager can truly perform his/her human resource management responsibilities by counseling, guiding and coaching the employee to improve job performance and/or broaden career aspirations.

In the final section, "Summary," an overall review of performance is required. A balanced, objective consideration is the determinant of this overall analysis. It should logically reflect the performance levels indicated above on the form. But it should not be the result of a mathematical formula.

Both reviewer and employee should sign and date the completed performance review. The employee's signature confirms the discussion only.

YOU THE TECHNICAL MANAGER

Technical knowledge: To what extent does this leader understand and apply technical competencies regarding workflow, equipment, systems, process, safety, etc.

```
0                           8                      12
|_____|_____|
```

0 — Is noticeably deficient in either skills or their application as measured by the feedback and business results.

8 — Demonstrates good skills, applies them well and trains employees so their technical knowledge meets the performance standards of their jobs.

12 — Indicates an exceptional understanding of the technical management of his/her department. Manager and employees frequently sought after as technical "experts."

Supporting comments:
_____
_____
_____
_____

Department knowledge: To what extent does this leader have and apply both formal and pragmatic technical/operational management knowledge required for the successful completion of his/her responsibilities? Does he/she understand the relationship between revenue generation and cost control?

```
0                           8                      12
|_____|_____|
```

0 — Sometimes caught "off guard" not knowing what employees are doing. Hasn't been keeping up to date with the Sherborne key results mission, spirit, etc. Frequently needs assistance in completing job responsibilities.

8 — Demonstrates sufficient current knowledge to generally work independently to produce agreed-to results. Rarely requires reminding of department concerns.

12 — Demonstrates thorough and current knowledge of all aspects of effective department management. Recognized as a resource person.

Supporting comments:
_____
_____
_____
_____

Customer service: Does this leader fully appreciate the value of customers/customer service and ensure that his/her employees treat each customer and their order/shipment as though they are the only reason why Sherborne exists?

```
0                          8                     12
|_____|_____|
```

0 — Customer service and quality, as measured by customer feedback, peer input, and manager's observations is low. Customer needs are not anticipated, employees don't go out of their way to accommodate customer deadlines, quality requirements, etc.

8 — Customers are treated "like kings" at all times. Feedback from all sources indicates high quality and customer service standards. Employees are well trained, and demonstrate a willingness to accommodate even the "difficult" customer.

12 — Positive feedback from other managers, peers and customers is frequently unsolicited. Department frequently used as a model. Customer service is pro-active.

Supporting comments:

_____
_____
_____
_____

YOU THE BUSINESS MANAGER

Business management: Does this leader actively participate in setting standards that makes the business (Sherborne) more successful? Are financial plans aggressive but achievable? Do actual results demonstrate a solid track record of financial success?

```
0                            8                    12
|_____|_____|
```

0 — Business expectations are not clear and/or are poorly communicated; hence, results are unpredictable. Achievement as measured against the application of business management, financial and/or budget plans is unacceptable.

8 — Regularly meets financial and budget targets. Demonstrates through actions that Sherborne business success requires involvement beyond current departmental activities. Variances to financial and/or budget plans are infrequent and do not repeat themselves.

12 — Demonstrates an enviable record of business acumen. Is sought after, by others, for advice on Sherborne business activities. Financial and budget plan results are "right on." A consistent producer with little or no follow-up required.

Supporting comments:

_____
_____
_____
_____

Key operating controls: Is this leader reacting promptly to the available financial data? Are the various operating reports used? Are expense items being controlled? Is he/she receiving value for the funds expended?

```
0                        8                    12
|_____|_____|
```

0 — Frequently operating costs are over budget. Value for money expended is below the norm. Operating controls, as a management tool, are sloppy; leader reacts only after being told.

8 — Sound day-to-day financial decisions are being made. When compared against the criteria, ratios, percentages, etc., are as planned. Variances, which occur infrequently, are documented and are not repeated.

12 — Expense items are always monitored closely, good value is received, negative variances are virtually non-existent. Leader demonstrates pro-active cost control behavior, and recommends improvements to the system. Subordinate leaders demonstrate a similarly high application of cost control practices.

Supporting comments:
_____
_____
_____
_____

Planning and organizing: How well does this leader plan, schedule, prioritize and lay out work assignments for himself/herself and employees? Does this leader predetermine a course of action so as to accomplish objectives?

```
0                        8                    12
|_____|_____|
```

0 — Frequently charges ahead without enough thought or planning. Is often confused by demands of the job, very often needs help setting priorities. Some of his/her employees are busy, while others aren't busy enough.

8 — Generally able to set priorities and to effectively plan the efficient utilization of resources. Usually meets deadlines with most problems solved. Usually knows where things stand. Short-term planning is good.

12 — Utilizes the broad view. Looks ahead. Anticipates what is coming. Sets long-range goals and priorities. Has a good feel for what is going on. Employees are well organized.

Supporting comments:
_____
_____
_____
_____

Decision maker and problem solver: Does this leader make sound decisions? Is he/she hesitant to make decisions that may be unpopular? Can this leader make quick decisions when needed?

```
0                            8                        12
|————————————————————————————|————————————————————————|
```

0 — Procrastinates when decisions are needed. Afraid to make unpopular decisions. Narrow-minded. Doesn't usually ask employees for their opinions before deciding. Unable to distinguish between problems and symptoms.

8 — Frequently makes the right decision. Sometimes makes decisions without all the facts. Occasionally consults others before deciding. Makes quick decisions when needed. Takes initiative to solve problems.

12 — Displays solid reasoning and analysis in making decisions. Objective. Gathers all the facts. Participative management style. Makes unpopular decisions when required. Is pro-active; anticipates problems.

Supporting comments:

_____
_____
_____
_____

Communications: How effective is this leader when communicating? Are his/her words, reports, memos, etc., clear and concise? Does this leader listen well? Are employees kept well informed?

```
0                        8                      12
|_____|_____|
```

0 — Reports usually need rewriting. Can't get ideas across effectively while speaking. Doesn't spend enough time listening — too busy talking. Next-level manager and employees often uninformed, e.g., expense items, why things are done. Information doesn't come up the organization readily.

8 — Generally has only rare and minor problems in understanding what is going on and/or getting information to others. Asks for clarification if in doubt. Messages are given to subordinate leaders who in turn communicate fully with their employees.

12 — Reports and discussions are routinely clear, concise and pertinent. Keeps everyone informed. An appropriate blend of listening and talking. Takes ownership of issues and communicates convincingly to employees and peers.

Supporting comments:

_____
_____
_____
_____

YOU THE HUMAN RESOURCES MANAGER

Role model: Does this leader establish and demonstrate high standards of conduct and business professionalism? Does he/she shape and model the Sherborne culture? Does he/she hold tenaciously to, and clearly demonstrate, the belief that excellence is achievable in their department? Is he/she a good leader?

0   8   12

0 — Says things but acts differently. Unpredictable. Loses temper. Moody. Too serious. Sometimes sloppy, negligent appearance. Not respected.

8 — Adheres to the Sherborne culture and conveys message to others. Leads by example. Looked up to by the better performers. Manages as a facilitator. His/her presence is evident in the department.

12 — Model for others. Contributes "added value" to the Sherborne culture, known as a "builder of leaders." Under control even when under stress.

Supporting comments:
_____
_____
_____
_____

Personnel management: To what extent does this leader select, train and develop employees; does he/she know their abilities, aspirations, etc? Are employees counselled effectively?

0   8   12

0 — Group/team just gets by. Not enough regular contact with employee. Doesn't know or assess them well, too

busy doing. Marginal delegator. Frequent complaints, low morale. Group not always cooperative. Not a good counsellor. Plays favorites frequently.

8 — Some interpersonal or operational problems develop but these are quickly overcome in a fair and participative manner. Counseling is an on-going process. Knows staff fairly well. Could delegate more.

12 — Gets the most out of his/her employees. Builds excellent team work. Group highly motivated, not afraid to discuss their weaknesses. Involves group in setting goals. Genuinely cares about staff. Excellent delegator. Good judge of people, knows their individual differences.

Supporting comments:
_____
_____
_____
_____

Staff performance and promotability: To what extent does this leader develop and motivate his/her employees? What percentage of the employees are assessed as "meeting job standards" or better? How many "new" leaders have been developed for other Sherborne departments?

0   8   12
|_____|_____|

0 — The performance review is seen as a "necessary evil." Employee turnover is higher than required. Few, if any, employees have been sought after by other leaders. Reviews are generally not completed on time. Senior manager spends excessive time on corrective reviews. Does not step up to performance problems.

8 — The performance review is used as a participative tool to develop employees. More than 75 percent of employees are assessed as "meeting job standards" or better. At least one employee is promotable and ready to fill a next level position.

12 — Performance appraisals frequently show signs of creativity and understanding of the "excellence" principles. Demonstrable examples of human and/or business growth resulting from the review process.

Supporting comments:
_____
_____
_____
_____

Causing constructive change: Does this leader consistently seek out opportunities to improve his/her human resource, business and technical responsibilities? Does he/she have a "sense" of the business and the role their department plays? Does he/she have a spirit of inquiry, knowing when, how and that change should occur?

```
0                        8                        12
|_____|_____|
```

0 — Status quo, accepts "we've always done it this way" rule. Expects management to cause change and take the risk. Will follow Sherborne policies and procedures if not personally threatening.

8 — Will follow manager's lead, infrequently needs a push. Causes change to occur but frequently makes unilateral decisions. Accepts responsibility for decisions taken within limits of job. Buys into ownership for improving performance — at all levels.

12 — Seeks out "excellence" opportunities and initiates change. Creatively and participatively resolves problems. Broad vision, sees the whole and accepts ownership to deal with all issues. Successful risk taker.

Supporting comments:
_____
_____
_____
_____

ADDITIONAL COMMENTS
(Include other performance factors that you wish to assess.)

_____
_____
_____

ACTION PLANS
In this space note the particulars of the action plans that have been agreed upon for the next review period that will lead to an improvement in performance or will upgrade this leader's competencies. The spirit of an action plan is best demonstrated when both leader and manager work together — remembering that buy-in is critical.

Specific Actions to Improve Performance:
_____
_____
_____

Target Dates/Milestones:
_____
_____
_____

EMPLOYEE COMMENTS
(on both the performance appraisal and the action plans)
_____
_____
_____
_____

EMPLOYEE'S SIGNATURE
I have read this appraisal. It has been discussed with me and I have a personal copy.

Employee:
Date:

SUMMARY
(To be completed after assessing performance factors recorded on the performance review.)

Overall assessment of performance. How well does this person perform his/her job function?

```
0                          8              12
|--------------------------|--------------|
```

0 — Unsatisfactory
4 — Needs performance improvement
8 — Meets performance standard
10 — Exceeds performance standard
12 — Outstanding

What are the strongest aspects of this person's performance?
_____
_____

Since the last performance appraisal this person's performance has
( ) Declined   ( ) Remained the same   ( ) Improved

Describe and explain the significance of this assessment to the employee and/or Sherborne.
_____
_____

In what areas does this person most need to improve present performance?
_____
_____

Interviewer's post-review notes
_____
_____

Next-level manager's signature/date:
General manager's signature/date:
Vice-president's signature/date:

TAKE ACTION!

1. Make a commitment to establish a climate that is conducive to change — a workplace that encourages, enables and rewards performance.
   - Ensure that the president of the company and senior management wholeheartedly endorse the employee development and appraisal program.
   - Recognize that the supervisor-employee relationship is critical and that the supervisor requires a genuine desire to understand, assess and help employees to develop.
   - Make sure that, as much as possible, supervisors understand human behavior, with all its complexities.
2. Establish specific performance standards and articulate them clearly.
3. Make sure levels of authority are clearly understood.
4. Prepare for performance appraisal discussion with employee.
5. Conduct the appraisal according to the steps detailed in Exhibit 11.1

12
MANAGING EMPLOYEE PERFORMANCE

A Positive Employee Relations program will be seriously handicapped if it does not have a comprehensive program for managing employee performance. The purpose of such a program is to assist all employees to perform at their highest level and in a manner that is consistent with company values, guiding behaviors, practices and job performance standards. The focus of the program, which must have as its cornerstone *consistency*, *fairness* and *impartiality*, is to enable employees to make responsible choices about their employment. The program assumes an adult-to-adult approach to interacting with employees.

Managing the performance of others is one of the most difficult and challenging leadership problems. A skill required of all supervisors, it is essential to productivity. A supervisor's ability to manage others is reflected in the organizational climate. In a unionized environment disciplinary issues (the results of "managing") constitute the largest single category of grievance cases going to arbitration. Setting up a comprehensive performance management program is of vital importance to the union-free employer.

What follows is a comprehensive program for dealing effectively with performance management. Any *responsible* performance management program must strive for crystal-clear communications.

▶ The employee must know the workplace expectations and know the consequences of unacceptable or inappropriate performance and behaviors.

Every step in the performance management program must be made clear both verbally and in writing. If the desired change in behavior or performance is not forthcoming, which sometimes happens, both management and employee have a clear understanding of the reasons leading to subsequent actions. If the employee being managed is unable or unwilling to perform at his/her highest level and in a manner which is consistent with company values, guiding behaviors, practices and job performance standards, termination of the employment relationship may be the only recourse.

WHAT DOES IT MEAN TO "MANAGE" PERFORMANCE?

Managing performance involves both regular performance appraisal and critical incident management. Regular performance appraisal tends to be scheduled at appropriate intervals to provide employees with summary feedback as to how they are performing their jobs, both from a functional perspective and from a behavioral perspective. An employee receiving a scheduled performance appraisal should never be hearing this feedback for the first time. Critical incident management arises when an employee acts so far out of line with the company values, guiding behaviors, practices and job performance standards that immediate action is required. Critical incidents can also arise around functional issues (how the job is performed) and from a behavioral perspective.

Approaches to managing performance

The objective is to develop in the employees attitudes and behaviors that conform to the values and guiding behaviors of the company. How can this be achieved?

On one hand, management can rule with an iron fist, punishing violators severely and, in general, forcing employees to obey and conform. This type of management, negative discipline, can be characterized as punitive, autocratic or simply rule-by-fear. It is also very parent-to-child oriented.

The Positive Employee Relations approach is to develop in people *a willingness and a desire* to conform to the values, guiding behaviors, practices and job performance standards.

▶ Employees should cooperate because they want to, not because they are afraid of the consequences of disobedience.

If employees "buy into" the values, live the guiding behaviors, conform with the practices and meet job performance standards, managing the performance of the employees is a relatively easy task. Unfortunately, however, the "buy-in" is not a simple achievement. For example, if one employs people with personal values that are in opposition to the company values, conflict or resistance is the only possible outcome. Further, if the supervisor does not behave in ways consistent with the company values or guiding behaviors, the employee will receive mixed messages. This need for consistency extends to the performance feedback and recognition systems. If supervisors and managers interpret the values, guiding behaviors, etc., differently, how is an employee to know which leadership person to emulate?

NEGATIVE DISCIPLINE

The problem with negative discipline is that it encourages only the minimum level of performance necessary to avoid punishment. Where such a management style is prevalent, employees are not given the opportunity to help formulate the workplace expectations, nor do they understand the reasons behind them. They know only that they will be punished for a violation. The rule-by-fear approach puts the emphasis upon avoidance of punishment rather than enthusiastic cooperation.

As a long-term management philosophy, rule-by-fear can have only limited success. This does not deny, however, that for certain employees, under certain circumstances, enforced authority may be the only answer. Some employees, as a consequence of their background and personality, may respond only to a supervisor who uses a get-tough policy. However, with more effective selection interviewing practices, these individuals can be identified *before* an employment offer is made.

RESPONSIBLE PERFORMANCE MANAGEMENT

Responsible performance management is a leadership practice that develops a willing adherence to the values, guiding behaviors, practices and performance standards of the organization. The employees, both as individuals and as a work team, adhere to the guiding behaviors and job performance standards because they understand, believe in and support them. It is an important ingredient in Positive Employee Relations.

The objectives of performance management

- To advise and inform, so as to assist the employee do his/her job better.
- To identify and turn around the employee's non-compliance (with values, guiding behaviors, practices and performance standards), not to condemn the employee.
- To encourage personal self-responsibility, not to harm the individual.

What a responsible performance management program does

- Emphasizes improvement rather than punishment.
- Results in the employee changing behavior to perform according to values, guiding behaviors, practices and job performance standards.
- Sustains the employee's dignity and self-respect.
- Provides for increased assistance if required.

Table 12.1 shows the elements of a responsible performance management program. Exhibits 12.1 through 12.4 give an example of a responsible performance management program and related documentation.

TABLE 12.1 — Elements of a Responsible Performance Management Program

Define policy and procedure	Top management must decide what kind of behavior it expects of its employees and how it hopes to achieve it — through a responsible and constructive form of performance management, sound leadership, and adequate employee training.
Communication of standards	Employees must have knowledge of the values, guiding behaviors, practices and performance standards for their position, before they can be held accountable.
Burden of proof	The principle that an individual is presumed innocent until proven guilty also applies to performance management. The burden of proof is on the employer to show that the employee is not meeting expectations.
Consistency and flexibility	Consistency means that all aspects of the program are applied uniformly to all employees; flexibility allows for the uniqueness of people and situations.
Reasonable guiding behaviors and workplace expectations	Guiding behaviors and workplace expectations should be reasonable and attainable.
Right of appeal	Employees must always have the right to present their side in a performance management issue. This is a basic tenet of a Positive Employee Relations program. (See Chapter 13 for positive ways of resolving outstanding issues.)

VALUES AND GUIDING BEHAVIORS

In some organizations, there are *too many* petty rules that tie everyone's hands and stifle initiative and morale. In such organizations, a rule becomes necessary when a certain type of behavior continually recurs and is being settled on an arbitrary basis. In this situation, management formulates a rule and decides on penalties so that everyone is treated alike. It is then necessary to make sure that the rules are communicated. However, in a Positive Employee Relations environment, values and guiding behaviors can take the place of rules.

Values reflect what the company stands for. The guiding behaviors are the actions that make the values real. Together they should be:

Easy to understand
An employee who cannot understand what a value is cannot follow it.

Important
A value must make sense to the employee and the guiding behaviors which support it must make a difference to the organization.

Easy to practice
A guiding behavior that cannot be followed is worse than no guiding behavior.

Actually practiced
Values and guiding behaviors must be practiced by everyone.

While rules are definite statements of what and what not to do — for example, "No smoking" or "No food or drink in the lab," or written regulations against gambling on the premises or leaving one's work station early — guiding behaviors are more general statements that ensure that employees will act in a responsible manner in the best interests of all the stakeholders in an organization. For example, if care and concern are values of the organization, "I will do no harm" could be a guiding behavior supporting that value. Such a guiding behavior covers a multitude of activities that would otherwise be called rules, such as no abusive behavior, no fighting, no drugs, no drinking, etc. Guiding behaviors tell people how they should conduct themselves as members of a specific group. It would be difficult to conduct a business without some common agreement on workplace expectations.

▶ Values and guiding behaviors must be clear and definite to avoid any misinterpretation.

WHEN GUIDING BEHAVIORS ARE NOT PRACTICED

When an employee does not practice a guiding behavior, it is necessary to consider both the guiding behavior and the employee. If the guiding behavior is not being followed by a large portion of the workforce, the emphasis of the investigation should initially be put upon the guiding behavior itself. If, however, the guiding behavior is not being practiced by only one or two employees, then the focus should be on the employee.

When there is widespread non-practice of a guiding behavior, chances are the guiding behavior itself needs to be amended. Determine if the guiding behavior is consistent with the company's values and Positive Employee Relations program. Supervisors should remember that even though they may not have the authority to change a guiding behavior, they can make a strong recommendation regarding its revision.

Exhibit 12.5 lists the questions you should ask about both the guiding behavior and the employee when an employee is not following the guiding behavior.

Functional performance problems

As we said earlier, performance management applies to both functional performance of the job and work behaviors. When an issue arises around functional performance, the approach is, in principle, the same as previously discussed (around behavioral issues). The supervisor identifies a performance problem — that is, a difference between the actual job performance and the expected performance.

After identifying the problem, the supervisor counsels the employee on the need to improve and ensures that:

- there are no work conditions or job-related issues preventing the employee from performing the work.

- proper on-the-job training has taken place.
- the employee has received regular performance feedback and appraisals.

Performance problems are easier to solve when desired performance and actual performance are expressed in specific terms. To state that one employee has a bad attitude or that another employee has a poor attendance record is not good enough. The supervisor must be able to state specifically what he/she expects from the employee, and in what way the employee is not fulfilling the expectation.

▶ The more clearly a problem is defined, the easier it is to solve.

If performance problems are expressed as generalized (for example, a poor attendance record) then the supervisor and employee are likely suffering from mis-communications. For example, what does "poor attendance" mean? Too many late arrivals? Leaving early too often? Extending the lunch break? Missing Mondays and Fridays on a regular basis?

Compare the problem to the standard so as to determine how serious it really is. Also, inquire from your peers and/or human resources, how a similar attendance problem has been handled by others in the leadership group.

WHAT TO DO

The leadership group has the primary responsibility for managing the performance of their employees. Even under the best conditions and with excellent supervisory leadership and employee training, somebody is going to step out of bounds every now and then. When this happens, the process of performance management goes into effect. Performance management is required when an employee fails to meet the agreed-upon and/or written standards.

▶ The performance management action should be directed at changing employee behavior; it is not meant as a punitive instrument.

Performance management should follow this progression:
- counseling interview(s).
- formal discussion of consequences.
- written statement of consequences.
- one-day suspension.

This sequence puts the onus on the employee to accept responsibility for the consequences of his/her actions. Rarely would an employee be discharged on the first occasion of failing to act in accordance with the values, guiding behaviors, practices and performance standards.

The one-day suspension is an extremely serious step as *the employee must decide during this period if he/she intends to act in accordance with the values, guiding behaviors, practices and performance standards. The employee has to understand that if he/she chooses not to act appropriately, then he/she is choosing to end the employment relationship.* It should be used only if, after counseling interviews and verbal and written discussions of consequences, there has been no change in performance. In essence this is a paid day off work, to be served off-site, so that the employee can think through his/her employment options. If the employee decides to change his/her behavior, returning to work should be viewed as an opportunity to start with a clean slate.

The issue of termination is outside the terms of reference of a performance management program. It is a final step that indicates the failure of all attempts to persuade the employee to change his/her behavior. Termination remains the ultimate consequence, but is being used less and less every day. Termination, from the standpoint of performance management, is not managing at all; it is the amputation, not the correction, of a problem.

In administering a performance management program, the leadership group must be constantly aware of the dual objectives of preserving the interests of the organization and protecting the rights of the individual.

Unless sound policies are adopted and orderly procedures followed, there is a danger that management will look at each case solely in the short term. The danger of short term thinking, when it comes to performance management, is that the leadership group gets caught up in sending a "don't do this" message. Over the long term, employees will interpret punitive actions as the result of managerial anger and frustration. This will create discontent among the employee population, when the aim of performance management should be to assist employees in making performance and behavioral changes.

EXHIBIT 12.1

RESPONSIBLE PERFORMANCE MANAGEMENT PROGRAM

Objective
The goals of this policy and its related procedures are to improve ongoing relationships between employees and management. We are concerned about the nature and quality of employee job satisfaction, individual/team morale and our product's quality. In short, the leadership group will operate Sherborne in a manner consistent with Positive Employee Relations; that is, fair, efficient, effective, equitable and perceived by employees as a good place to work.

Philosophy
As an enlightened employer, Sherborne understands and supports the philosophy that each employee is a mature, responsible and self-reliant person who is interested in meeting job performance standards and workplace expectations and deserving of fair rewards in the form of recognition, income and potential advancement.

The following are our assumptions about performance management:

- This policy will, to the best of our ability, be administered fairly and equitably throughout the company.
- Performance management is designed to assist development, not as punishment.
- All Sherborne employees will meet and maintain the performance standards for their position, and will adhere to company values, guiding behaviors, practices and performance standards.
- Employees affected by this policy will always have the right to appeal any decision through the leadership group or an alternative dispute resolution process.

To maintain a productive working environment and to ensure that Sherborne maintains its operating license(s), policies, procedures and practices have been established by the company and government regulatory agencies in Canada, the United States and the United Kingdom.

Responsible performance management has been established to be *assistive* and *responsible* rather than punitive. It has also been designed to be *fair* and *consistent*. It is, however, a formal method of performance management because non-compliance with our values, guiding behaviors, practices and performance standards may have serious consequences for Sherborne employees, the products we manufacture and the company.

Causes for performance management

There are two basic areas that account for nearly every type of performance management problem:

- Behavior that does not conform to our values, guiding behaviors and practices.
- Functional work performance that does not meet performance standards.

SETTING THE GROUNDWORK

The following are guidelines, not hard and fast rules. They have been developed to assist you to determine the appropriate performance management response. As such, they must be tempered with judgment, fairness and common sense.

Tell them what you expect

People cannot be faulted for failure to comply with values, guiding behaviors, practices and performance standards if they don't know what they are (workplace expectations). For example, if a guiding behavior is "I will not smoke in non-smoking areas," then "no smoking" signs should be posted to identify such areas. Similarly, supervisors must clearly instruct employees on work methods, quality criteria, work deadlines and other performance expectations.

While all values can and should be clearly articulated, not all guiding behaviors, practices and performance standards can be written down. Many are communicated by on-the-job training. Others are just common sense.

The general rule is that supervisors must communicate work performance and behavior expectations to an employee *before* trying to manage non-compliance.

Before a supervisor begins to take action under the responsible performance management program, it is important for the next-level manager to be involved. This will provide Sherborne's Positive Employee Relations program with two important checks. First, that the supervisor has had an opportunity to think through the problem and develop a reasonable solution, and second, that the employee's interests will be protected from the risk of actions taken without careful consideration.

Seek an explanation
When an employee is found to be not practicing a company value, guiding behavior or practice, or when job performance does not meet performance standards, the supervisor will meet with the employee to explain the nature of the problem, seek an explanation or justification of the problem and counsel the employee on how to improve the situation. Before, or at the beginning of the counseling interview, the supervisor will establish *beyond a doubt* whether or not the employee *knew* that he/she was not practicing the value, guiding behavior or practices, or not meeting job performance standards. For example, had the employee been properly instructed and/or trained with respect to job responsibilities?

During the interview, the supervisor will listen objectively to the employee's explanation. If the supervisor decides to accept the employee's reasons or decides that the employee has accepted the responsibility for changing his/her behavior or work performance as required, the supervisor will inform the employee accordingly.

If the employee knew the guiding behavior or performance standard and if the explanation is not satisfactory, or if the supervisor believes this preliminary discussion alone will not result in changed behavior or performance, the supervisor should immediately take further action.

It may be difficult to decide what further action to take. In coming to that decision, it is essential to know what the alternatives are. These are described below.

PERFORMANCE MANAGEMENT ALTERNATIVES

Counseling interviews

A counseling interview should be initiated by the supervisor as soon as it appears that a problem exists. The supervisor should first discuss the problem with the employee in a helpful and non-threatening manner. The goal of the interview is to help the employee recognize that a problem exists and to help the employee develop an effective way to improve his/her work performance or behavior.

When meeting with the employee, a supervisor should follow this format:

- Review the problem in terms of the relevant company value, guiding behavior, practice or performance standard versus what actually transpired.
- Review the justification for the relevant value, guiding behavior, practice or performance standard.
- Encourage the employee to participate in the discussion. Ask for the employee's comments and reasons and *listen to what the employee has to say*.
- Review with the employee the changes he/she must make, and the timeline for making these changes. Share your confidence in the employee's ability to improve.

Step 1 — Formal Discussion of Consequences

- Review with the employee the value, guiding behavior, practice or performance standard. Ensure that the employee fully understands the purpose as well as the benefits of compliance. Express confidence that, henceforth, the employee will be able to practice the relevant value, guiding behavior, practice or performance standard. Advise the employee that this is a discussion and the first step in the responsible performance management program.
- Seek employee agreement as to action plans.
- Prepare a written memo to file. The purpose of the note is to confirm that the verbal discussion took place and to provide a record for future reference. Typically, this memo will include:

- Date of interview.
- Date of non-compliance and nature of non-compliance; that is, not wearing glasses, interviewed and advised of non-compliance, Step 1.
- Statement of agreed-upon action plan to change performance or behavior.
- Signature of supervisor.
- Give one (1) copy to the employee.
- Forward one (1) copy to human resources/employee's personnel file.

Step 2 — Written Statement of Consequences

For an unacceptable reoccurrence of a repeated minor non-compliance or for a first major non-compliance:

- Interview and advise the employee as in Step I.
- Depending on the nature of the matter, ask if the employee enjoys the work that Sherborne has to offer, feels he/she can meet the performance expectations and is willing to accept Sherborne's values, guiding behaviors and practices. If not, suggest that the employee may wish to look for another job or a different type of work. However, encourage the employee to remain with Sherborne. Stress that it is necessary for the employee to adapt to the requirements of Sherborne.
- Complete and distribute the *written statement of consequences*. (See Exhibit 12.2 for sample Step 2 letter.) Distribute as in Step 1. Ask the employee to sign the letter (indicating receipt only).
- Prepare and sign three (3) copies of a letter confirming the conversation and distribute as follows:
    - One (1) copy to the employee. If the employee will not accept the letter, send by *registered/certified mail* to his/her home.
    - One (1) copy for the manager's file.
    - One (1) copy to human resources/employee's personnel file.

The purpose of asking the employee to sign the written statement of consequences is to acknowledge its delivery, not to admit to the facts. If the employee refuses to sign, hand it to the employee in the presence of another supervisor and have that supervisor sign as a witness.

Step 3 — Further Statement of Consequences
Depending on the seriousness or the amount of repetition of the non-compliance, a further written statement of consequences may be appropriate.
- Interview, advise and notify as in Steps 1 and 2.
- *This interview, advice and notification are to be scheduled with the next-level manager being present.*
- Make abundantly clear the seriousness of the situation. Tell the employee that another occasion of non-compliance will lead to further consequences which could include termination of the employment relationship.
- Complete and distribute the *written statement of consequences*. (See Exhibit 12.3 for sample Step 3 letter.) Ask employee to sign. (See comments on employee signature under Step 2.)
- Prepare and sign three (3) copies of a letter confirming the conversation and distribute as follows:
    - One (1) copy for the employee. If the employee will not accept the letter, send by *registered/certified mail* to his/her home.
    - One (1) copy for the manager's file.
    - One (1) copy to human resources/employee's personnel file.

Step 4 — Suspension
Depending on the seriousness and reoccurrence of the non-compliance, a suspension of varying lengths of time may be appropriate.

- Interview, advise and notify as in Step 3.
- *This interview, advice and notification is to be reviewed or confirmed by the vice-president and a representative of the human resources department.*
- Direct the employee to go home for the remainder of the work day to underline the seriousness of the non-compliance. Ask the employee to consider seriously whether he/she

wishes to abide by Sherborne values, guiding behaviors, practices and performance standards. Depending on the seriousness of the matter, the number of hours remaining in the shift and the apparent willingness of the employee to change his/her behavior or performance, you may inform the employee before leaving that he/she will receive full pay for the shift. This is a last expression of Sherborne's hope that the employee will decide to stay and meet the workplace expectations.

- Make abundantly clear the seriousness of the situation. Tell the employee that any further instances of non-compliance will indicate to the company that the employee no longer wishes to be part of the Sherborne community. The employee in effect will be choosing to end his/her employment relationship with Sherborne.
- Complete and distribute the *written letter* confirming the suspension. (See Exhibit 12.4 for sample Step 4 letter.) Ask employee to sign. (See comments on employee signature under Step 2.)
- Prepare and sign three (3) copies of a letter confirming the conversation and distribute as follows:
    - One (1) copy for the employee. If the employee will not accept the letter, send by *registered/certified mail* to his/her home.
    - One (1) copy for the manager's file.
    - One (1) copy to human resources/employee's personnel file.

Termination of the Employment Relationship

We assume that an employee who returns from a suspension makes a decision that he/she wants to stay at Sherborne and acts accordingly. In the event that subsequent events prove this to be incorrect, or in a situation where an employee's act of failing to practice the company's values, guiding behaviors, practices and performance standards is so contrary to the company's interests that sustaining employment is impossible, then termination of the employment relationship is the only possible outcome. Follow these steps:

- Interview the employee *in the presence of the vice-president and the human resources manager.* Consult with the human resources department to ensure that every step has been taken to support our values on fairness and equity.
- Terminate the employment relationship and give the employee a letter which recites the previous responsible performance management record and the culminating incident.
- Note this action on the employee's personnel file.

DECIDING ON PERFORMANCE MANAGEMENT ACTIONS

Alternative performance management actions have been spelled out on the previous pages. The question that remains is: "Which one to use and when?"

This is important because if the consequences of an employee act are disproportionate to the act, the supervisor is branded "unfair," and soon morale and motivation suffer. Too often, supervisors *anticipate these problems and end up "doing nothing."* That is equally unfair. It is unfair to other employees who perform well and meet workplace expectations, and unfair to the company because productivity suffers. Furthermore, it is unfair to the supervisor who becomes known as a "softie."

Before making a decision, a supervisor should use the following resources:

- other supervisors and managers who have experienced performance management problems.
- their next-level manager and his/her manager.
- the human resources department.

In selecting the appropriate performance management action, keep these points in mind:

- If you tolerate non-performance of work or inappropriate behavior for a period of time, it becomes more difficult to manage later because your tolerance has set a precedent.
- Performance management actions could be found to be unjust and could be reversed by the issue resolution committee, an

outside government agency or court if it is used inconsistently (that is, treating similar cases differently).
- Accurate and detailed record-keeping is very important.
- It is not enough just to note for yourself instances of unsatisfactory performance or behavior. You cannot just save these up and suddenly terminate the employment relationship for an accumulation of instances of non-compliance. You must communicate your dissatisfaction and take performance management action progressively. The best practice to follow here is: when an incident occurs, address it at that time.

RECOGNIZING GOOD PERFORMANCE

Managing performance is not just a case of assisting employees to change their job performance or behavior when it is not satisfactory. It is equally important to allow the employee an opportunity to "clear the record." If an employee improves performance or behavior and solves the problem that caused the performance management action in the first place, the employee is more likely to maintain good performance if given an opportunity for a fresh start.

If the employee's performance improves after performance management, the following time frames are appropriate:

Performance Management Action	Becomes Inactive After
Formal discussion of consequences	3 months
Written statement of consequences	6 months
Further statement of consequences	9 months
Suspension	12 months

When performance management action is taken, the employee should be told it will become inactive after the appropriate time has passed, provided no other problems arise. After the time has elapsed, take the following action:

- Advise the employee that the previous performance management action is now inactive.
- Reinforce and encourage continued appropriate behavior and job performance.

The original correspondence, issued to the employee after the performance management action and/or suspension, should not be removed from the personnel file; it is a permanent part of the employee's record. You should, however, amend the file in the following ways:

- Write "inactive" and the date on the original correspondence.
- Write the employee a memo indicating that the previous action is now inactive because of behavior and/or performance improvement. Give the original copy of the memo to the employee and place a copy in the personnel file.

Giving Positive Feedback
One of the best ways to prevent performance management problems is to recognize good performance. Give verbal feedback regularly and sincerely. Too often we forget to say "thanks." There are many opportunities when a written note or memo can be used to give an employee formal recognition, for example, when an employee has:

- done something above and beyond the call of duty.
- performed competently and diligently over a period of time.
- taken immediate action in a crisis or emergency situation.
- developed a cost-saving or work-saving idea.
- provided special training or assistance to other employees.
- participated in outside activities that reflect well on Sherborne.
- maintained a good attendance record.
- maintained high quality and production standards.

EXHIBIT 12.2

SAMPLE LETTER FOR STEP 2:
WRITTEN STATEMENT OF CONSEQUENCES

<u>SHERBORNE COMPANY</u>
15 BOND ST., WINDRUSH, ONTARIO

Date
Name and address of employee

Dear (name of employee):

This letter will confirm our conversation of (date of interview). At that time, I reviewed with you the need for our values, guiding behaviors, practices and performance standards to ensure the safe, orderly and efficient operation of our business. This is for the benefit of you and your fellow employees.

We discussed and agreed upon the following issue(s) and resolution(s). You were then advised of the performance required of you in your job. (*This language will vary with the nature of the problem.*)

Your personnel record since (date) reads as follows:
(Summarize previously written letters of consequences.)

On (date of incident) you left your work area without notifying me or any member of the leadership group. I could not accept your excuse for non-compliance with our guiding behavior of keeping leadership informed of your whereabouts. We discussed this incident on (date).

On (date of the Step 2 interview) I reviewed your record with you and again advised you of our workplace expectations. We again discussed the benefits of your practicing the values, guiding behaviors, practices and performance standards that are required of you in your job.

This is formal notification to advise you that this behavior is unacceptable. Should there be any further non-compliance with our guiding behaviors, there will be more serious consequences.

Yours truly,

Supervisor's name and signature

I acknowledge having received this letter.

Employee's signature

Date

EXHIBIT 12.3

SAMPLE LETTER FOR STEP 3
FURTHER STATEMENT OF CONSEQUENCES

<u>SHERBORNE COMPANY</u>
15 BOND ST., WINDRUSH, ONTARIO

Date
Name and address of employee

Dear (name of employee):

This letter will confirm our conversations on (date of Step 1 and Step 2 interviews). At that time, I reviewed with you the need for our values, guiding behaviors, practices and performance standards to ensure the safe, orderly and efficient operation of our business. This is for the benefit of you and your fellow employees.

We discussed and agreed upon the following issue(s) and resolution. You were then advised of the behavior required of you in your job. (*This language will vary with the nature of the problem.*)

Your personnel record since (date) reads as follows:
(Summarize previously written letters of consequences.)

On (date of incident) you were found sleeping on the job, and away from your work area. This behavior is clearly contrary to our guiding behaviors and there is no reasonable explanation for it.

During the interview of (date of Step 3 interview), I reviewed your record with you and again advised you of our workplace expectations. We again discussed the benefits of practicing the values, guiding behaviors, practices and performance standards required of you in your job.

This is further formal notification of consequences to impress upon you the need for you to act in a manner that is consistent with our values, guiding behaviors, practices and performance standards. We certainly hope that you will choose to behave in the appropriate manner; otherwise we will be forced to conclude that you do not value your employment with Sherborne and we will act accordingly.

Yours truly,

Manager's name and signature

I acknowledge having received this letter.

Employee's signature

Date

EXHIBIT 12.4

SAMPLE LETTER FOR STEP 4 NOTIFICATION OF SUSPENSION

<u>SHERBORNE COMPANY</u>
15 BOND ST., WINDRUSH, ONTARIO

Date
Name and address of employee

Dear (name of employee):

This letter will confirm our conversation of (date of Step 1, 2 and/or Step 3 interviews). At that time, I reviewed with you the need for our values, guiding behaviors, practices and performance standards to ensure the safe, orderly and efficient operation of our business. This is for the benefit of you and your fellow employees. You were advised on the workplace expectations required of you in your job. (*This language will vary with the nature of the problem.*)

Your personnel record since (date) reads as follows:
(Summarize previously written letters of consequences.)

On (date of incident) you were using profane and abusive language. During the interview (date of Step 4 interview) I reviewed your record with you and again we discussed our guiding behaviors. In an effort to point out to you the seriousness of the situation, a suspension of one (1) day will be recorded against you. However, since our purpose is to communicate the seriousness of this matter and not to exact a monetary penalty, you will not be required to serve a suspension without pay.

It is our hope that you will decide, after all, that you seriously wish to work at Sherborne and abide by our workplace expectations.

However, should you fail in the future to meet fully the duties and responsibilities required of you in your job, we will have no choice but to conclude that you have chosen to end our employment relationship with you and will act accordingly.

Yours truly,

Vice-president's name and signature

I acknowledge having received this letter.

Employee's signature

Date

EXHIBIT 12.5

ISSUES ARISING FROM NOT PRACTICING GUIDING BEHAVIORS

When investigating a guiding behavior, there are several questions that should be considered:

- What is this guiding behavior intended to accomplish?
- Is the guiding behavior realistic?
- Is it easily understood?
- Is the guiding behavior out-of-date?
- Can the guiding behavior as currently stated be practiced under prevailing circumstances?
- Are the consequences of not following the guiding behavior either too light or too severe?
- Do the employees living the guiding behavior consider it to be reasonable?
- Is the guiding behavior being practiced consistently?
- Do the people involved know about the guiding behavior?
- Does everyone understand the value behind the guiding behavior?

In investigating the violator, the following questions should be asked:
- Does the employee understand the guiding behavior?
- Does the employee know the "why" of the guiding behavior?
- Is the violator a new employee?
- Is the employee trying to get attention by violating the guiding behavior?
- Does the employee think the guiding behavior should not apply to him/her in particular and, if so, why?
- Does the employee feel the guiding behavior is unjust?
- Are there circumstances beyond the employee's control that caused him/her to violate the guiding behavior?
- Did the employee violate the guiding behavior for the fun of it?
- Is the employee doing this out of resentment?

TAKE ACTION!

1. Determine company values, guiding behaviors practices and performance standards.
2. Articulate these as clearly as possible.
3. Be aware of the dual objective of preserving the interests of the organization and protecting the rights of the individual.
4. Define policy and procedure, using Exhibit 12.1 (Responsible Performance Management Program) as a working model that can be adapted to suit your organization.
5. Communicate the workplace expectations.
6. Make sure you have an appeal process in place, such as that described in Chapter 13.
7. Provide employees with an opportunity to clear their record.
8. Give positive feedback to good performers both verbally (on a regular basis) and in writing on a more formal basis.

13
ISSUE RESOLUTION

It is inevitable — necessary, in fact — that from time to time employees will have issues that need to be resolved. These issues may center on differences of opinion, conflict or problems between employee and supervisor or between co-workers. From the employee's perspective, it is important that the presence of issues be viewed as a positive force that enables growth. Satisfactorily resolving issues reinforces the employee's feelings of belonging and commitment to the organization.

▶ An important element of a Positive Employee Relations program is to provide employees with a healthy way of resolving outstanding issues.

WHAT HAPPENS WHEN ISSUES GO UNRESOLVED

Differences of opinion arise when we view a set of facts differently from someone else viewing the same facts. Conflicts arise when we perceive that someone is attempting to block our efforts or obstruct the attainment of our goals. Problems occur when there is an unacceptable discrepancy between the way things are and the way we want them to be.

Unresolved issues can result in increased absenteeism, higher turnover, reduced productivity and, in extreme situations, industrial sabotage. Employees who experience issues at work may be absent more often because they periodically escape from the workplace for a "mental health day" or they may have a higher incidence of illness due to stress. In a buoyant job market, rather than suffer in silence when their efforts are thwarted, the best and the brightest voice their opinions by seeking employment elsewhere. Employees who cannot leave may slow their productivity to a minimum in an act of passive aggression. The most dysfunctional response is, figuratively or literally, to throw a wrench into the works. Sabotage may be more common than most managers imagine. It can take very subtle forms that cannot be detected, such as the withholding of information.

A staggering amount of time is spent by supervisors and managers dealing with unresolved issues. In a recent American survey, participants indicated that they spend about 20 percent of their working time resolving some form of conflict. That's one day a week!

Dissatisfied employees who see no management-supported alternatives frequently choose to organize collectively because a union can give them a voice to address issues. Many of the traditional approaches to resolving issues are embedded in collective agreements. Grievance/arbitration clauses, for example, provide a mechanism for employees to raise concerns about the terms and conditions of their employment without fear of reprisals.

▶ For employers, the unionization of their workforce is the ultimate sign of the failure of management to address employee issues in a proactive and responsible manner.

EXTERNAL RESOLUTION OPTIONS

Many employee/employer disputes are referred to third-party forums. Most of these forums have been introduced as part of government legislation designed to protect an individual's rights. In most jurisdictions, a human rights or employment equity commission (agency or tribunal) is made accessible to employees who feel they have been discriminated against for reasons such as race, color, gender, religion, disability, etc. Similarly, governmental agencies (with scope for health and safety, labor or industrial relations) can hear complaints from employees who believe their employers have taken reprisals against them for exercising a right granted to them by employee rights legislation.

These forums are imperfect and usually carry very high costs, not just in financial terms. Both the manager and the employee pay a high emotional price when a complaint must be referred to a government agency for adjudication. Merely being accused of a breach of prevailing legislation can stigmatize a supervisor. Employees with significant concerns can become disenfranchised as a result of the often lengthy investigative process in which ownership of the complaint can shift to the governmental agency that has jurisdiction.

Government agencies face an overriding mandate to enforce the enabling legislation. Consequently, the process becomes issue-focused and usually results in a situation in which there is a clear winner and a clear loser. This, of course, does nothing to further an ongoing relationship between the disputing parties. However, in most instances the employment relationship has been damaged beyond repair before the complaint ever reaches the third party for investigation.

The recent past has taught us that the employment relationship is subject to ongoing change. Governmental agencies and forums have a history of lagging behind marketplace realities. This creates lengthy delays that leave many employees with only one choice: sue their employer. Wrongful dismissal cases have steadily increased over the years. Government-supported dispute resolution mechanisms available to employees appear to offer no solace. Employees are forced to quit or the employer is forced to terminate the employment contract as an immediate solution to unresolved conflicts. In either case, the organization is the ultimate loser: its investment in the employee is forever lost. The root cause of the problem may go undetected, in which case the problem is likely to be repeated. The hurt feelings persist and may proliferate among other employees.

It is understandable why many employees seek third-party representation in the form of a union. Joining a union provides employees access to the *perceived protection* offered by a collective agreement. It offers them due process in the form of a grievance/arbitration process. However, for an enlightened organization that embraces Positive Employee Relations, this does not have to be the case.

ALTERNATIVE ISSUE RESOLUTION PROCESSES

This book firmly supports the position that the supervisor must be responsible for settling any issues arising among employees. That is why we strongly advocate the implementation of a Let's Talk© program (see Appendix D), which strengthens the relationship between supervisors and their employees. However, when a supervisor is unable to resolve an issue for an employee, alternative issue resolution mechanisms are required.

Intervention by human resources or an external ombudsperson

Intervention by the human resources department or an external ombudsperson can be effective when the processes used are designed to get at *root causes*. A significant part of their mandate is precisely to manage the issues so that there is enough impetus for creativity but not so much that it detracts from the overall effectiveness of the organization. For example, job descriptions and the performance management processes help eliminate role ambiguity and reduce goal incompatibility, which are two common sources of issues that arise.

In many organizations the human resources professional is called upon to take a more direct role in handling internal issues. However, as with line managers, many human resources people are not trained in the skills of mediation and process facilitation. As a result, they may focus on the symptoms rather than the root causes. The issue may appear to be resolved, the intervention withdrawn, but the heart of the issue remains. And this can lead to resentment towards the human resources representative who intervened, for failing to get results.

Moreover, in this role the human resources representative must be seen as independent and neutral, by no means an easy task. When investigating complaints, the human resources person is frequently perceived as an inquisitor working to develop management's case, rather than as a neutral fact finder. Some organizations circumvent this problem by establishing an internal or external ombudsperson, separate from the human resource department, to handle internal complaints.

Open-door policies

Open-door policies are completely internal processes that, for many organizations, have proven successful at reducing the dissatisfaction associated with unresolved disputes. Sometimes introduced as part of a union-free strategy, an open-door policy invites employees to raise complaints or concerns through the organization's chain of command, ostensibly without fear of reprisal. Usually a member of the human resources staff helps the employee frame his/her complaint and offers advice on how to present the issue.

Certain limitations may, however, diminish the effectiveness of the open door. For example, in organizations where authority is highly centralized and distributed among only a handful of senior managers, complaints through the open door may be considered as a sign of disloyalty. In these "authority cultures," employees fear retribution for speaking up, perceiving that senior management wishes to avoid criticism at all cost. Compliance, rather than speaking up, is viewed as the way to achieve promotions and success. In most environments employees are reluctant to raise a complaint if the source of the dispute is their immediate supervisor.

Employee hotlines

These 24-hour-a-day phone services provide employees with quick responses to employment-related questions, which range from run-of-the-mill questions regarding employee benefits or company policies, to more serious questions, such as how to handle sexual harassment. The hotline operator offers advice and counseling. These services are completely confidential and may be offered as an extension to an employee assistance program. Some organizations offer this service through their human resources departments, although doing so may create problems with employees' perceptions of confidentiality. Moreover, this may not be the most cost-effective option.

Hotlines provide only advice, and refrain from active intervention in issue resolution. But often the quick response and independence of the advice serves to prevent many conflicts from escalating. As well, even though the employer is not made aware of any specific complaints, the service provider submits a report on the number and type of inquiries made. This allows the employer to gauge employee morale on a continuous basis and therefore creates an opportunity to address common issues before they escalate into serious problems.

▶ A well-planned and administered hotline is a perfect complement to a Positive Employee Relations program.

One noteworthy downside is that it is not always possible for the hotline counselor to deal with the issue while maintaining confidentiality. In the case of a harassment complaint, for example, the issue cannot usually be addressed unless the complainant is willing to come forward and confront the problem openly. In some cases, the counselor may be able to persuade the employee to seek the assistance of the human resources department. An alternative step would be for the counselor to refer the complainant to an independent ombudsperson who can investigate the matter and mediate any dispute. For smaller employers who cannot afford full-time human resources staff, the cost advantages of an employee hotline can be significant. But even for larger employers, the cost advantages and continuous coverage are advantages that may not be possible using in-house staff.

OTHER INTERNAL MECHANISMS

Several other internal mechanisms can be established to provide employees with alternative issue resolution options that allow them to have their concerns fairly and expeditiously heard. When properly designed and introduced, these alternatives are also more effective than other forms of issue resolution. Using collaborative approaches and rational decision making methodologies, they focus on real problem solving rather than merely settling the specific (or narrow) issue before them. The presence of a neutral third party removes the threat of obvious vested interests in the results. Participants perceive a level of fairness absent in traditional processes.

▶ The win-win orientation of the process is particularly important in ensuring that all parties are satisfied that their concerns were given due consideration.

One of the key aspects of most issue resolution mechanisms is that the parties to the issue are the "process owners." Participation must be completely voluntary to ensure compliance and buy-in to the results. In this way the processes are beneficial to the ongoing relationships between the parties. These alternatives tend to be more efficient because they make it possible, with focused resources, to expeditiously handle issues. Fewer dollars are spent when matters are dealt with quickly. Speed also ensures minimal disruption for the employee and the organization. Two examples of such alternative issue resolution processes are relationships-by-objectives and peer review panels.

Relationships-by-objectives

This is the more commonly recognized name for a conflict management intervention called inter-group mirroring. With the assistance of a facilitator, two conflicting groups are brought together to discuss their differences and improve their ongoing relationship. Each group independently creates a list of their perceptions of the other group and, in particular, the manner in which they believe the other group is frustrating their work efforts. These perceptions are then shared and solutions are explored. The parties are not allowed to debate the relative merits of each other's perceptions. Instead, they must treat them as genuine and focus on solutions.

Peer review panels

In recent years a new internal process has emerged to help employers and employees resolve issues on their own. Peer review panels have become prevalent among many leading union-free employers. Essentially, they are internal arbitration boards that are convened to hear employees' complaints. Like external arbitration boards, they can only interpret the meaning of established policies and procedures. They cannot "add to, subtract from, or amend" the terms of employment set out by the organization's policy manual. However, they can decide if a disciplinary sanction was justified, including dismissals, or can substitute the penalty with a lesser sanction.

Peer review panel members are trained both in aspects of the company policies and in employment law. An employee's concern is typically heard first through the chain-of-command in an open-door process and referred to the panel for final disposition only if the matter remains unresolved. To ensure impartiality, a roster of potential panel members is maintained so that those selected to hear the issue have no immediate connection to either of the parties to the conflict.

▶ Peer review panels have proven to be quite successful, but demand a high degree of commitment, especially from management, to make them work.

SETTING UP AN ISSUES RESOLUTION PROGRAM

Including employees in the resolution of their own concerns or issues is consistent with Positive Employee Relations. Leaders, whether at supervisory or management levels, are not perfect in carrying out their responsibilities. When employees have the right to constructively voice their concerns, exercising that right does not hinder the operations of the organization.

In effect, the openness of this process gives a voice to the employee's dissatisfaction. This can eliminate smoldering resentment before it becomes outright discontent.

▶ A meaningful and constructive process provides options that reduce employee frustration, alienation and turnover.

Our process of choice is a three-stage issue resolution program that requires the employee to first give his or her immediate supervisor an opportunity to deal with the issue. The supervisor has a specific time frame in which to respond to the employee. If no response is forthcoming or if the response is not satisfactory to the employee, then the employee may proceed to the second step with a request that the supervisor's manager consider the issue. At this stage, the employee must put his or her concern in writing and the response must also be put in writing. As well, at this stage, we advocate the compulsory involvement of human resources. If the employee is still not satisfied with the resolution of the issue, then the employee may submit the issue to an employee panel (which, unlike a peer review panel, is not necessarily composed only of peers). The employee panel makes a recommendation of resolution to the most senior manager responsible for that facility or business unit.

If such a policy is to be adopted, several administrative matters must be established, such as time frames between stages, composition of the employee panel, operating guidelines of the employee panel, and so on. The program is detailed in the sample issue resolution policy, and accompanying documents, included as exhibits 13.1 to 13.4.

EXHIBIT 13.1

ISSUE RESOLUTION POLICY

Sherborne Company is committed to the timely and efficient resolution of employee issues for the betterment of all stakeholders, in a manner that respects the needs of all stakeholders. An issue resolution process (IRP) has been created and is available to all employees. *No employee may be penalized in any way for using the issue resolution process. Any employees who believe they are being penalized in any way because they have used the issue resolution process should immediately advise the human resources director, who will investigate and take corrective action as appropriate.*

Assistance to employees

While employees are encouraged to take responsibility for presenting their issues through the IRP, at any step, an employee may request assistance from any employee (a peer, a human resources representative or a supervisor/manager). Such assistance may take the form of helping the employee to verbalize his/her issue or to prepare a Request for Resolution Form or Request for Further Consideration Form.

PROCEDURE FOR USING THE ISSUE RESOLUTION PROCESS

Step 1

When an employee has an issue concerning a decision relating to his/her individual treatment, the employee should bring that issue to the attention of his/her immediate supervisor. In doing so, the employee should:

- declare that he/she is starting the issue resolution process; and
- present all facts or circumstances that are relevant to the issue in a forthright manner.

The immediate supervisor should respond to the presented facts in a non-judgmental way, seeking out additional information or assistance if required. The employee should always receive a response from the immediate supervisor within two (2) business days of having raised his/her issue, or within a timeframe agreed to by both the employee and the immediate supervisor.

While it is desirable that all issues be brought first to the attention of the immediate supervisor, if the nature of the issue is such that the employee is unable to reasonably bring the matter to his/her attention, the employee may speak with a human resources representative or proceed directly to Step 2.

The issue resolution process may not be used to obtain a decision. It may be used only to request reconsideration of a decision once the decision has been made.

Step 2
If the employee is not satisfied with the resolution from Step 1, the employee should detail his/her facts and circumstances on a Request for Resolution Form and provide copies to his/her immediate supervisor, the next-level manager, and the human resources department. The forms should be submitted within seven (7) calendar days of response from the immediate supervisor. If the issue is not submitted to the next-level manager within seven (7) calendar days, the issue will be considered to be resolved. (Blank Request for Resolution Forms may be obtained from the human resources department.)

An employee who does not submit a request for resolution form within seven (7) calendar days, who subsequently decides he/she cannot accept the resolution arrived at in Step 1, must repeat Step 1 prior to moving on to Step 2.

Upon receipt of a Request for Resolution Form, the next-level manager will accept responsibility for discussing the issue with the employee. He/she will also discuss the issue with the immediate supervisor and the human resource representative to ascertain any additional relevant facts. The next-level manager will provide a written resolution to the issue and explain the reasoning/facts underlying the resolution. The written response must be provided within five (5) business days of receipt of the Request for Resolution Form.

Step 3
If the employee is not satisfied with the resolution provided by Step 2, he/she may request that the issue be considered by either:

- the employee panel, or
- the human resources director.

Employees wishing to proceed to Step 3 should complete a Request for Further Consideration Form. Completed forms should be submitted to human resources in a sealed envelope within ten (10) business days of receipt of the written response to the Request for Resolution Form (from Step 2). If the issue is not submitted to the employee panel within ten (10) business days, the issue will be considered to be resolved. (Blank forms may be obtained from human resources.)

All issues must be received by the human resources department one (1) week before the next scheduled meeting day of the employee panel to be considered at that meeting. Requests for Further Consideration not received one week before the next scheduled meeting day will be deferred until the following meeting. A schedule of meeting days will be posted. While every attempt will be made to adhere to the posted schedule, occasionally it may be necessary to reschedule meetings.

In completing a Request for Further Consideration, the employee should state why the resolution provided by the next-level manager (Step 2) is not acceptable. The form should also include any further additional information that the employee may wish to be considered. The employee should expect to speak to the employee panel.

After considering all the facts, the employee panel will recommend a resolution to the senior manager for implementation. The senior manager will advise the line management of the resolution, while the employee panel will advise the employee of the resolution both verbally and in writing. All resolutions are final and binding. All resolutions will be determined and communicated no later than 17 days subsequent to the Step 3 meeting at which the issue is initially considered. This time frame allows the senior manager an opportunity to discuss the recommended resolution with the employee panel. The employee panel may also present to the senior manager issues which, while presented as individual issues, in fact may represent broader, systemic (business-wide) issues.

Emergency/urgent resolutions
If the nature of an issue is such that an urgent resolution is necessary, the employee should discuss the issue with the human resources manager or with his/her next-level manager, indicating the reason for the urgency.

EXHIBIT 13.2

REQUEST FOR RESOLUTION (Step 2)

Employee name:
Supervisor/manager name:
Current date:
Date first discussed with supervisor/manager:

Brief statement of the unresolved issue:

_____
_____
_____
_____
_____
_____
_____

Relevant facts:

_____
_____
_____
_____
_____
_____
_____

Desired resolution:

_____
_____
_____
_____
_____
_____
_____

(Use back or attached additional page(s) if you require more space for any section above.)

EXHIBIT 13.3

REQUEST FOR FURTHER CONSIDERATION (Step 3)

Employee name:
Supervisor/manager name:
Next-level manager name:
Current date:
Date first discussed with immediate supervisor:
Date of response to completed Request for Resolution Form:

Reason why Step 2 resolution is not acceptable:

_____
_____
_____
_____
_____
_____

Further relevant facts (optional):

_____
_____
_____
_____

Please indicate whether you would like your issue considered by the employee panel or by the human resources manager (check one):
     ( ) employee panel
     ( ) human resources manager.

Requested Employee Panel meeting date (check one):
     ( ) next scheduled meeting
     ( ) other date (refer to posted schedule).

Please attach a copy of Request for Resolution and written response from Step 2.
   (Use back or attached additional page(s) if you require more space for any section above.)

EXHIBIT 13.4

MEMO TO EMPLOYEE

To: (Employee name)
From: Employee panel

Subject: What you can expect from the employee panel

You have asked the employee panel to consider an issue that is unresolved for you. We thought it might be helpful if we explained what happens at the employee panel meeting and what you can expect from us.

First of all, let us state our goal:

To resolve a personal issue of an employee in a manner that is respectful of the employee needs and Sherborne needs and is consistent with existing policies, procedures and practices, and in line with the values and guiding behaviors of Sherborne.

Our role is to ensure that you have been treated with fairness and equity and any decisions or actions taken or planned with respect to you have been in accordance with the relevant policies, procedures, practices and principles (the Positive Employee Relations program) of Sherborne. We do not make decisions. We make recommendations.

We cannot recommend changing a past or planned action simply because you don't like it. In fact, we may not like it either. If the past or planned action is inconsistent with the Positive Employee Relations program, of if you have not been treated with fairness and equity, then we will recommend a change in the past or planned action or decision. However, as long as your situation has been treated with fairness and equity and any action or decision taken or planned is consistent with the Positive Employee Relations program, then we cannot recommend changing the past or planned action or decision. In some instances, where appropriate, we may recommend that a policy, procedure, practice or principle be reconsidered and perhaps changed.

Before we meet with you, we will have reviewed the Request for Further Consideration that you submitted (including the attached request for resolution and the next-level manager's response), as well as any relevant documentation, be it a policy, procedure, practice or principle, or a similar issue brought to us previously. We need to be sure that we know and understand all the relevant facts. Meeting with you will give us an opportunity to ask you questions about anything we don't understand. It will give you an opportunity to tell us, in your own words, what the issue is and what resolution you are seeking.

You are a very important part of the process. We are not here to judge you. We are here to learn and assess the facts relating to your issue. Our personal opinions are irrelevant. We will be objective and impartial in assessing your particular issue.

As you know, there will be five panel members to meet with you. If you would like to bring a friend with you to the meeting, you are welcome to do so.

We will give you the opportunity to ask any questions you may have.

After meeting with you, we will meet with your supervisor and your next-level manager (separately). Our purpose in meeting with them is the same as our purpose in meeting with you — to ensure that we have a thorough and complete understanding of all the facts relevant to your issue.

If necessary, we will meet with any other person who has information or input that is relevant to the issue.

Once we have met with everyone, and we are assured that we have all relevant facts, we will evaluate the information we have received. We will determine if you have been treated with fairness and equity and if any actions or decisions taken or planned are consistent with Sherborne's values and guiding behaviors. We will present our conclusion and recommendations to the business leader shortly after our meeting.

We will give you a response as soon as we can, but not later than one day after our next planned panel meeting.

We hope this letter has provided you with answers to any questions you may have about what you can expect from the employee panel, but if it hasn't, please feel free to ask us when we meet with you on [date and approximate time].

TAKE ACTION!

1. Always start by encouraging the supervisor and employee to resolve the issue without intervention. Implement a Let's Talk© program to strengthen the relationship between supervisors and their employees. See Appendix D.
2. Consider the pros and cons of available issue resolution processes and determine which process(es) would be suitable for your organization, either alone or in combination. These include:

   - intervention by human resources or an external ombudsperson.
   - open-door policies.
   - employee hotlines.
   - relationships-by-objectives.
   - peer review panels.
   - three-stage process outlined in exhibits 13.1 to 13.4.

3. Educate supervisors and all levels of management regarding the importance of your company's issue resolution process in maintaining Positive Employee Relations. Make it very clear to them how the process works and also that no employee should ever be penalized in any way for using the process.
4. Make sure that employees understand that the issues resolution process exists, and how and when to use it.
5. Encourage employees to seek assistance internally, if they wish, for presenting issues through the issue resolution process.

14
EMPLOYEE RETENTION

Some employers believe that a high level of turnover is a major part of their union-free strategy: employees are not on the payroll long enough to become involved in any union activity. Fortunately, most employers would agree that this tactic is poorly thought out, costly, leads to decreased productivity and quality and is very short-sighted. Such a practice would be the antithesis of Positive Employee Relations.

Employees leave for many reasons. A reasonable amount of employee turnover can be expected for reasons over which the employer has little or no control. For example, individuals may return to college or university, relocate to another community, get married or change their life priorities. People may leave because another organization offers more money and good job prospects in a field in which your business is not involved. These reasons are understandable and, as long as the turnover percentage is not too high, should not cause a great deal of concern. Similarly, when an employee who has been identified as having "less than standard" performance levels leaves, there is little cause for concern.

WHY GOOD EMPLOYEES LEAVE

However, "good" employees are hard to find. Retaining their commitment should be of great concern to the organization. For when good employees leave, this sends at least three messages throughout the informal communication channels:

- Management could not get along with these talented people and did not treat them well enough for them to stay.
- Management pays only lip service to pronouncements about being competitive in its salary and benefit programs.
- The organization's ability to "walk the talk" about its values (the bedrock of the Positive Employee Relations program) is just not there.

Such messages running through the rumor mill, reinforced every time a good performer leaves, deal a body blow to the Positive Employee Relations program. So the question is, "Why do good performers leave?"

We should begin by exploring why people leave jobs. More specifically, why do people leave jobs for reasons that are ostensibly in the employer's control? The reasons can be categorized around three topics, in order of priority: career, relationships and economics.

CAREER

The concept of career embraces everything that's involved when employees perform their jobs, including the boundaries in which they carry out their responsibilities and their opportunities for advancement or progression. A manager should not start with the false premise that the concept of career applies only to individuals in technical, professional and/or managerial roles.

▶ Employees' aspirations have nothing to do with their job title, their salary grade, or whether their pay is calculated hourly or annually.

Overqualified employees are rarely content for long. Employees who have been hired to perform jobs that are below their skill or competence level and/or experience and potential level, are likely to become bored fairly quickly. And, if there are no realistic opportunities for progression or advancement, the likelihood of boredom will increase exponentially. These circumstances will lead to a turnover statistic.

If we follow the selection and interview pattern outlined in Chapter 8, this risk would be identified in advance so that some accommodation could be made to reduce the risk. For example, such employees could be offered accelerated learning opportunities, or be partnered with peers who would positively challenge their skills, etc.

Potential problems associated with overqualified employees will, in all likelihood, show up in the probation period. Watch for indications of boredom or restlessness. Their presence in an overqualified employee places the supervisor at a critical juncture when the probation decision must be made. If the role/responsibilities cannot be made more challenging, then the employee will become another turnover statistic, and on his/her *own* time schedule.

The reverse of this situation occurs with employees whose skills, competency and/or potential are below that required for the position. This situation should never occur unknowingly. An effective interview should have identified this imbalance and ruled out the candidate. And, if the candidate slipped through because of a poorly conducted interview, his/her performance and behavior should have been noticed by an alert supervisor long before the end of the probation period.

Under-qualified employees pose a variety of problems. First, they will be frustrated by their inability to achieve the performance standards of their position. They will eventually become demoralized and feel alienated from the organization. (This is an ideal profile of someone who would be ripe to sign a union membership card.) Finally, if their demoralization is not addressed, it will infect other employees.

Poor match between skills and job

When job responsibilities are poorly matched with the candidate's skills, competency, behavioral requirements and potential, there is a high risk of turnover. To confirm the employment interview results, we recommend the use of an assessment tool that allows for measurement of the job as well as the candidate and the subsequent determination of "fit." Please refer to Appendix D for an explanation of the Activity Vector Analysis (AVA) and how it clearly identifies fit.

Lack of clarity around decision-making roles

Lack of clarity around decision-making roles can be another source of career dissatisfaction. Examine the job in question and determine if the decision-making ingredients are correctly assigned. As managers, we have a strong propensity to want to do things right, both for our careers and for our sense of security. Consequently, we regularly retain decision-making; for example, approval levels, signing-off authority, etc.) within the scope of our positions. We tend to narrow the decision-making potential of positions reporting to us by the amount of decision-making we wish to retain. Jobs that have been restricted in this manner can be a detriment in many ways. For example, if the position's title is supervisor but the next-level manager retains all the decision-making authority, is the supervisor's role really that of an "assistant-to"? If so, candidates for this position who have relevant experience and potential will likely become a turnover risk because someone didn't analyze the job well enough.

In summary, the reasons why career can become a key reason for employee turnover are:

- interview results that lead to a poor selection decision.
- a probation system that does not properly identify individuals with behavioral or performance problems (compared to the realities of the position).
- an incomplete or inaccurate picture of the position, particularly with respect to levels of responsibility, authority and accountability.
- supervisors or managers who do not have a strong enough personal commitment to Positive Employee Relations, so that self-interest overshadows the organization's long-term development.

RELATIONSHIPS

People also leave jobs because of relationships with peers, including those reporting to them and those to whom they report. The latter tends to be the most critical issue.

Relationship with supervisor

If an employee's relationship with a direct supervisor or manager is not built on a foundation of mutual respect and trust, it is doomed to repetitive cycles of dysfunctional behaviors. In the context of Positive Employee Relations, this explains why the main reason for unionization is the employee's perception of a supervisor's attitude and leadership practices. As we move higher up the organization's structure, where unionization is not seen as a viable option, lack of respect for one's manager leads, at best, to voluntary termination and at worst, to long-term regrets, personal bitterness, unacceptable performance and, in extreme cases, "get even" behavior such as industrial sabotage or embezzlement.

When characterized by little or no mutual respect or trust, an employee's working relationship with his/her supervisor is forced into uncomfortable values and norms that often cause the employee to behave in ways that satisfy the supervisor to the exclusion of the employee's own beliefs. In such a stilted relationship, creativity, innovation, and free and easy dialog become much more difficult. The employee must then guard against spontaneity as this may overstep the unwritten norms of the relationship. The absence of respect and trust often leads to relationships based on fear.

Mentoring/coaching relationships

Mutual respect is essential for the success of coaching and mentoring programs. Without it, why would anyone place their career progression in the hands of their manager? Respect transcends one's level of performance. Regardless of how successful the "junior" is in performing his/her responsibilities, if the relationship doesn't move beyond the simplistic black or white of performance, the "senior" is not going to give his/her wholehearted commitment. The investment in coaching and mentoring is both professional and personal, and without the give and take inherent in relationships based on respect and trust, the dynamic will not work.

▶ Without respect, trust will not flourish. And without these two ingredients, the relationship will be mediocre at best.

Peer relationships

From a different perspective, the relationship issue also includes employees' interactions with peers. Most people seek collaboration, not competition, with their colleagues.

▶ Competition belongs in the marketplace, not between individuals mutually working towards organizational goals.

A work environment where competition is supported by senior management frequently leaves employees on their own, with little support, no advice on past experiences, no synergy. This describes a workplace where "information is power" and there is no benefit in sharing that information, not even for the good of the organization. Why? Because the organization is always a secondary priority. An individual's career, aspirations and achievements are his/her first priority. Competition within the organization causes team players to leave.

Hostile relationships

Regarding relationships with one's staff or direct reports, the relationship issue takes on a slightly different perspective. If the leader (supervisor, project leader, etc.) cannot make a difference because of hostilities between staff/employees and management, and if the time and energy determined to effect a turnaround is significant, this can cause a newly hired leader to leave.

Whether in a leadership position or not, most employees would want to leave a work environment that is hostile to management, internally competitive, or lacking in respect and trust among peers. They may stay long enough to gain specific experience, training, a job title, but they'll always be on the lookout for something better. Another turnover statistic waiting to happen.

In summary, the reasons why relationships are a key factor for employee turnover are:

- a lack of mutual trust and respect with the direct manager.
- the absence of coaching, mentoring and support to justify placing their career in the hands of their employer.
- internal competition rather than collaboration, synergy and teamwork.
- a hostile work environment.

ECONOMICS

In the case of a newly hired employee, compensation should never be the primary cause of termination. One can reasonably assume that the "hire rate" was acceptable or the employee would have negotiated further. An employer who lowers the hire rate in a labor market where there are more candidates than jobs is buying a short-term gain that will lead to long-term pain. The ethical reality of such a situation is so poor that turnover may be the employer's naive strategy for union avoidance. Such behaviors are grounded in greed, not Positive Employee Relations.

In most organizations, sound compensation practices are based on internal comparisons of positions (job evaluation) and a study of going rates in the community (wage comparison studies/surveys) in order to determine salary ranges (minimum to maximum rates).

▶ Economic-driven employee turnover in organizations with generally sound compensation practices usually signal that the salary rates have not been determined accurately.

If an organization with generally sound compensation practices faces economic-driven employee turnover, then the following questions should be addressed in order to correct the problem:

- Are the salary/wage ranges based on a fair comparison of the industry and the labor market geography?
- At what point did the employer decide to draw the comparison line — at the 50th percentile or at the 75th percentile?
- Are salary determinations made equitable based on a reasonable assessment of performance and potential?

The technology to determine marketplace wage/salary ranges is well within the capabilities of most organizations. However, it requires a judgment call that is usually made by the senior executive or the management team regarding which percentile to benchmark. Objectively, this judgment call is linked to the organization's stated values, its business plan and the caliber of human resources it wishes to recruit and retain. However, the decision regarding percentile is often influenced more by short-term financial results than by a long-term business strategy. Lowering the percentile (and thereby lowering next year's wage/salary range) from the 75th to the 50th will positively impact the bottom line. It will, however, negatively impact employees' bottom line (or take-home pay). If there is a positive "good will" balance in the organization's "trust and respect" account with the employees, the event may pass with little more than a brief explanation. If, however, the "trust and respect" account is in arrears, employees will likely have little sympathy and support for such a move and the top performers will begin to think about leaving. This is another example of an outcome that leads to mediocrity.

Performance reviews

One of the main reasons why employees "fire their employer" is the process used to determine the worth or value of last year's performance. The process, in such circumstances, is disrespectful and/or insensitive to the individual's perception of his/her contribution. Assuming that most employees, most of the time, are willing to perform their job responsibilities well (or at least as well as they have been trained to do), a performance review that is singularly tied to their wage/salary adjustment is problematic. Why? Many organizations determine the annual increase in their compensation structure, based on many financial and economic factors, before they investigate the human resource contribution. This means that an employee who performed at an above-standard level of accomplishment may receive an increase of one or two percentage points above the cost-of-living (or inflation rate) increase. The manager may well sympathize with the employee that such an increase, compared to the level of performance, is less than appropriate.

From the employee's perspective, an annual performance contribution that is assessed at "above standard" is an endorsement by management of a personal and professional accomplishment. To then be told that the reward for such achievement is only a percentage or two above the norm for most employees is demoralizing. Without an intervention by senior management, this employee has a limited number of options:

- leave and find a better paying job.
- stay and try for more financial rewards next year.
- stay, become dissatisfied, and turn against the organization.

In two out of three scenarios, the employer loses.

In summary, the reasons why economics become a key reason for employee turnover are:

- Wage scales or salary ranges are not competitive in the labor market or the industry.
- The level of competitiveness within the labor market (for example, the 50th percentile, or 75th percentile) has not been harmonized with the employees' level of contribution and the inclusive economic realities of the organization. (Employees are stakeholders too.)
- Wage/salary increases are perceived to be too low for the accomplishments demonstrated by the employee over the last period.
- The organization's compensation plan has been developed and is administered with little or no connection to the requirements of hiring and retaining the best.

HOW CAN YOU KEEP YOUR BEST EMPLOYEES?

Having looked at the problem of employee retention from the perspective of the employee's career, relationships and economics, what can be done in a Positive Employee Relations environment to address these issues?

Start with the values of the organization. Your values statement will provide bridging points at which to present your organization's strategy to retain those employees with high performance levels and evident prospects of future potential. Starting with your values ensures a degree of congruity that is needed to be seen as credible rather than as just another "smoke and mirrors" show by management.

The pro-active management style that is part of a Positive Employee Relations program depends on understanding that the organization benefits in direct relationship to its "investments." These investments can be with a single stakeholder or combination of stakeholders. These may, for example, take the form of long-term investment in market research, product development and customer care. Similarly, a well thought out and integrated plan for human resource management will be more successful at building union-free relationships than a poorly conceived plan or no plan at all. Such a plan should include the following cornerstones:

- Respect, dignity and honesty in all employee dealings is the best way to ensure that management is treated with respect, dignity and honesty by the employees.
- An organization on a continuous improvement path towards excellence will achieve success only if the employees it hires and retains have the competencies and desires to walk along the same path.
- All organizational relationships that stand the tests of adversity and time are relationships between people — which means that "who I am" and "what I achieve" are intersecting circles.

Given these building blocks, employee retention can be significantly enhanced if the organization ensures that:

Selection, placement, orientation, training and assessment processes are of the highest possible caliber.
Anything less, and you employ the wrong people, beginning a process that will not lead to excellence. If our most valuable resource is "the

people who work with us" then, arguably, you cannot invest too much time in a good selection process. Similarly, leaders and human resource staff who lack interviewing, counseling, coaching and performance feedback skills are doomed to lower the standard of excellence. Lowering the performance standard, mediocrity and good people leaving the organization all fall within the same cycle.

Performance feedback is tied into values.
Providing clear, objective performance feedback that is consistent with the values of respect and dignity means being honest and sensitive in the performance assessment interview(s) while, at the same time, acknowledging that the employee may have valuable insights that can modify the leader's initial observations. Subsequent to this they can jointly arrive at conclusions.

All leaders are held accountable for performance standards and behaviors that exemplify the organization's values and beliefs.
The commitment of all leadership is critical on this point. Arguably, it is in the spirit of the values that we find more humanity and hence, quality. Without such a commitment by leadership, employees have little reason to let down their guards and expose personal views and perspectives. Then the supervisor will be unable to get close enough (quickly enough) to understand each employee's individual motivations and ways of behaving. Without this information, the likelihood of responsible coaching and mentoring is remote.

The maximum amount of responsibility, authority and accountability is retained within each job.
Do not move it up the organization to the next level; keep pushing these factors and their consequences — problem-solving and decision-making — down the organization.

Jobs that are routine and repetitive lead to idle minds; and this, in turn, leads to thinking that does not support the organization's values or its wish to remain union-free. Narrow, boring jobs should, wherever possible, be automated. A robotic arm has the "mindset" to do repetitive work; the human brain has been developing for a million years to create robotic devices (for example), not just to routinely affix part A to part B for 40 hours per week.

▶ Bright, capable and competent employees do not generally leave positions that challenge and excite their brains.

Payroll costs are recognized as an investment, not an expense.
By compensating good performers there is always the value-added factor that commitment will increase and turnover will decrease. By linking holistic jobs (built on problem-solving, decision-making) and self-responsibility with good selection practices and inspirational leaders, above-average salary scales naturally follow.

Retaining good people is relatively easy with these cornerstones firmly in place and operationalized. Any individual who has not met the performance and values standards should be removed in a manner that is consistent with the organization's Positive Employee Relations program.

TAKE ACTION!

1. Determine the sources of dissatisfaction that are causing your employees to leave. Explore factors related to career, relationships and economics.
2. Starting with your values statement, develop a strategy to retain those employees who have demonstrated high performance levels and evidence of future potential.
3. Be pro-active. Ensure that:

   - selection, placement, orientation and assessment processes are of the highest possible caliber.
   - performance feedback is tied into values.
   - leaders are held accountable for performance standards and behaviors that exemplify the organization's values and beliefs.
   - the maximum amount of responsibility, authority and accountability are encouraged within each job.
   - payroll costs are recognized as an investment, not an expense.

15
CREATING A DECERTIFICATION CLIMATE

You've worked hard to put into place an enlightened set of Positive Employee Relations practices. But you started out at a disadvantage. Your company was already unionized. So you've wasted your time, right? There's nothing you can do to change things, right? You're stuck with a union, right?

Wrong, wrong and wrong! The Positive Employee Relations practices that will keep a non-union organization union-free can be useful tools in creating a climate where unionized employees will reconsider this decision about certification.

Decertification is the process of returning to a union-free environment. The reality is that decertification proceedings are becoming more and more common and, once begun, are often successful. This is especially true in the United States. But even in Canadian jurisdictions, which have a more favorable labor environment, decertification elections are successful about half the time.

However, *employees must initiate this process*. Management intervention is almost entirely forbidden and usually accompanied by stiff penalties. As a result, most managers are reluctant even to participate in a strategic decertification discussion within the management team. They fear that any discussion, let alone action, will result in their being charged with an unfair labor intervention. This pervasive fear calls into question how eager managers will be to promote the very beginnings of the decertification process. But there are policies and practices management can put in place to make decertification more attractive to employees than unionization.

▶ It is possible to encourage employees to opt for decertification without contravening labor legislation or the collective agreement.

Most often, the decertification election has been viewed as management's oasis in a unionized desert — just be thankful it's there and don't bother to consider where it came from. But this naive attitude is no longer acceptable. By putting in place a Positive Employee Relations program you implicitly decided that what motivates your employees' actions is important to you.

▶ The principles inherent to your Positive Employees Relations program are the precise values that your employees will want you to demonstrate before they vote for decertification.

ENCOURAGING DECERTIFICATION

Why?

At the outset, we should be clear as to why decertification is attractive. First, you eliminate the financial costs of unionization. More importantly, however, the leadership group regain control of the business. You re-establish an environment where you can have direct communications with your employees.

You should know that...

- Decertification comes down to who has more credibility, you or the union.
- Influencing people is about values and leadership.
- Decertification will cause change and the transition will be less painful if there is consensus within the management group.
- Decertification is about a fundamental realignment of influence and power — the union will resist.
- A "plan to regain employees' respect" is not a quick fix — it may take up to five years to bring about such a culture change.
- A "plan to regain employees' respect" is no different than "managing for excellence." The benefits affect all aspects of the business.

STRATEGY

The strategy for encouraging your employees to consider decertification sounds simple: *offer more to your employees than the union does*. That's the strategy the union used when it was certified — it offered employees more than you did.

Offering more can mean a number of things: more pay, more autonomy in the workplace, being treated more like an adult, being given more information by management so that employees aren't always the last to know, etc. This may sound simple, but it isn't. It is an involved process that requires complete management commitment.

TACTICS

Reverse the reasons for unionization

Re-train, provide coaching and mentoring opportunities and, if this does not succeed, replace supervisors and front-line managers whose presence is exacerbating the situation and whose attitudes will prevent you from implementing your program of Positive Employee Relations.

Begin company-wide internal marketing of what you are offering employees

Have department meetings to discuss all the information to be disseminated so that there aren't any surprises waiting for your supervisors and managers. Please refer to Chapter 6 on how to become an "employer of choice."

Raise the standards for recruitment

Hire employees who respond more to your offerings than to those of the union. These employees, responsive to your attempts at creating a new corporate culture, will be important when decertification becomes an issue. The Activity Vector Analysis, which should be administered to prospective employees as part of your hiring process, can help you determine the outlook of a prospective hire. See Appendix C for more about the AVA.

Apply the principles of continuous improvement to your employee relations

Always keep in mind that yesterday's achievements are tomorrow's minimum standards. This, in other words, is the principle of providing *more* than the union does.

ELIMINATING THE OLD PARADIGM

We have spent a considerable amount of time discussing the values, policies and practices that will eliminate the need for a union. But a company that is already unionized will likely be dominated by a different set of beliefs — those practices that led to unionization in the first place. Before you can create the conditions for decertification, you must understand why your employees unionized in the first place.

▶ Before you can create the conditions for decertification, you must understand why your employees unionized in the first place.

Consider the following scenario:
1. Entrepreneur/manager builds a business where production is paramount.
2. Supervisors are given a production focus and only limited "people training."
3. Hiring is frequently done at the last minute on the principle that any "warm body" will do; the jobs have been engineered so that any "dummy" could do them.
4. Employees begin to feel used by the company.
5. Employee dissatisfaction increases and creates opportunities for union organizers.
6. Managers now think of employees as workers, "alive equipment" and not as employees.
7. The union and its message gains credibility.
8. Employees now see management as the enemy.
9. Management has succeeded in institutionalizing an adversarial mentality.
10. Unionization is just waiting to happen.

This is quite a company we've created. It started out with all the best intentions — with a product or service that its founder believed it could provide better than anyone else. The entrepreneur never wanted to become embroiled in labor-management disputes. Now look what it's costing: 25-30 percent of the annual payroll to deal with these issues. With a $5-million payroll, that's $1.25 million each year. And the employees aren't any better off. They owe 2.5 hours of pay each month in union dues. With an average wage of $20/hour, that's $600 a year for each employee!

But costs aren't even the key issue in this illustration. What's more important is the working climate that these insensitive employee relations practices have created:

- excess control by management
- reduced productivity
- diminished work quality

- poor communication
- job dissatisfaction
- increase in grievances
- unscheduled downtime
- tense working relations
- poor morale.

From my experience, clients do not go out of their way to create this situation. Few entrepreneurs want a dissatisfied and disgruntled work force. No matter how you view this, it's a lose-lose scenario. So why does it happen? The simple answers are:

- lack of awareness.
- lack of a long-term perspective.
- an insatiable quest for more money and/or more power: in a word, greed.

Creating and managing a business is a "technical" process. That is, the product is a manufactured or processed item; the business systems, policies, practices and procedures are understandable enough to write down; the day-to-day operational management of the business is numbers- and control-oriented; what we make and how we make it is all task-driven or right-brain thinking.

Now we inject people into the equation. They are all different, unpredictable and don't all have the same learning abilities, skills and competencies. They have different needs, wants and aspirations. They have feelings and emotions that can't be left at home when they come to work. And they come in different sizes, ages, genders, colors and ethnic backgrounds. So what's an entrepreneur to do?

Most entrepreneurs are going to attempt to deal with and treat employees in a paradigm similar to the way the rest of the business is run. Establish policies, practices and procedures and expect everyone to follow them without disagreement, disloyalty or dissension. But it does not work that way. People are not "technical" items, nor are they extensions of machines who obediently follow the pace of the technical process. To behave as though they are, by initiating and supporting policies that encourage this perspective, indicates that the entrepreneur or the management team is not in touch with the employees' paradigm, and/or is thinking only about short-term gains over long-term benefits.

▶ No action (including the thought underlying the action) is without consequences.

Every action has a reaction. This is as true in the human realm as it is in the scientific realm. Managing people as though they were technical systems or processes leads to dissatisfaction and eventually to alienation. These negative outcomes are opportunities for the union organizer. In the vast majority of cases, unions sell their services because management was unaware of the need to rethink how they lead (not manage) their employee population.

It is not difficult to see that our entrepreneur would have preferred a different set of outcomes:

- clarity of mission and purpose.
- people-skilled managers.
- a climate of creativity and innovation.
- open and direct communications.
- loyal and committed employees.
- better employees attracted and retained.
- reduced waste and fewer accidents.
- quality service and products.
- a customer-first attitude.

What is less clear is how we move our company from its current state to our preferred (and, hopefully, decertified) state. What is required is a change in thinking throughout the entire company.

▶ A new paradigm must evolve that places Positive Employee Relations at the forefront.

RECLAIMING THE POSITIVE ORGANIZATION

At the heart of this new paradigm are the values of your company. As outlined in Chapter 1, values are the essence of every organization. The more positive the values embraced by your company, the more your company's employees will feel encouraged to share those values. As you attempt to re-position your company within the minds of your employees, recall, from Chapter 1, the Seven Core Values of the Positive Employee Relations organization:

1. Spirit of Partnership.
2. Solid Belief in Decency.
3. Commitment to Self-knowledge and Development.
4. Respect for Individual Differences.
5. Health, Safety and Well-being.
6. Appreciation that Change Is Inevitable.
7. Passion for Products and Process.

Your new corporate culture can best be summarized by examining the differences between it and the existing (unionized) culture, as outlined in Table 15.1.

TABLE 15.1 — What Changes Are Needed?

Old Paradigm	New Paradigm
Short-term goals for the corporation and the human resources.	Long-term vision for the corporation and the human resources.
Rigid culture.	Flexible culture.
Management's role is to determine direction and control.	Management's role is to inspire everyone, including themselves, to live values that enrich the business and its stakeholders.
Focused solely on competition.	Recognition of cooperation, co-creation and contribution.
Aggressive behaviors.	Supportive behaviors, such as trust, integrity, collaboration.

To reclaim a Positive Employee Relations position, you must eliminate the conditions within your organization that led to unionization.

▶ Management will have to do business differently in order to encourage decertification.

The new corporate values will have to permeate all business activities. You will need to acknowledge that decertification will result from the adoption and implementation of your corporate values. And, finally, you cannot overlook the importance and necessity of managerial and supervisory commitment to these goals.

DOING THINGS DIFFERENTLY

In creating a decertification strategy, it is important to recognize that decertification has nothing to do with the relationship between your employees and their union. It has everything to do with your relationship with your employees. As this relationship improves, the union will lose credibility, influence and perceived cash-benefit value. Your actions will be responsible for the transition from a unionized organization to a union-free one. You must manage the transition.

Managing the change to a new culture

In implementing the following ten steps, you should set a decertification time frame, fully aware that the process is a long one and may easily take up to five years.

1. Don't let the existing culture interfere with the creation of a new culture.
2. Focus your vision on new business processes, not old and established relationships.
3. Make the culture change obvious.
4. Make significant changes in your recognition systems to reflect the new culture.
5. Champion the new vision from the senior management level.

6. Change the locus of decision making from management's sole responsibility to a collaborative model that recognizes employee contributions.
7. Crank up the communications. Let all your employees and supervisors know about the changes taking place and how they will benefit.
8. Be willing, if training, coaching and mentoring fail, to replace managers and supervisors who cannot work within the new culture.
9. Recruit new supervisors and managers to a higher standard.
10. Train everyone.

Hiring practices

In your new organization, it must be clear that getting hired is difficult. There should be a rigorous process of screening applicants to determine who is best able to perform the tasks of the job and operate within the new corporate culture.

 A probation period is not an alternative for a good selection interview.

But interviews and all other selection instruments cannot contravene legislation or the collective agreement. The following employment practices should be components of your new organization:

- Train all interviewers.
- Use a behavioral model and specifications as criteria to objectively assess candidates. (Please see Appendix C for information about the Activity Vector Analysis.)
- Have high achievers do peer interviews.
- Interview, test, reference check and, if in doubt, interview again.
- Make supervisory involvement and approval mandatory.
- Reward supervisors who hire good employees.

Communications

Chapter 10 outlined the importance of communications to Positive Employee Relations. In a unionized environment, effective communications are just as important, perhaps more so. Claiming that "employees wouldn't understand" as a justification for poor communications is unacceptable.

▶ Clear, candid communications are pivotal to gaining respect in the workplace.

Avoiding issues or conflicts resolves nothing. The keys to good communications for supervisors and managers include:

- Opening your eyes and ears: listen, question, then listen some more.
- Saying what you mean.
- Encouraging feedback.
- Resolving conflicts before resentment sets in.
- Remembering that communication is leadership. Leadership is communication.

The following three communications programs can be implemented to reinforce your new culture and support your wish to see a two-party (rather than a three-party) workplace. Additional programs can be developed by referring to the upward and downward communications techniques outlined in Chapter 10.

Let's Talk© program

The Let's Talk© program is for employees. They set the agenda and whatever they wish to talk about is acceptable. Through face-to-face communication, Let's Talk© helps develop a supportive relationship between employee and supervisor. They jointly resolve issues of concern to the employee, through scheduled and planned meetings.

A sample employee's guide to the Let's Talk© program is included in Appendix D.

Lunch with the president

Lunch with the president is a program that opens unfiltered lines of communication between senior management and employees. It reinforces the benefits of company-wide synergy and demonstrates the human side of an authority figure. Additionally, this process can be used as a supervisory audit to determine whether supervisors are satisfying their internal customers.

This program consists of an informal luncheon, scheduled monthly, with no agenda and no minutes taken. Employees are selected randomly, with approximately eight to ten employees at each lunch. This event is a good opportunity to acknowledge anniversaries or product/service accomplishments. These lunches reinforce the culture and values of the organization and encourage an open exchange of information. No topics are excluded from the discussion, except personalities, and this rule is agreed to in advance.

All-employee meetings

These meetings ensure that messages are heard by all. They allow for employee accomplishments to be recognized and influence the corporate culture by demonstrating that management is walking the talk. Meetings are scheduled every month, near the end of the day (or shift) with social time to follow. They focus on presentations by the president and others (including employees) regarding the status of the business, financial reports, quality issues, customer feedback, etc. Recognition of events and special contributions are also included. During the social time after the meeting, employees and management talk about any other issues.

Recognition

Your recognition and rewards system is another area where the new corporate culture can be demonstrated to your employees. Recognition must be meaningful to employees. It should reinforce the values that make your organization a better place to work, and at the same time be fun. Programs of this sort provide management with an opportunity to move away from the parent-to-child model of employer domination and employee dependence.

Earmark the behaviors to be rewarded, such as sales, production, quality, innovation, safety, team building and internal customer success stories. Monetary rewards can be used (if they are distributed in a manner that is seen to be fair and reasonable by the majority of employees). Remember to design your recognition program with employee involvement. Here are some examples of possible rewards:

- gratitude: you cannot overdo "thank you."
- special clothing with company or event logo.
- media coverage.
- the opportunity to train others.
- recognizing employees through "way to go" awards. Any employee can give other employees such awards thanking them for their support.
- a "brag sheet," at the employee entrance, listing individual employees' outstanding efforts.
- thank-you notes sent by the company president to employees who excel.
- providing the "employee of the month" with a reserved parking space, or a donation in his/her name to that person's favorite charity.

Leadership and supervisory training

The importance of supervisory leadership to your decertification wishes (and the selection and training of effective supervisors) cannot be overemphasized. Influence (as opposed to power that is denoted by a title) is earned by leading employees, not granted by management.

▶ Leaders are defined by their followers. In fact, the followers grant them leadership.

It is not easy for supervisors to realize that leadership springs from accepting imperfection and the paradox that their influence increases as they relinquish some power. Sharing power helps prevent poor decisions, because power built on fear is an expression of intimidation, not leadership.

Managing only the technical component of a supervisory position, however, is not enough. Managers must buy into the new business vision, be positive role models and be held accountable for their "people" decisions. Additionally, senior management needs to acknowledge that learning and applying core competencies in both the human and technical part of the supervisor's job must be aligned with the performance appraisal and compensation process. Above all, remember that supervision equals leadership.

▶ If the group hasn't succeeded, it's likely that the leader hasn't supervised.

Implement the following supervisory training practices as part of your decertification campaign:

- Assess supervisors before promotion to determine their people versus things orientation.
- Use a training needs instrument for pre- and post-assessment of the value of the training.
- Create training workshops to accompany all human resources policies and procedures.
- Conduct training during workday/shift and on a continuous basis.
- Incorporate employee perceptions (from focus group meetings or perception surveys) into training design and content.

REGAINING LEADERSHIP

Once you have begun to implement a new set of values and establish a corporate culture based on Positive Employee Relations, you will be able to re-assert management's leadership role in your organization. Remember that decertification is about management demonstrating its ability to lead. The best way to do this is by institutionalizing your new corporate values. Promulgating a new business vision and proclaiming an Employees' Charter of Rights will help you begin to regain control of your workplace from the union. You will also find that neither the new business vision nor the Employees' Charter of Rights contravenes labor legislation or your collective agreement.

New business vision

A new business vision may assert that the financial bottom line follows everything else. Profit is like breathing: it's required. As a company we do not spend a lot of time on profit. What we pay maximum attention to is creating a workplace environment where people can do the work that produces the bottom line. We are concerned here about the humanness of the work process.

Employees' Charter of Rights

An Employees' Charter of Rights may recognize that as a management team, we are committed to the survival, growth and development of the company. We believe that this can be achieved only if we — all managers and supervisors — respect your:

- thoughts, feelings and fears.
- unique strengths and differences.
- desire to participate and contribute.
- need for recognition of achievements.
- desire to learn and develop.
- desire for a safe and healthy workplace.
- personal and family life.

FROM MANAGING TO LEADING

It's one thing to proclaim a new corporate culture, but quite another to see it take hold and play a part in changing employees' attitudes towards management and the union. In order to ensure the effectiveness of management's new policies and practices, we need a series of indicators, or signposts, of success. These indicators are signals that front-line supervisors have moved from managing to leading.

Indicators that show we've changed how we do business

- Systems to encourage both upward and downward communication are in place and used effectively.
- Customer complaint resolution includes the employees as equal partners.
- Employees are encouraged to sign up for "pre-supervisory" training workshops.
- Plant facility changes, manufacturing process changes, etc., are discussed openly and employee input is deliberately sought before the changes are implemented.

Indicators that middle/senior managers are seen as positive role models

- Communication becomes more open and shop floor problems are given the importance of customer problems.
- Better (more qualified) employees are being hired, trained and coached.
- Front-line supervision is reinforcing the new values.
- People skills are being rewarded.

Indicators that the quality of front-line supervision is visibly upgraded

- Supervisory training results in positive changes on the shop floor.
- Team leaders and supervisors become coaches, trainers, mentors.
- Supervisors are held accountable for delivering quality Positive Employee Relations.

Indicators that assumptions regarding hourly "workers" and salaried "staff" have equalized

- All workers are employees.
- Benefit programs are the same for all.
- Hiring, discipline, performance management policies, etc., are the same for all.
- Everyone attends the same social events.
- Parking, cafeteria facilities, etc., are the same for all.

A SCENARIO

Think back to the old paradigm scenario outlined earlier, where an enthusiastic entrepreneur with little or no interest in employee relations created an organization that was ripe for unionization. Now examine the following scenario. The new paradigm has been implemented through the practices of Positive Employee Relations and institutionalized in the new business vision and Employees' Charter of Rights. The result is that the tables have been turned on the union. Its security value and usefulness have been threatened and its traditional practices don't allow for an effective response to management's new approach.

1. The union will likely feel threatened by initiatives such as the new business vision and the Employees' Charter of Rights.
2. Management can predict the union's response. We have seen the aggressiveness and intimidation before.
3. Initial union reaction will be posturing, along the traditional adversarial lines.
4. Management's response must be: "Let's talk: we believe we are treating our employees well."
5. The parties meet.
6. Management's response to specific issues raised by the union is developed in light of the business vision, Employees' Charter of Rights, and the existing collective agreement.
7. Meetings will likely resolve nothing of significance in the union's eyes (because their power base is eroding).

8. Management meets with the union only to discuss specific issues, not to debate the merits of management's new business paradigm.
9. A "battle" between management and union officials will ensue for credibility, respect and influence.
10. Employees who are pro-company are already on-side, while the unionists among the employee population will likely never be won over. Those on the fence, however, will recognize that this "test of wills" is about management wishing to create a better workplace without charging any dues or fees and the union being unwilling to let go of its power and revenue stream.
11. Management must, at all times, walk the high road. Follow the letter of the collective agreement, but establish a "higher spirit." If management does this, it will demonstrate that it is the best party to represent employee interests. The union will slowly lose its credibility, influence and reason for being. Once this happens, the success of the employee-initiated decertification campaign is all but assured.

In summary, while only the employees are permitted to run a decertification campaign, the employer can, through Positive Employee Relations, regain the employees' respect and create a working environment that makes the union redundant. Why would employees prefer to pay a union to protect their interests if their employer has been able to demonstrate, by living its core values, that a positive relationship with its employees is as important as a positive relationship with its customers? However, this is by no means a "quick fix." It requires patience, integrity and commitment on the part of all management. The regaining of trust is a gradual process, but it can be done.

TAKE ACTION!

1. Review the Seven Core Values of the Positive Employee Relations organization.
2. Examine the difference between the existing (unionized) paradigm and the new paradigm of a Positive Employee Relations culture.
3. Strive for consensus within the management group so that senior management can champion the new vision.
4. Examine the reasons for unionization and develop a plan to reverse the conditions that caused employees to choose third-party intervention.
5. Begin company-wide marketing of what your company is offering employees.
6. Raise the standards for recruitment and hire employees who respond more to your offerings than to those of the union.
7. Apply the principles of continuous improvement to your employee relations.
8. Manage the change to a new culture according to the steps detailed in the section "Doing Things Differently."

EPILOGUE

Now that we have traveled down this path together, let's reflect on what Positive Employee Relations means in the management of your human resources.

Positive Employee Relations as discussed throughout this book is a set or behaviors, based on mutually agreed-upon values, that respond to a wide range and varying degrees of employee relations issues. These values underpin each and every one of our financial, marketing, production and human resource decisions. They are our guideposts as to appropriate versus inappropriate, ethical versus unethical, just versus unjust behaviors and actions.

The values, though agreed-upon within one's organization, are frequently the result of the thoughts of only a very few people. For example, in a highly centralized and autocratic organization, mutual agreement can be reached by potentially two or three people and subsequently be promoted to and by the whole management team. In a more participative and consensus-driven organization, agreed-upon values can actually be the result of an in-depth inquiry by a large number of people. The method and process by which we articulate our values is an insight into the bedrock of our beliefs.

Value-based decision making is older than the free enterprise system as we know it in the Western world. Values are as old as society's first communities and, if viewed in this broader perspective, have been attached to political and economic systems and not the other way around. But, over many millennia and many political, economic, social and technological revolutions, we in the business community frequently contruct a paradigm around the idea that business values are different from, and in many cases, more important that personal values. For example, business values are frequently articulated as profitability, competitiveness, leanness, and personal values as respect, collaboration and integrity.

The thought processes that many leaders undertake to separate these two types of values (and there are more categories, e.g., religious values) are in my opinion somewhat flawed. Why? First, because I believe the thought processes are done at an instinctive or subconscious level. There is no debate or in-depth inquiry — just a pre-conditioned or socialized reaction. Second, if we believe that one's life can be lived to its fullest potential without a rigorous examination that results in a harmonious blend of all the varieties of value experiences, we have missed one of life's greatest lessons. A person divided by their own conflicting values is not whole and hence cannot think or behave holistically. My experience is that the *quality* of our life (what we think about, how we behave to ourselves and others, the degree of our generosity, etc.) is more precious than the *quantity* of our life (how much we purchase, who we manipulate to get personal advancement, whether we apply our religious values just on Saturday or just on Sunday, etc.). Why? Because all other values are secondary to the values of self-respect, self-esteem, self-actualization and the good we do for others as a result of the good we do for ourselves.

By attempting to think of ourselves as part business and part personal and part this or that, we are creating our own fragmented existence. This, in turn, leads us to say we are under too much pressure, too stressed out, not multi-tasking fast enough and we have less and less quality time with our children every year.

What happens next is we either break or we give up one of the parts. In the business world (note how easily our everyday language causes us to think in fragments), to break is translated into a variety of occurrences, from an emotional breakdown, to a stroke or heart attack, to the addictive breaks of drugs or alcohol. We can also break by not keeping up with, for example, the amalgam of rapid technological change and younger and more energetic people pushing for our jobs.

If we don't break then we will likely give up one of the parts (the business part, the personal part). The consequence: broken lifelong relationships, estranged relationships with children, obsessions about career and career advancement, obsessions about competition and winning at all cost — the list goes on.

So, my argument is that we can lead lives of great *quantity* and convince ourselves that we are leading lives of great sophistication and importance because of our acquisitions. We can live in the fast lane — touching only the surface. Or we can lead lives of great *quality* and be actively concerned about our thoughts and motives and the behaviors and actions they cause us to undertake. Quality, in whatever aspect of life we choose to consider, is always the winning strategy.

In painting a dual factor model (quality versus quantity) I run the risk of it being dismissed because of its simplicity. However, that would be your choice. Just as it is your choice to become attached to the business part, the personal part or some other combination of parts that constitute your life. It is your choice — but you have options. More options than you, at any one time, could articulate. Once your choice is made let it be known to every fibre of your being that you have made a choice. It was not your parents' choice or your partner/spouse's choice. It was your choice. For in this act of awareness are the seeds of self-respect and self-esteem which quickly grow into self-responsibility. For without these attributes we miss the quality and just skim the surface of life.

Let's call for the question: What does Positive Employee Relations mean beyond the union-free issue? I believe it means that each and every leader, regardless of his/her organizational position, has an obligation to know his/her personal values system before accepting the responsibility and obligation of leading others. For without this self knowledge, the leader's guidance, coaching, decision making, have a questionable foundation. So, Positive Employee Relations means that every leader starting with the chairman and the CEO owe it to themselves, first and foremost, and then to their organizations to appreciate what values they are using to guide their lives. In this knowing is *integrity*. As we have seen throughout this book — integrity is what carries us forward as whole rather than broken leaders. And with this integrity we give to ourselves and to our organizations the benefit of our self-understanding, our wisdom and our compassion; and what we get back from those who choose to follow us is their self-understanding and their integrity.

Just imagine the collaboration, synergy, innovation and creativity from an organization that is rooted in the values of self-understanding, integrity and compassion. In such an organization the extent of integration between all employees and all leaders would be such that Unions Are Not Inevitable!

Lloyd M. Field, Ph.D.
Waterloo, Ontario, Canada
October 2000

A
Employee Perception Survey

ADMINISTRATIVE SCHEDULE

1. Communications

A letter or memo should be circulated (for example, via pay envelope) to all employees, outlining the survey's objectives and encouraging employee participation.

One week prior to the survey date a memo from the consultant should be circulated.

A few days prior to the survey a final memo should be circulated detailing the survey timetable, indicating where the survey will be conducted, and assigning the survey groups.

2. Conducting the survey

All groups should participate in the survey within the same timeframe (ideally one or two days). The selected groups from normal organizational units will be identified by a code number.

Individuals within the survey groups will be asked to maintain their confidentiality. The survey will require about 45 minutes to complete.

Any number of employees can complete the survey during the same timeframe. However, the groups must be accurately coded.

3. Survey process

When the surveys have been completed, the responses will be compiled in statistical format. This data will provide a breakdown of how each individual, by group, responded to the questions.

By interpreting these results, key trends can be identified, that is, areas of employee concern and areas of satisfaction. To amplify these trends and obtain specific details, the consultant will take the survey results back to selected employee groups and ask for their interpretation.

4. Employee feedback

Statistical data on approximately 10 to 15 questions will be shown to selected survey groups at feedback meetings. These groups will be asked to respond, in detail, to concerns or problems represented by the statistical data. Then they will be asked to discuss, among themselves, ways and means of effecting change; that is, what improvements they would like to see and how the department or company might go about implementing these changes. The feedback meetings will take about one-and a-half hours per survey group.

5. Recommendations

Based on the information obtained through the feedback meetings and supported by the statistical data, the consultant will prepare a detailed report. This report will outline the employees' comments as they relate to each trend, as well as specific recommendations for change.

SHERBORNE COMPANY

To: All Employees
From: William Burford
Date: November 1, 20__
Subject: **Employee Perception Survey**

It has been our philosophy to encourage and provide frequent opportunities for communication within the Sherborne Company. We believe this ensures that our employee relations programs and practices are sensitive to your needs.

At the same time, we recognize that a number of different attitudes and opinions about our company, our jobs and our surroundings may exist. Only when we, as an organization, have a good understanding of our employees' feelings about these issues can we make any change.

To help us continue to be aware of our employees' feelings, we have asked Jay Martin of Performance House Ltd., Human Resource Consultants, to conduct an employee perception survey. We feel that it is one of the more effective and accurate ways to obtain your opinions and views about your job and Sherborne. This perception survey will involve all employees and it will cover a broad range of work-related topics. The survey is confidential and no individual will be identified. The consultants have designed the format and will be administering it as well as interpreting the results.

The survey will be conducted on December 3, 20__. While answering the questions is, of course, entirely voluntary on your part, we urge you to use this opportunity to register your views. *Employees participating in the survey will be made aware of the results and the action plans to follow.* To provide all employees with an overview of the survey results, a special employee relations bulletin will be published.

SHERBORNE COMPANY

To: All Employees of Sherborne Company
From: J. Martin, Performance House Ltd.
Date: November 20, 20__
Subject: **Perception Survey Update**

Our consulting firm has been asked to conduct a confidential employee perception survey, to tabulate the results, and to present these results for discussion.

An employee perception survey offers employees the opportunity to assess their jobs, their company and their surroundings frankly and honestly. The management at Sherborne is very interested in what the employees think about the company and its operations. They believe, as we do, that your ideas will be helpful in making Sherborne a better place to work.

This survey will give you the opportunity to tell us what you like and don't like about your work and where you feel improvements can be made. The information you provide will help your company correct or improve existing policies and practices and build upon those which are considered good.

We have designed the survey questions and will be processing the results in such a way that no one can be identified. We will return to discuss these results with you.

Although participation in the survey is completely voluntary, we sincerely hope that all of you will give the Sherborne Company the benefit of your ideas.

We plan to be in the conference room to conduct the survey on December 3, 20__, with the feedback meetings scheduled for the week of January 28, 20__. Your department manager will advise you of the precise time and location of the session in which you will participate.

EMPLOYEE PERCEPTION SURVEY

Confidential

Introduction

This survey has been designed to help your company management review its policies and practices. Your views and opinions are important and will help management make sure that the programs and procedures at Sherborne meet your needs as well as the company's goals.

Please be frank and honest in answering these questions; write what you really feel.

Here are some simple instructions to follow:

- <u>DO NOT SIGN YOUR NAME.</u> Put your group number at the top of the next page. (This will be provided to you by the survey administrator.)
- Please provide only one response to each statement. If you wish to provide additional information, or explain your answer, please do so using the back of the survey pages. (Be sure to indicate which answer you are explaining.)
- REMEMBER, THIS IS NOT A TEST. THERE ARE NO WRONG ANSWERS. <u>YOUR OPINION IS THE RIGHT ANSWER.</u>
- If you feel a statement does not apply to you, or if you have no opinion, leave it blank.
- When the word "manager" is used in a statement, it means your immediate boss. (See listing on white board.)
- When you have completed your survey, please put it in the attached envelope, seal the envelope and turn it in to the survey administrator.

We will provide Sherborne with a report that will categorize answers by groups of employees. Rest assured that the report we provide to Sherborne will not identify any specific employees.

Thank you for taking the time to complete this survey.

Employee Perception Survey

In accordance with the instructions of the survey administrator, please indicate your group number.

Place a checkmark (✓) in the column you feel most closely reflects your opinion. Remember to use only one checkmark for each question. (If you wish to expand upon your answers, please use the back of each page, but indicate the question upon which you are expanding.)

ABOUT THE COMPANY	STONGLY AGREE	AGREE	DISAGREE	STONGLY DISAGREE
For anyone who does the type of work I do, I think Sherborne is a great place to work.				
Sherborne has a good future.				
Sherborne gives a high priority to its employees.				
Sherborne makes an effort to understand its employees' point of view.				
Sherborne is focused on high standards in everything it does.				
Sherborne is concerned about safety in the workplace.				
I would encourage my friends to come to work at Sherborne.				

ABOUT MY SUPERVISOR	STONGLY AGREE	AGREE	DISAGREE	STONGLY DISAGREE
My supervisor treats me with respect and fairness.				
My supervisor treats other employees with respect and fairness.				
My supervisor provides me with good direction about my work.				
My supervisor is very supportive of me as a person.				
My supervisor is trying to help me grow and develop.				
My supervisor recognizes when I need training and ensures that I get training opportunities.				
My supervisor gives me regular feedback about my performance.				
The feedback I receive from my supervisor is helpful and constructive.				
My supervisor asks for my input about my job.				
My supervisor is available to discuss any problems I may have.				

	STONGLY AGREE	AGREE	DISAGREE	STONGLY DISAGREE
My supervisor is responsive to my problems.				
My supervisor is loyal to and supportive of Sherborne.				
My supervisor is a good communicator.				
My supervisor handles himself/herself in a professional manner.				
My supervisor is concerned about safety in the workplace.				
I believe that my supervisor cares about our customers and how we treat them.				
ABOUT MY JOB				
I understand my job responsibilities.				
My job allows me to do the best I possibly can.				
I enjoy my job.				
My work schedule (hours of work) is reasonable and considerate of my needs.				

	STONGLY AGREE	AGREE	DISAGREE	STONGLY DISAGREE
The *quantity* of work I am expected to perform is reasonable.				
The *quality* of work I am expected to perform is reasonable.				
I have the supplies, equipment and information that I need to do my job properly.				
I believe that my job is important to the success of Sherborne.				
I believe that the management at Sherborne thinks my job is important.				
I am encouraged to make suggestions for improvements.				
I have job security.				
ABOUT MY CO-WORKERS				
My co-workers are co-operative.				
My co-workers and I get along well with each other.				

	STONGLY AGREE	AGREE	DISAGREE	STONGLY DISAGREE
At Sherborne we work as a team.				
I get assistance from my co-workers when I need it.				
ABOUT MY WORK SPACE				
I work in a pleasant environment.				
I work in a safe environment.				
Sherborne provides satisfactory facilities for its employees (lunch room, washrooms, etc.).				
My work space is well-lit.				
My work space is well-ventilated.				
The noise level in my work space is acceptable.				
The temperature in my work space is properly controlled.				

	STONGLY AGREE	AGREE	DISAGREE	STONGLY DISAGREE
ABOUT MY COMPENSATION				
I am fairly paid for the work I do.				
I am paid a competitive salary.				
I receive a good benefit package.				
Sherborne has a good vacation policy.				
How well I perform affects my compensation.				
ABOUT COMMUNICATIONS				
Sherborne keeps me informed about what is going on in our company.				
Sherborne keeps me informed about what is going on in our industry.				
When changes are necessary, they are always explained to me.				
The rumor mill is my best source of information at Sherborne.				

	STONGLY AGREE	AGREE	DISAGREE	STONGLY DISAGREE
My supervisor is my best source of information at Sherborne.				
I am informed about various company policies and procedures.				
I am informed about the company's benefit programs.				
Doing this survey was a really good idea.				
ABOUT OUR CUSTOMER SERVICE				
We provide the best possible service to our customers.				
I would recommend to my friends that they should purchase their "widgets" from Sherborne.				
We are always friendly and courteous to our customers.				
We make doing business at Sherborne a pleasant experience.				
There is nothing that we could do to improve our customer service.				

	STONGLY AGREE	AGREE	DISAGREE	STONGLY DISAGREE
The way in which I do *my* job has an impact on customer satisfaction.				
The long-term success of Sherborne is dependent upon how well we provide customer service.				

Please use the space below to provide your answers to the following questions

If I could, I would change the following things at Sherborne:
___
___
___

The things I like best about working at Sherborne are:
___
___
___

What I would do to improve working at Sherborne are:
___
___
___

I would like to make the following additional comments:
___
___
___

B
A Supervisor's Guide to Remaining Union-free through Positive Employee Relations

This appendix provides the reader with an extensive and detailed guide to what a supervisor or manager can and cannot do during a union organizing campaign.

It is based on generally accepted practices under labor and industrial relations legislation in Canada, the United States and the United Kingdom. In all these jurisdictions, the decision to join a union or not join a union is an employee and not an employer decision. When leaders respect this employee right and provide a workplace environment supported by Positive Employee Relations values and behaviors, the perceived value of a union will diminish dramatically.

This appendix is a guidebook for the union-free employer. Any reader who becomes involved in a union organizing campaign should seek advice from a competent and experienced labor relations counsel/attorney.

I. Introduction

Unions organize employees by capitalizing on management's mis-management. Most union campaigns are initiated by employees who seek out a third party because of poor management practices. On the other hand, when supervisors effectively carry out their people-management responsibilities and realistically examine and respond to problem areas, the need for employees to seek outside assistance is eliminated.

Compensation is not the only issue that creates employee dissatisfaction and makes unionization attractive. Compensation is far down the list of reasons why employees join unions. Employee dissatisfaction can frequently be traced to other areas, such as problems that arise when employees perceive that their supervisors are unfair or disrespectful in the manner in which they handle performance matters, recognition and the performance appraisal program. Whatever the cause, the key to Sherborne's Positive Employee Relations is conscious attention — now — to the employees you supervise. In this way we will avoid future problems. This is the goal of our Positive Employee Relations program.

The most frequent employee relations topic that gives credence to unions is the poor handling of employee complaints by a supervisor. You should respond to every employee complaint promptly, in private, and on a one-to-one basis. You should take the necessary time to listen to every employee's complaints fully and objectively. If an employee's complaint is unsubstantiated, explain why it is. If it is factual, admit it and thank the employee for bringing it to your attention. Then follow up: your best intentions will be meaningless unless prompt action is taken to correct the cause of the employee's complaint. Remember, if employees feel they cannot openly bring complaints to your attention, they will turn to a union to provide this service for them.

Face-to-face communication is another critical element of Sherborne's Positive Employee Relations program. Ensure that you promote and maintain meaningful two-way communications with all your employees. It should be part of your supervisory practice to talk with every employee in your department daily if possible, and not less than every second day.

Get to know your employees as individuals. Discover what motivates them by talking about their work, performance achievements, personal interests and career goals. Involve your employees in department goal-setting and decision-making. Seek their advice and listen to their suggestions.

When you build on employee involvement and mutual trust, you enhance Sherborne's ability to retain its right to deal directly with our employees.

Below we have listed several further suggestions to follow when dealing with your employee group:

- Make "fairness and equity" the watchwords in your relationship with your employees. Before taking any negative action (e.g., discipline) ensure that your actions are impartial and consistent with previous employee relations practices. When in doubt, review your intended plans with human resources.
- Treat your employees as you treat your customers; make them feel truly important, like "internal customers." Philosophically, you should follow the motto used by a major Canadian foundry: "Our product is steel: our strength is people."
- Remember that your daily behavior is a role model for others to follow. Your conduct has a direct impact on your employees' feelings of self-respect and well-being.
- Respond to your employees' desire for information. Communicate openly and willingly about Sherborne — its operations, markets, upcoming changes, general business plans. It is always beneficial to handle employee concerns about rumors and misinformation from a base of accurate information.
- Inform your employees that discrimination of any kind is totally unacceptable. All human rights legislation prohibits discrimination based on race, religion, creed, ancestry, citizenship, place of national origin, color, gender, sexual orientation, age, record of offense, marital status, family status and handicap. The basis upon which Sherborne operates is that those who perform well and produce quality "widgets" receive preference in consideration for promotion and advancement — it's performance on the job that counts.
- Communicate all the details about Sherborne's wage, salary and benefit programs. Since these issues are frequently of concern to both employees and their spouse/partner, ensure that both parties are fully informed. This will be an ideal opportunity to create a bridge between the workplace and the family.
- Create a work climate and environment that is open, friendly and responsive to your employees' needs. Provide positive recognition when work is well done and when employees give extra of themselves.

II. Communicating our Positive Employee Relations program

We must communicate to our employees Sherborne's policy on unionization. Our policy is abundantly clear — legislation provides that every employee is free to join the trade union of his/her choice. This same legislation also provides that every employee is free not to join a union. Sherborne Company believes that by reason of its employee relations policies, and the mature way in which supervisors lead their teams, employees have no reason to seek third-party intervention. Further, employees are often misled about the significance of union membership and do not understand that by joining a union they are entering a complex legal and contractual relationship with an entity that has nothing to do with Sherborne, its profitability, its productivity and the creation of jobs. As a company, we believe strongly that the needs of every employee can be met and served fully and promptly without the necessity of outsider involvement. As a supervisor, you must understand, accept and communicate this policy.

As a supervisor, you are the individual best trained to communicate certain facts to our employees in the event of union activity or attempts to organize the workplace. In fact, as a supervisor, labor relations legislation gives you the right to express your views and opinions. However, it is abundantly clear that there is a very narrow interpretation placed on the notion of your "freedom of speech." It therefore becomes very important for you to be aware of what you should and should not say.

Any comments or opinions expressed by a supervisor that are likely to frighten a reasonable employee from becoming involved in, or continuing to be active in, union affairs will be seen as intimidating or threatening, and therefore a breach of the legislation. Remember, as a supervisor, you speak for Sherborne and we are bound by your behavior (which includes what you say and do). While you are not expected to become an expert on the law, you are expected to know what you can and cannot say to employees with respect to their right to join or not to join a union.

The first point to note is that any initiatives with respect to discussions about trade union activity should come from the employees and not from the supervisor. In other words, if union activity begins to take place in the workplace, it would be wrong for a supervisor to approach employees in order to discuss the subject. Almost certainly, however, one or more employees will approach the supervisor and seek opinions and information from that supervisor about union organizers. Wait for the employees to make the first move.

Second, try to avoid dealing with a so-called "captive audience." Don't call a meeting of your team during working hours or at any other time, for the purpose of initiating discussions about union activity, particularly in circumstances where it appears that their absence from the meeting would be noted. It is always better to speak to employees about unionization on an informal basis, preferably with one other member of supervision present. Discussions of this nature are less likely to lead to legal problems than are situations where a supervisor addresses a number of employees in his/her office.

You must always indicate to an employee who approaches you that the decision as to whether or not to join a union is entirely up to the employee to make and that Sherborne respects the rights of employees to make such decisions. You can, however, express the view that you hope the working environment at Sherborne is such that employees don't feel that it is necessary to bring in an outsider or third party. There is nothing improper or illegal in giving a candid answer to a request for an opinion. If you are asked, for example, "Do you think we need a union here?" there is nothing wrong in saying "no." On the other hand, you must be very careful to avoid expressing opinions that contain a veiled threat or that might be seen as threatening or intimidating. Examples of management "opinions" that have been found to be improper are:

- "If a union is certified, the company will refuse to bargain with it."
- "If a union is certified, the company will be unable to afford its demands and will have to close down."
- "If the company knows which employees are signing union cards, there will be trouble for them."
- "If a union is certified, the company may have to lay off employees."
- "Employees should consider an employee association rather than a trade union."
- "Certain of the company's competitors have come to be unionized and they are now worse off then they would have been if they had remained non-union."

Keep in mind that employees who approach you will also be seeking information about the union. You should encourage employees to read carefully the union's constitution and to ask questions of the union organizers. You can remind employees that the constitution of the union is, in essence, a contract, and that the terms of the contract into which they enter with the union are contained in the constitution. You may suggest to them that they demand a copy of the constitution from the union's organizers.

It is important to remember that you and your fellow supervisors are the individuals who are expected to be the "eyes and ears" of the company with respect to matters of this nature. You are expected to keep senior management advised on what is happening in the workplace and to communicate the views of the employees. Don't be afraid to take the initiative. Remember that you are the company's main communication link with our employees and your strong Positive Employee Relations stand will go a long way to ensure that our employees do not perceive the need for third-party representation. Remember that the communication link is a two-way street. You must keep your manager and human resources advised of all critical incidents and employee concerns that might have broad, company-wide implications.

In summary, if our employees believe and see evidence that you (and your fellow supervisors) are concerned about their interests and views as employees, they will remain union-free and not be subject to the "collectivism" imposed by third-party bargaining agents.

Finally, a cautionary note. As supervisors you should be wary of being "set-up" in a union organizing campaign. It happens quite often that the union organizer will approach a member of management hoping to extract from him/her an improper or threatening reaction. If you are suspicious, avoid saying anything at all, or at least be sure you have another member of management present as a witness to what you say. An easy example of a "set-up" is where an employee comes to you and says: "The union organizers have been to see me. I didn't sign a union card but I know they had a meeting with Mary, Tom and Charlie and they all signed union cards." It is very likely that the individual who shares this information with you has, in fact, signed a union card. The reason he/she is telling you about the transaction is that he/she wants to assure you that he/she has not, in fact, done so. Subsequently, should it become necessary to discipline that individual, you will find that a complaint has been made that you have taken reprisals against him/her because you believe that he/she has been involved in union activity. (It doesn't matter that he/she told you exactly the opposite — his/her evidence will be that he/she told you something entirely different — and if you don't have a witness to support your testimony, you've got a problem!)

III. Positive Employee Relations and your role as a supervisor

Our current union-free status is of great importance to you and your fellow supervisors. For example, if our employees were to select a union to represent them, you would see a dramatic change in the nature of interpersonal relationships and the trust level between employees and supervision. In other words, the overall "climate" would probably change dramatically. In management's view this would not be a change for the better. Additionally, supervising a unionized group of employees is like attempting to build team trust and mutual goal commitment while bargaining across a negotiating table.

Supervising under a Positive Employee Relations program, and thus remaining union-free, will enable you to achieve both business and personal goals without third-party interference in the following decision-making areas:

- wage increases
- job transfers
- work schedules
- overtime requirements
- employee discipline
- employee complaint resolution.

Sherborne Company considers your supervisory ability to be a valuable asset. Your career as a supervisor has been built largely on the very functions that a union would like to take over. Giving up your management rights to a union shop steward not only harms the company but will materially affect your ability to do the job and reduce your level of job satisfaction.

Professionally carrying out your human resource responsibilities will further our business objectives and promote a healthy and satisfying employee relations atmosphere. The maintenance of an atmosphere which encourages employees to remain union-free calls for the best efforts of everyone on the management team.

IV. Indicators of union activity

It is essential to be both attentive and observant in this area. You should be able to recognize the common signs which frequently signal that a union organizing drive is underway. The following are some of the key indicators:

- Eye contact is lost with employees.
- Employees talk in out-of-the-way places or disperse when you approach.
- Strangers appear to linger on company property or in work areas.
- Union literature appears on the premises or in the parking areas.
- Employees use labor relations terms normally not heard in the workplace, e.g. "unfair labor practices," "demand for recognition," etc.
- Complaints are made by employee delegations and/or committees rather than the usual single employee approach.
- Unusual questions are more frequently and aggressively asked at staff/departmental meetings.
- Union organizers visit or write employees at their homes.

The above list is only a beginning. Your judgement, instinct and human resource skills are critical in observing union organizing activity. Apart from any consideration of union activity, good human resource practices require that you be sensitive to any unusual conduct that may indicate friction between you and your employees. This sensitivity is essential in the early detection of an organizing attempt.

If you have reason to believe that union activity is underway, you must act immediately. Many constructive and proper measures can be taken as soon as an organizing drive is detected. Take the following action steps:

- Immediately contact human resources and your manager.
- Do not remain silent. Provide your employees with relevant and useful information to respond to the organizer's strategy. What you say and how you say it should be approved by human resources *before* you respond.
- Emphasize the company's benefit programs, and make sure your employees know and understand all about them. Make sure they understand the company's policies on wages and that Sherborne's wage scales are competitive in the industry. Push the positive aspect of employment at Sherborne Company as being open, friendly, supportive and without cost (i.e., union dues).

V. The distribution of union literature

What are union membership cards?
In an organizing campaign, unions seek to have employees sign union membership cards. These cards may be distributed separately or attached to union literature. A signed union membership card is a legal document through which employees assert that they want a particular union to be their collective bargaining agent.

Not only that, it constitutes a contract between the employee and the trade union. As with any other contract, all the fine print must be read. For employees to understand completely the legal obligations incurred by signing a membership application form, they must read the union's constitution and the by-laws of any local union that is organizing. They should also find out what they have to pay in union dues.

The critical language in a typical union membership card reads as follows:

"I hereby authorize [Name of Union] to represent me and, on my behalf, to negotiate and conclude any and all agreements as to wages benefits, hours of work and other conditions of employment."

Union certification
Signed membership cards are essential to the success of a union organizing drive. It should be understood the purpose of applying for certification is to obtain the exclusive right to represent a group of employees.

There are three possible ways for a union to acquire the exclusive right to represent a group of employees as their bargaining agent. The certification guidelines are established by different government agencies in different countries. For example, in Canada, labor matters fall under provincial law, so we have ten different Labor Acts and one for federal jurisdiction. In the United States, the National Labor Relations Act covers all 50 states; however in some employment situations, state law may override the national Act. In the United Kingdom, a single Act covers industrial relations throughout the country.

Legal implications of signing a card

The employees usually do not know the legal implications of signing a union membership card. They do not realize that the signing of a card binds them contractually not only to the trade union but to each and every other employee who has signed a card. In addition, once a union becomes the bargaining agent it may legally require a "union security clause" which would require all employees to pay dues to the trade union or lose their jobs. Further, once employees become union members they may be subject to extensive contractual obligations, including the paying of dues, special assessment fees and fines.

Union misrepresentation to influence employees

You should also be prepared to anticipate union misrepresentation. The following are examples of false statements that frequently circulate during an organizing drive:

- "You must sign the card. Everyone else has."
- "Sign now or you won't have a job after we win."
- "It will cost you more if you don't join now."
- "This card is only to get more information."
- "This card is only to get an election."

By understanding and exposing the fallacy of these statements you can help every employee to make an informed decision. We are confident that, given correct and truthful information, employees will refuse to sign cards or at least will defer signing until they are informed of all the implications involved in unionization. In short, practice good Positive Employee Relations and demonstrate initiative by promptly speaking out. Remember: if in any doubt, check with human resources before addressing these false statements.

Canvassing and distribution by non-employees

During an organizing drive, union representatives may attempt to visit Sherborne Company premises to canvass union membership cards or distribute literature to your employees. Therefore, identification and proper handling of visitors is extremely important. Union representatives are not allowed on company premises unless invited by a member of the senior management team. They are, however, allowed to be on public property adjacent to the company's facility.

It is a company rule that no unauthorized visitor shall come inside working areas, or engage in canvassing or distribution of literature inside working areas. If you observe this conduct, immediately take the following steps:

- If possible, ask a witness to approach the canvasser with you. Our security personnel are available to assist you.
- If possible, escort the canvasser to a private area.
- In the presence of your witness, advise the canvasser of our no-trespassing policy and ask him/her to leave. Be polite but firm.
- If necessary, escort the canvasser outside the working area to an entrance or exit.
- If the request is refused, ask another supervisor to immediately notify human resources while you remain with the canvasser. Assistance will be provided.

Your vigilance in the enforcement of our no-trespassing rule is an important factor in preserving a working environment free of union disruption. However, you should also be aware of three key elements in the enforcement of the rule:

- Enforce the rule without exception. The company's rule applies to all unauthorized visitors, not just union representatives. This includes, for example, those canvassing for community charity groups.
- Request the identity of the visitor; get a business card if possible.
- Follow up by immediately reporting the incident to human resources. You and your witness should then make a written record of the incident.

Solicitation and distribution by employees

An employee cannot be disciplined or terminated for exercising his/her lawful right to join a trade union and to participate in its lawful activities, including signing up other people to membership. It is understood that while at work he/she is expected to work. Accordingly, if you find that employees are engaging in canvassing and union organizing on company premises during work periods, you are entitled to stop them from doing that. You should indicate to such employees that they are not authorized to engage in that activity and that they are at the place of work for the purpose of working. If the employee continues to engage in such conduct in spite of the warning, you should report this to human resources immediately.

Engaging in union activities on company premises during working hours includes oral communication about union matters, efforts to persuade employees to sign membership cards, and discussions about unionization. Such activities are generally permitted, however, when the employee is not working, i.e., lunch or coffee breaks. This point varies significantly by jurisdiction and advice should be obtained from human resources before any action is taken.

Administer the "no solicitation and no distribution while on work time" rule with an even hand. Remember, you ought not to be in a position where you are dealing with unauthorized union solicitation or distribution any differently than you deal with any other kinds of unauthorized solicitation and distribution. Follow normal past practice and if you are not familiar with such practices, notify human resources before you act.

If you do not apply the rule even-handedly, the company runs the risk of having these rules invalidated when they are applied against union activities. If the rules are applied consistently, the company will retain a valuable asset in its efforts to prevent union disruption in the workplace.

Act Quickly

It is your responsibility to take prompt action if prohibited canvassing and distribution occurs or is attempted. Regardless of whether a Sherborne employee or an outsider is involved, you should immediately inform the canvasser of our policy and remain until the prohibited conduct ceases.

Remember: notify human resources and your manager promptly in the event that you observe any activity which leads you to believe that a union drive is underway.

VI. Communicating with your employees

Legislation not only protects an employee's right to organize, but also expressly protects his/her right to oppose or refrain from union activities. As discussed earlier, you have a critical responsibility in communicating facts about unions which will enable employees to evaluate intelligently whether to support, oppose or refrain from union activity.

You may discuss unions generally or the particular union engaged in the organizational drive. Explain the significance of signing union membership cards, clarify misrepresentation of facts by the union, and describe the benefits Sherborne employees now enjoy.

Employee inquiries whether to sign union membership cards

Often employees will seek your advice about the union and whether they should sign a membership card. This is an excellent opportunity to express our position with regard to unions. State that while it is the employee's own decision whether to sign a union membership card, if you were the employee, you would not. Explain the basis for such an opinion. Specifically:

- Employees should think carefully before signing or they might unknowingly forfeit their valuable right to a secret ballot election.
- Once the union is the legal bargaining agent it will require a "union security" clause with the company. Such a clause may require an employee to join the union or lose his/her job.
- Union membership will obligate employees to abide by lengthy union constitutions and by-laws. Violation of those by-laws may result in union fines or even dismissal from the union.
- Employees now enjoy competitive wages and benefits without the union. At present, an employee's take-home pay is not subject to union initiation fees, dues, fines or assessments. Also, an employee's income can't be cut off for an undetermined period by a union strike.
- Signing a union card is a commitment to the union before hearing all the facts. For example, have you reviewed the union's constitution?

Revocation of signed cards by employees

If you have communicated the facts about union membership cards, some of your employees may approach you and ask how they may revoke cards they have signed.

You cannot, under any circumstances, tell these employees what they can do in terms of revoking cards. The best thing for you to say is, "Under our laws, I cannot give you that advice. I suggest you contact the government agency for information."

Communicate all the facts you can about unionization

There are many other subjects that should be communicated to your employees which demonstrate Sherborne's sincere belief that they will not benefit by belonging to a union. You might state:

- It is preferable to deal with management directly — one-to-one — rather than have intermediate union officials or other outsiders (e.g., government) interfere in the resolution of an employee's problem.
- No employee has to sign a union card or vote for a union to safeguard his/her future job opportunities at Sherborne.
- No union can obtain more than the company is able or willing to give.
- No union can guarantee anyone's job — good work performance and successful marketing and production of our "widgets" ensure job security.

Tell employees of their rights to privacy

It is also important to let employees know that they have the legal right to be left alone. Be prepared to inform employees of their right to privacy by saying:

- Employees are not required to talk to organizers, attend union meetings, or listen to union canvassing of any kind. And they cannot lose their jobs for refusing to do so.
- Employees are not required to allow union organizers to visit their homes.
- Employees are not required to give anyone their names and addresses. If they do so, they should understand that this could result in a visit or a call from an organizer in their homes.

Remember, the examples furnished in this guide are just a few of the statements that can and should be expressed if the question of unionization arises. Communicate with your people. There is much to say on this important subject and it is up to you to do it. Remember that your statements must never interfere with the fundamental principle that an employee has the right to join or not to join a union — it's his/her choice. Management must not intervene in this "right" by means of 1) intimidation, 2) undue influence or 3) coercion. Stating objective information that will help employees better understand Sherborne's employee relations track record is within our management rights. If in any doubt, please contact human resources for clarity.

VII. Avoiding unfair labor practices

Throughout this guide we have emphasized your responsibility to take positive steps in the event of a union campaign. However, there are certain legal rules which should guide your conduct in order to avoid any improper activity. It is critical for you to know exactly what rights employees have during a union organizing effort and what rights the company has. Here are some important guidelines for you to follow.

- Your employees are entitled to discuss union matters or hand out union literature when they are not scheduled to work. The interpretation of non-work time includes rest periods, lunch periods, washroom breaks and before/after work. You are not allowed to prohibit this activity.
- Your employees are entitled to hand out union literature in non-work areas during their own (non-work) time. Non-work areas are normally considered parking areas, plant entrances, hallways, washrooms and cafeterias.
- Your employees may wear union buttons or other union insignia while at work. However, you may remove union stickers or literature affixed to walls, machines and/or other company property.
- You may listen to any information an employee wishes to volunteer about the union. However, you may not call employees into any private office in order to make statements opposing the union. Likewise, interrogating employees about the union is prohibited.

- You may not knowingly permit or encourage employees to take part in anti-union activities or distribute anti-union literature on company time or premises while denying pro-union employees similar rights to engage in pro-union activities.
- Above all, you should answer all employee questions fully and completely. If you don't know all the correct answers, ask your manager or human resources. And then get back to the employee with an answer promptly.

VIII. Conclusion

As a Sherborne Company supervisor, you are the key to the success of our Positive Employee Relations program. If you create and maintain a work environment that responds promptly and sensitively to your employees' needs, a union organizing campaign will never succeed. However, if union activity is detected, your prompt and skillful response is the indispensable factor in stopping the union drive. A union-free future for Sherborne employees depends on the professionalism of its supervisors.

No one knows your employees as well as you do. You are the primary source of information regarding Sherborne Company, as well as the company's primary source for knowing your employees' concerns. That is why you should be familiar with all company policies, benefits and practices. You should keep yourself sufficiently informed and knowledgeable enough to answer questions so that you can ensure your credibility with employees. It is no exaggeration — the supervisor is the most important individual in a union campaign. If your employees perceive you don't care how they vote, they are most likely to vote for the union. Remember, your primary responsibility during an organizing campaign is to make Sherborne's position known in a positive, effective and, above all, legal manner.

C
Activity Vector Analysis

SAMPLE INDIVIDUAL PROFILE: JOHN SMITH

Introduction

Activity Vector Analysis (AVA) is a scientifically developed, reliable and valid methodology to measure the behavioral demands and the suitability of people to perform effectively and productively in jobs. It is not a test. It does not measure technical knowledge, skills or education. It usually takes less than 20 minutes to complete. However, the results gained from AVA-based assessments can enhance the success and productivity of the individual, thereby improving results for the organization.

The Job Activity Rating (JAR) system is a facilitated process to determine the priority expected results and frequent demands of specific jobs and assists in the development of behavioral job descriptions.

The AVA Individual Analysis is a process to identify the natural behaviors of individuals to determine those that are most likely to be top performers in a specific job and/or task.

The Job Expectation Analysis is a process to identify an individual's perception of the behavioral demands of a job or their own behavioral paradigm of the role they themselves wish to perform.

Interpretation

The enclosed AVA Individual Profile is based on information provided by John Smith. Its accuracy is dependent on the accuracy of the information provided. The process is designed to assess one's natural ability to meet the behavioral demands of a role as defined by the Job Activity Rating.

Behavioral research validates the fact that people are most successful and contented when they do what comes most naturally to them. Once we understand the key dynamics of John's natural behavioral style and motivators, we can proceed to identify needs and develop strategies to drive change. Learned behaviors can develop from understanding, training and experience.

Performance achievements are also dependent on an individual's "desire" or "wanting" to perform their responsibilities and role in a manner that is consistent with: (1) the behavioral demands as determined by the employer and (2) the individual's own natural behavioral style.

The Activity Vector Analysis process measures five basic drives found in all individuals to different degrees. The combination of these drives can result in hundreds of different personality styles which provide unique insights into leadership, motivation, communication, stress, decision-making and conflict resolution. The five vectors are assertiveness, sociability, work pace, structure and principles.

Behavioral overview — general comments

This section provides a narrative description of the natural behavior style of John Smith. It is based on the responses provided by John. It does not include information from the assessment as to how John may be modifying his behavior to meet the current needs of the job or how he may be perceived by others.

John's response to the AVA identified the following adjectives that may describe him. These can be verified by checking with friends or colleagues.

- Calm
- Serene
- Methodical
- Patient
- Predictable
- Composed
- Fair-minded
- Consistent
- Focused
- Tolerant
- Down-to-earth
- Controlled

John's response to the AVA yielded the following insights into his natural behaviors.

- Possesses a high degree of emotional control.
- Accepts most situations with patience — doesn't get ruffled.
- Behaves in a deliberate and unhurried manner.
- Is perceived by others as amiable, warm, and accommodating.
- Adapts easily to routine and repetitive activities, can be habit bound, develops a rhythm and works at a steady pace.
- Has the ability to "stay put," possesses a high degree of "sit-ability."
- Displays predictable, regular behavior.
- Enjoys being part of a group or team; generally, the most valued group for John is family.
- Possesses good listening skills, and responds in a composed, unperturbed and non-judgmental manner.
- Displays excellent emotional control — slow to anger, "high boiling point," long-fuse. If John does become angry, he can hold a grudge for a long time.
- Remains calm, unemotional, detached in a turbulent situation.
- Maintains stable performance under pressure and/or opposition.

John tends to be calm, open-minded, easygoing and tolerant. He accepts most situations with patience and he is generally poised and reserved. John favors a conservative approach to issues in both his job and his personal life. He is consistent and prefers little unexpected change, but he has a tendency to be tolerant if normal "pressure situations" occur. He can maintain an empathic and accommodating manner with people. He is a cooperative, collaborative person.

John uses his time and ability well and can show persistence in reaching either short- or long-term goals. He makes his ideas known in a diplomatic manner and strives to understand others' points of view in a conflict or disagreement. He shows objectivity and empathy by actively listening and responding non-defensively to the views of others. He has an easygoing, non-antagonistic approach to providing positive feedback to subordinates. He expresses his ideas well one-on-one and in group settings. His need for harmony within the group is important. He will give attention to satisfying each individual's needs and will reward others for their work efforts. John may place importance on working on tasks that are methodical in nature. However, his patience, tolerance and empathy are not without limit and he can "explode" at the end of a long fuse. He prefers to perform his job in a relaxed and strain-free manner and tends to function best when he perceives the work environment as a comfortable one.

John can concentrate carefully on work assignments for long periods. He places an emphasis on quality. He tends to have firm emotional control and is patient in teaching and working with subordinates to improve their contribution to the organization. He is able to analyze information systematically to identify problems or patterns, and can use his diagnostic skills by asking key questions before coming to a conclusion or decision.

Due to John's consistent nature, he may become stressed when faced with too much unexpected change. He prefers taking a thorough, methodical approach, and having enough time to complete projects. If this is not the case, John may become anxious and nervous. He may also feel stress if forced to make quick decisions. Consequently, he may hesitate as he weighs the options which may lead to an occasional missed opportunity.

In a management role, he combines his non-threatening approach, high tolerance level and good listening skills with the patience to teach and work with subordinates. John is able to be sensitive to the needs and feelings of others, supporting their efforts to overcome obstacles blocking their successful performance. He tends to reach decisions through use of a participative management style.

Personal leadership style

When leading or directing the activities of others, John will demonstrate a personal leadership style that is distinctive. The responses provided by John indicate the following insights into leadership style.

- Is fair-minded, respectful, trustful, sincere, amiable, respectful and composed.
- Places emphasis on listening and deciphering information presented and then takes required actions in an organized, composed manner.
- Is consistent, predictable and composed.
- Bases decisive action on "the tried and true," or defers action in novel situations until more information gathering can be done.
- Is good at developing subordinates over a period of time.
- Is patient and understanding when developing subordinates.
- Understands the value in providing others with positive feedback for their achievements.
- Is sensitive to the needs and feelings of others, supporting their efforts to overcome performance obstacles.
- Reaches decisions through use of a participative management style.

Strengths relative to the behavioral demands of the role of Lead Hand

Leading research validates that people are most successful and happy when they do what comes most naturally to them. An individual's behaviors take on meaning when compared to the benchmark behaviors required for success in a role. The following provides insights into John's behavioral responses to the demands of the Lead Hand role.

- Listens long and hard to ascertain goals and needs — accepts most situations patiently; behaves in a deliberate and unhurried manner.
- Prefers organizations that recognize loyalty and teamwork.
- Uses a reserved but warm approach focused on facts rather than emotion.
- Communicates in a telling rather than selling style.
- Probes with "how" and "when" questions to understand and explain the processes.
- Builds rapport through thoughtful questions and warm concern at a low-key, methodical pace.
- Has difficulty planning for situations where there is insufficient information about expectations.

Behavior modification strategies for peak performance

Ironically, strengths can become weaknesses when overused or used in inappropriate circumstances. The following are areas that John should be aware of and use strategies to increase effectiveness.

The AVA revealed that John is in fact attempting to alter his natural behavior based on his perception of the demands of his role. He is clearly stepping up his assertiveness to a higher level. Also he is attempting to demonstrate a higher sense of urgency than is his natural tendency. Likely each of these is desirable in the role.

Also reflected in the responses is a strong desire to follow procedures and policies to the letter and possibly to micro-manage others. These may be issues depending on the demands of the role.

Other issues based on the AVA responses:

- The tendency for thoroughness can turn off superiors focused on the big picture rather than the details.
- The desire for structure may limit ability to change direction and respond flexibly to superiors who are impatient and demanding.
- May be wary of change.

- Needs to understand that obtaining results through others and the development of subordinates depends also on the ability to communicate well and inspire others.

Coaching strategies

Because people are different, there is a need to personalize dialogues and motivational strategies in order to be successful. Based on the natural behavior of John, these coaching tips when utilized by management have potential for positively impacting his performance.

- Create an orderly work environment by helping to prioritize work demands.
- Provide systematic and exhaustive training focused on all phases of the job with thorough follow-up and review.
- Communicate in a friendly, one-on-one manner on a regularly scheduled basis to try to draw out concerns.
- Be prepared to provide support and advanced communication in periods of change and instability.

Graphical representation

The graphical representation is intended as a visual aid to identifying variances (or "gaps") between natural and desired behaviors. Learned behaviors develop from understanding, training and experience. Strategies can be developed to drive change in one's personal or work life based on this understanding.

The graphical representation shows relative strengths of the drives within an individual. The measures are not absolutes and do not correlate to those of any other individual. Interpretation does not come from looking at individual vectors but from the relationship each has to the others and from additional factors not reflected on this graph.

For this reason, we suggest they be kept confidential and used only as a visual aid to understanding.

Terms used in the graph are as follows:

Energy

The degree of physical and mental readiness of an individual to meet, respond to and sustain the demands of the work environment in which he/she functions.

It measures the stamina, alertness and awareness an individual has to respond to events occurring around him/her. It represents the endurance or vitality an individual possesses to effectively carry out work responsibilities and assignments. It represents potential to execute behaviors over a sustained period of time.

Assertiveness

The degree of ability to take initiative and/or risk in favorable or unfavorable situations.

Measurement of the ability to be proactive in one's work environment and to take action to achieve a desired result.

```
     Passive <——— ASSERTIVENESS ———> Aggressive
     cautious                           decisive
   conservative                        competitive
     helpful                           demanding
```

Sociability

The degree of ability to approach and actively engage people in a work environment.

Measurement of the need for an individual to seek out and depend on people to achieve goals and objectives.

```
     Reserved <——— SOCIABILITY ———> Outgoing
   introspective                      friendly
     skeptical                       personable
    analytical                       persuasive
      serious                         trustful
```

Work pace
The pace at which an individual responds to, engages in and completes work assignments.

The measurement of a preferred work pace in which an individual approaches and processes work responsibilities.

```
       Impatient <——— RESPONSIVE ———> Patient
     sense of urgency                methodical
       multi-tasking                  tolerant
         reactive                    consistent
        spontaneous                  predictable
```

Structure
The degree of need for structure, reassurance, conformity and direction before taking initiative.

The measurement of an individual's need for systems, procedures, policies and dependence on higher authority in his/her decision-making process.

```
      Independent <——— APPROVAL ———> Dependent
       self-reliant                   cooperative
         positive                      compliant
        big-picture                 detail-oriented
         confident                 process-dependent
```

Principles
The degree of values, ethics, integrity, conscious restraint and maturity an individual brings to the workplace.

The measurement of the consideration an individual gives to the consequences of his/her decisions and actions. The ability to perceive situations from other perspectives.

```
        Immature <——— VALUES ———> Mature
     inconsiderate                     considerate
     thoughtless                       objective
     self-serving                      moralistic
       impulsive                       judgmental
```

Activity Vector Analysis

Gap analysis — John Smith

The following provides a description of the "gap" between the natural behaviors of John Smith and the behavioral demands of the Lead Hand role.

- Requires the awareness of and the need for better management of energy to meet the demands of the Lead Hand role.
- Requires taking greater initiative to be in control of job responsibilities and the outputs of subordinates.
- Requires taking a proactive approach and more readily engaging people/subordinates, to deal with unfavorable issues/situations.
- Requires being more open to the ideas and suggestions of others.
- Requires more focus on and attention to desired end results.
- Requires less dependence on systems, procedures, precedents and policies in his decision-making process.
- Requires less dependence of higher authority in managing day-to-day Lead Hand responsibilities.
- Requires greater attention and adherence to the values, ethics, principles and standards of the organization/Lead Hand role.

APPENDICES

Sherborne Company

John Smith

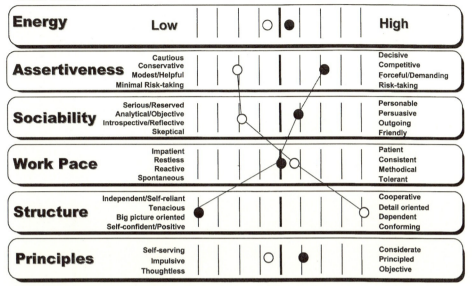

● – "Ideal" Lead Hand – Job Profile

○ – John Smith

D
Let's Talk© — An Employee's Guide to Effective Communications

SHERBORNE COMPANY

Date: January 13, 20__
To: All Employees

We are very pleased to provide you with this employee's guide to Let's Talk©, a unique employee communications program.

The goal of Let's Talk© is to provide each and every one of you with answers to all of your questions concerning your relationship with Sherborne. This is a special communications program, designed to emphasize the importance we place on open dialog between all employees and their supervisors.

Let's Talk© has my personal support. This guide explains the program and how it works. Please use Let's Talk© to the fullest. We believe it will make your career with Sherborne more enjoyable.

Yours very truly,
W. H. Burford
General Manager

INTRODUCTION

At Sherborne we value your input. We are interested in hearing your ideas about how your job can be done better. After all, once you have been trained on the job and have been doing it for a while, you may have some ideas about how your job can be changed to improve it. We want to hear from you. So we have designed a special program—Let's Talk©—to ensure that we will hear what you have to say.

The idea behind Let's Talk© is a basic one. To maintain our position as a major North American supplier of widgets, Sherborne requires the cooperation of you and your fellow employees. Maintaining an atmosphere in which you can perform well and work creatively is a goal we share. This requires frequent and direct one-to-one communications and that is what Let's Talk© is all about.

The initial phase of Let's Talk© is a confidential discussion that you have with your supervisor. We have included suggestions on how to make the conversation meaningful for both of you. The ongoing phases consist of the many brief personal contacts that you have with your supervisor every day.

Sherborne's continued success depends upon the commitment, resolve and good working relationship between you and your supervisor. We believe that making this special Let's Talk© program part of everyday communications will noticeably enhance our working relationships.

WHAT IS LET'S TALK©?

Definition

Let's Talk© is a communications program directed at discussing any items that you have established on the agenda for regular meetings with your supervisor. Follow-up actions will be handled by your supervisor or, where appropriate, by yourself.

The Objective of Let's Talk©

The purpose of Let's Talk© is to assist you in developing a strong and supportive working relationship with your supervisor so that each of you:

- understands the other.
- talks freely with each other.
- gains a broader perspective of each other's point of view.
- knows the scope of your job.
- works together effectively to get the job done.

The benefits to you

Let's Talk© provides you with an opportunity to express your feelings, to offer suggestions and to question matters affecting you and your work. It offers, on a regular basis, an opportunity for you to express your thoughts and opinions about the company, jobs, policies and procedures.

When used properly and consistently, Let's Talk© creates an open-door climate and encourages you to become more involved. In turn, you develop a greater sense of "belonging" and gain an additional feeling of purpose in your career.

To your supervisor

Let's Talk© is an approach to enhancing communications within Sherborne. It is a way for your supervisor to develop a working relationship with you so that both of you get to know each other on a personal and individual basis.

It is a way of building and maintaining trust and confidence between you and your supervisor.

It is a means of communicating Sherborne's objectives and your supervisor's departmental goals. It can help your supervisor accomplish his/her job responsibilities by reducing, and hopefully eliminating, friction and disagreement.

It helps us respond to your comments and feelings, both positive and negative, as they arise. Let's Talk© will help Sherborne give its employees the individual attention and recognition that are so important to us all.

How Let's Talk© works

Timing
Every three months, your supervisor will prepare a schedule of planned individual talks for you and all employees in your department. (However, you can talk to your supervisor at any time; you do not need to wait for a scheduled talk.) Each discussion will likely take between 30 and 45 minutes.

The Let's Talk© schedule will operate for nine months of the year. The remaining three-month period will be devoted to the annual performance appraisal.

Let's Talk© agenda
The Let's Talk© agenda form is designed to encourage discussion about issues important to you. It allows you to specify the topic(s) you wish to discuss.

Your supervisor will give you an agenda to complete prior to your Let's Talk©. Additional blank copies of the agenda are available in the cafeteria. Complete and return it to your supervisor at least two days before your meeting. This will enable you both to be better prepared. It will not only stimulate meaningful discussion but will help to relieve the tension that can be present in any face-to-face meeting.

Having your Let's Talk© and writing it up
Each Let's Talk© discussion you have should be looked upon as another opportunity to resolve issues or concerns while building a better and more stimulating career with Sherborne. It is impossible to anticipate all of the topics that you or your supervisor might raise, so we encourage you both to talk openly and freely.

However, Let's Talk© can become a most meaningful experience for you and your supervisor if you keep the following points in mind.

Both of you can stimulate the conversation by using such phrases as: How About...? Do you agree...? Is it really...? How do you feel about...? Why do you say that...? It is correct that...? Above all, be flexible: listen, think and consider the other person's point of view.

Sherborne has carefully advised each supervisor:

- To avoid dominating the discussion.
- To be prepared for negative comments.

- To keep an open mind and give serious consideration to all comments.

We have also counseled supervisors:

- To be receptive to your ideas.
- To explore them thoroughly.
- To give recognition when the opportunity presents itself.

A word about *trust*. Employees need not fear that any issue or topic raised during a Let's Talk© will be used against them. This is a commitment. If you have any concerns in these areas, we encourage you to discuss them immediately with your supervisor or any member of management.

Concluding your Let's Talk© session

When either you or your supervisor have talked through the issues and the discussion is winding down, it is time to conclude the Let's Talk© session.

As part of the closing, your supervisor will summarize the discussion and review the timetable for any action steps both of you have agreed to undertake during the talk.

Action plan/action steps

During the course of your Let's Talk© session, you and your supervisor will determine action steps to be taken to resolve any concerns raised or to answer any questions. In total, these steps represent the action plan resulting from the Let's Talk© session. As you agree on each action, record it on the action planner.

Action steps must be taken promptly after the talk. The responsibility for most action will probably fall on your supervisor. However, it is likely that some of the action steps may also be yours.

You and your supervisor will decide the following:

- *What* has to be done.
- *Who* should be involved.
- *How* it will be done.
- *When* it will be completed.

Your supervisor will ask you to sign the action planner at the end of your Let's Talk© session and will give you a copy. Another copy of the planner will be sent to the human resources department. This will be used to audit the program and ensure that you and your supervisor are getting the most from these discussions.

Conclusion

Let's Talk© is really about how we can work together more effectively. In other words, it is about communications. Planned communication, about issues you choose, is the primary aim of the Let's Talk© program. By providing you and your supervisor with an opportunity (and a format) to discuss any issues of interest to you, Sherborne believes it is making a significant contribution to the quality of everyone's working life.

Like any communications effort, the success of this program depends on the enthusiastic support and commitment of all parties involved. We are solidly behind Let's Talk©. Once you have seen what Let's Talk© can do for you and your relationship with your supervisor, we know you will give it your support and commitment as well.

LET'S TALK© AGENDA

Employee:
Department:
Supervisor:
Let's Talk© Date/Time:

Forward a copy to your supervisor two (2) days prior to your Let's Talk© meeting.

Please check (✓) the items that you would like to discuss under each general heading. If there are other topics you would like to talk about in this Let's Talk© session, please do not hesitate to write these down in the section for additional comments.

1. Communications

- ❑ What's the future for Sherborne?
- ❑ Where do I fit into Sherborne's future?
- ❑ Quantity of information
- ❑ Working relationship with supervisor
- ❑ Working relationships with others
- ❑ Being treated with courtesy/honesty

2. Recognition

- ❑ Recognition for accomplishments
- ❑ Being treated fairly
- ❑ Performance appraisal feedback
- ❑ Available job opportunities
- ❑ Further job responsibilities wanted
- ❑ Skill/job training

3. Quality/productivity

- ❑ Planning work
- ❑ Productivity
- ❑ Quality of workmanship
- ❑ Quality of systems, procedures
- ❑ Tools, equipment, supplies
- ❑ Suggestions for improvements

4. Wages/benefits

- ❑ Health and benefit plans
- ❑ Life insurance/pension plan
- ❑ Sick leave/bereavement
- ❑ Disability/WCB benefit
- ❑ Wage levels/increases
- ❑ Payroll deductions
- ❑ Vacation pay/procedure

5. General

- ❑ Parking
- ❑ Lunchroom
- ❑ Hours of work
- ❑ Working conditions
- ❑ Quality of parts
- ❑ Safety and housekeeping
- ❑ Office equipment

Additional topics/comments:

_____

_____

LET'S TALK© ACTION PLANNER CHART

Employee _____
Let's Talk© date/time _____

Based on the discussion, what Action Steps are necessary? Indicate who will complete the Action Steps and the planned completion date. Record any follow-up comments and the actual completion date.

	ITEMS/ACTIONS TO BE TAKEN	WHO WILL COMPLETE	PLANNED COMPLETION DATE	FOLLOW-UP NOTES/DATE COMPLETED
A				
B				
C				
D				
E				
F				
G				
H				

Supervisor/date _____
Employee/date _____

Next scheduled Let's Talk© date/time _____

E
Sherborne Employee Handbook

CONTENTS

1: The beginning
- Welcome
- History of Sherborne Company
- Our Mission
- Direct and One-to-One
- Our Values

2: Communications
- Introduction
- 01-2-1   Communication Meetings
- 01-2-2   Shift Communication Meetings
- 01-2-3   Problem Handling Procedures
- 01-2-4   Issue Resolution Committee
- 01-2-5   Telephone Calls
- 01-2-6   Open-Door Policy

01-2-7	Let's Talk© Program
01-2-8	Dialog with the President
01-2-9	Sherborne Newsletter
01-2-10	Memo to Employees
01-2-11	Bulletin Boards

3: Your career with Sherborne
Introduction

01-3-1	Equal Employment Opportunity
01-3-2	Immigration Law/Compliance
01-3-3	Respecting Others at Sherborne
01-3-4	Probationary Period
01-3-5	Employees Hired for Temporary Assignments
01-3-6	Performance Appraisal
01-3-7	Staffing of Vacant Positions
01-3-8	Reporting Relationships
01-3-9	Transfers
01-3-10	Seniority
01-3-11	Training
01-3-12	Workplace Harassment
01-3-13	Job Security
01-3-14	Human Resource Files
01-3-15	Retirement

4: Absences and timekeeping
Introduction

01-4-1	Attendance/Punctuality
01-4-2	Leave of Absence
01-4-3	Bereavement Leave
01-4-4	Jury and Witness Duty
01-4-5	Medical/Dental Appointments
01-4-6	Maternity/Paternal/Adoption Leave
01-4-7	Workers Compensation
01-4-8	Canadian Citizenship

5: Money matters
Introduction

01-5-1	Wage Rates

APPENDICES 393

    01-5-2   Pay Day
    01-5-3   Hours of Work and Overtime
    01-5-4   Time Cards
    01-5-5   Travel Reimbursements
    01-5-6   Report In/Call-In Pay
    01-5-7   Vacation/Statutory Holidays/Paid Holidays
    01-5-8   Benefits

6: Health and safety matters
    Introduction
    01-6-1   Protective Equipment
    01-6-2   Joint Healthy & Safety Committee
    01-6-3   Reporting Accidents
    01-6-4   Safety Rules
    01-6-5   Motorized Vehicles
    01-6-6   Housekeeping
    01-6-7   Smoking
    01-6-8   Refusing to Work

7: Living our values
    Introduction
    01-7-1   Outside Employment
    01-7-2   Business Ethics/Solicitation
    01-7-3   Leaving Sherborne
    01-7-4   Letters of Reference
    01-7-5   Termination
    01-7-6   Guiding Behaviors
    01-7-7   Performance Management
    01-7-8   Recognizing Achievement (Employee Recognition Program)

Listening to you

Final thought

Employee acknowledgment

KEEPING YOUR HANDBOOK UP TO DATE

The breakdown of the policy numbering is as follows:

e.g.: 01-3-11

01 = Year: 2001
3 = Section 3: Your Career
11 = Policy 11: Training

SECTION 1

The beginning

WELCOME
Prepared for: (name of employee)

WELCOME. We are very pleased that you are a member of the Sherborne family. Along with your fellow employees, you will play an important role in the success of our company.

At Sherborne, we believe that one of the best ways to encourage cooperative effort is to give each person the information needed to understand the general objectives of the company and the reasons why our practices and procedures exist.

To maintain a positive working environment, we have developed guiding behaviors that we expect all employees to practice. These are not meant to restrict the rights of any particular person, but to protect the rights and increase the safety and happiness of all.

Please review this Employee Handbook and ask any questions you may have. Your supervisor will be happy to help.

This is going to be the start of something great!

History of Sherborne

Sherborne was established in 19(xx). We are a privately-owned company which provides [insert company's history].

Our mission

We believe that Sherborne's success is dependent on the individual success of each of our employees. We believe in Positive Employee Relations. By pulling together, we will all win.

The Mission of Sherborne is:

- To produce the world famous "widgets" that meet customer requirements, on time, in a cost-effective manner, having due regard for the needs of all our stakeholders.
- To be the "employer of choice" within our community.
- To demonstrate our respect for the environment.
- To ensure a healthy and safe workplace.

Direct and one-to-one

The working conditions, wages and benefits we offer to employees are competitive with those offered by other employers in this area and in the same industry. As an open company, we encourage employees to discuss any concerns about jobs or compensation levels directly with their supervisors.

The experience of Sherborne shows that when employees deal directly with supervisors, the work environment will be positive; communications will be clear and useful and the work will be satisfying. We are committed to our employees and we pledge to respond effectively to employee concerns.

We affirm our commitment to maintaining Positive Employee Relations in our workplace. For those employees who may consider union representation in the future, we urge careful consideration of all issues involved including cost of union dues and the effect on existing working relationships which a union may have. We firmly believe that after you carefully consider the policies and programs in this handbook, you will recognize that a union is not needed to make Sherborne a good place to work.

This company supports the preservation of direct relations with employees. We encourage employees to use and preserve their right to speak openly, and for themselves, in the workplace.

Our values

1. We value our employees as partners in our business.

Guiding behaviors that will demonstrate that Sherborne "lives" this value include:

- We will communicate with employees.
    - We will listen to our employees, seeking understanding.
    - We will speak to our employees (keep them informed).
- We will have a mechanism for resolving issues that results in fair and equitable solutions.
- We will compensate our employees fairly, recognizing the value that each contributes to the organization.
- We will treat out employees with respect and dignity.
- We will treat others as we ourselves wish to be treated.
- We will take the time to learn about the needs of others so that we may respond to them as they would wish.
- We will recognize that there is more than one right way.

2. We value trust and integrity in all of our relationships.

Guiding behaviors that will demonstrate that Sherborne "lives" this value include:

- We are measured by our own performance.
    - No one grows on the back of another employee.

- Ours will be a non-political environment. (No one is out to get anyone else.)
- We believe that all our employees will act in the best interests of the company.
- We will admit our own mistakes.
  - We will take responsibility for our own mistakes.
  - We will learn from our own mistakes.
- The company will not blame people for mistakes.
  - We will learn from our mistakes, understanding what went wrong, to avoid a re-occurrence.
- We will treat others as we ourselves wish to be treated.
- We will hold confidential matters to be confidential.
- We will be truthful in all our dealing with others.

3. We value our employees as partners in our business.

Guiding behaviors that will demonstrate that Sherborne "lives" this value include:

- We will empower our employees:
  - through training in production processes and decision-making.
  - through assignment of responsibility, authority and accountability.
  - through knowledge.
- We will seek employee input to solve business problems.
- We will provide our employees with meaningful work, either in basic assignments or through cross-training.
- We will foster personal growth and development through regular performance feedback and training.
- We will recognize people as experts in their field (once they are appropriately trained).

4. We value our customers as an essential element of our business.

Guiding behaviors that will demonstrate that Sherborne "lives" this value include:

- We will communicate with our customers to ensure we understand their needs.
    - We will solicit customer input when we are solving problems related to their product.
    - We will be responsive to needs that our customer express to us.
- Employees will be trained so that they will be knowledgeable in discussions about the customer's product, both with the customer and with other employees.
- We will demonstrate our commitment to the success of our customers as well as ourselves by ensuring that they receive only quality products, on time, at the agreed-upon price.
- We will be flexible in our relationship with our customers.

5. We value the demonstration of leadership in our employee relationships.

Guiding behaviors that will demonstrate that Sherborne "lives" this value include:

- Each of us is responsible for the consequences of our own actions.
- We will take the initiative to anticipate problems and lead to their resolution.
- We will take the initiative to offer help where it is needed.
- We will put our values into action.

6. We value the demonstration of teamwork in our employee relationships.

Guiding behaviors that will demonstrate that Sherborne "lives" this value include:

- We will work together to accomplish our jobs.
- We will recognize the contribution of others to our own work.
- We will perceive ourselves as steps in a total process, each interdependent upon what went before and what comes after.

7. We value creativity and ingenuity in our workforce.

Guiding behaviors that will demonstrate that Sherborne "lives" this value include:

- We will ask others to look for better ways to do our job.
- We will look for ways to do other jobs better.
- We will consider new ideas with an open mind, never saying "it can't be done" before all options are explored.
- Creative and ingenious ideas will be recognized and rewarded.

8. We value a safe and healthy workplace.

Guiding behaviors that will demonstrate that Sherborne "lives" this value include:

- We will adhere to safe workplace rules and procedures.
- Safety will not be compromised for productivity.
- We will be concerned for the general health and well-being of our workforce.

9. We will ship only quality "widgets" and continually strive to improve upon them.

Guiding behaviors that will demonstrate that Sherborne "lives" this value include:

- Quality will be measured.
- Quality will be recognized.
- We will be open to new ideas from any source to improve quality.
- We will not be satisfied with less than the best.

F
Life Management Skills Workshop

With the advent of the global economy and its consequences for employees, we know that there is an ongoing need for people at all levels of the organization to understand the self-responsibility revolution. Employers would like to see:

- Greater employee productivity.
- Increased employee retention.
- Greater value for both their payroll and benefit costs.

These are not new employer aspirations, but with new technology, organizational restructuring, mergers and world-wide competition, their importance has reached the top of the corporate agenda. Most employers are addressing this need with skills training—more computer applications and more computer-based training. However, more computer skills do not necessarily translate into life management skills or the capability to think and behave with more "self-responsibility."

By linking the completion of a newly hired employee's probation period with the opportunity to participate in a life management skills workshop, the employer is sending a clear message about the importance of self-responsibility. And he/she is also celebrating the importance of a key rite of passage for any employee. In my view, this approach should win an award for its brilliance. Here, in one program, an employer can achieve the following three advantages:

1. Celebrate the transition from probationary status to full-time status. In almost all organizations this event passes without recognition. Frequently managers even forget to use it for its evaluative purposes — not a good idea if getting hired should be difficult because your organization only employs those who demonstrate they match the profile.
2. Educate employees in how to manage their life goals and resources. This is an ideal template for self-responsibility. Because life goals change regularly, learning how to objectively and realistically manage one's own affairs is easily transferred to the regular needs that an organization has to change its direction, systems and processes.
3. Establish early in the employee's career with your organization that you, the employer, view the employee as a responsible adult who has to manage his/her career and financial affairs independent of you. You are concerned enough (within your values) to provide the life management skills training and signal that dependence on the employer is not always in the employee's best interests.

This voluntary employee benefit program is designed to help the employer in several other ways as well. For example, by:

Increasing participation and contributions to employer-sponsored retirement plans.

- Meeting the fiduciary responsibility of a retirement plan sponsor.
- Supporting early-retirement and down-sizing programs.
- Providing financial education for employees, which translates into reduced use of benefits and sick leave.

One of the better recognition ideas, this life management skills workshop uses a unique, lifestyle-driven approach to life-management planning. The employees determine their own lifestyle-based goals and objectives before considering their financial situation.

A step-by-step process guides them through the development of their goals and objectives. Using a straightforward educational software program, participants build a "model" of their future, and learn about the financial impact of their lifestyle and investment decisions. They can then readily identify the dynamic relationship between their lifestyle choices and their financial decisions and situation.

Generic in nature, the program does not recommend specific financial products, but discusses them in general terms and educates the participants on their use. For example, asset allocation is described using asset classes and not specific investment vehicles. Finally, it is neutral with respect to the retirement decision. It neither encourages nor discourages a participant from deciding to retire. It gives participants unbiased information and a process to come to their own conclusions, based on their personal circumstances and feelings about the issue.

THE PROCESS

The learning process in this workshop is one of self-discovery designed to meet the needs of the participant and the organization in the areas of change and goal management. It provides participants with a framework within which to visualize their hopes, dreams, goals and aspirations for the next stage of their life.

It consists of preparatory exercises supported by an inter-active workshop session and extensive self-education materials. Participants may model any number of life alternatives, measuring their life goals against the financial reality. This process educates them on the dynamic relationship between their life choices and the financial implications of those choices. In doing so, it creates an atmosphere of self-responsibility in the employee population.

THE APPROACH

In traditional retirement planning situations, the first question is typically: "Can I afford it?" However, the real questions require far more soul-searching:

- How will I spend my time?
- What do I really like to do?
- What will keep me motivated?
- How will I react to not having a job?
- How will my family be affected by my retirement?
- Are my finances capable of supporting my lifestyle?

Participants visualize the lifestyle issues before dealing with the financial consequences of those dreams. Experience suggests that successful transition planning is 70 percent lifestyle related and only 30 percent financial. Finding the balance between these two aspects is the key to successful planning.

Employees are eager for solid information they can trust. This learning experience provides a transition management process which, when properly followed, allows participants to control their life's agenda whether they are developing new personal skills, considering a second career or arranging a savings program with financial intermediaries.

THE COMPONENTS

There are six components to this life-management workshop:

1. Employee Introductory Meeting
2. Life Choices — self-preparation
3. Financial — self-preparation
4. "Getting the Life You Want"
5. Modeling — self-education
6. Reference Library — self-education

THE OUTCOME

An employer who provides life management education to the employee population sends a very powerful message about the organization's values and culture. Employees receive a clear acknowledgment that they must take greater responsibility for their lifestyle decisions and for developing the financial resources to achieve these goals, in a framework of personal or self-responsibility for all their work/career decisions.

This is the new economic reality of a global marketplace. Life-long learning translates into "value added" benefits for both the employee and the employer. Employees do not expect life-time employment and employers can no longer provide such assurance. An employee's profession or career receives the primary focus. And, with changing technologies and marketplaces, this benefits both parties. By devoting themselves to their profession (versus seeking job security from their employers), employees live out the self-responsibility component of the equation.

By providing employees with the tools to understand and better achieve their lifestyle goals, an employer demonstrates that its employees are its greatest resource. Once this becomes known, the employer is on the path to becoming an employer of choice. And tying this message to completing a probationary period and hence being embraced as a full-time employee—with all its "rights and responsibilities"—is an outstanding example of celebrating an important event and demonstrating that, to be successful, people have to take ownership of their own behavior and performance.

For further information on this program, please contact:

Av Lieberman
President
The Retirement Education Centre Inc.
275 Lancaster Street West, Unit #1
Kitchener, Ontario, Canada
N2A 4V2

phone: (519) 576-1575
fax: (519) 576-5934
toll free: (800) 637-6140

email: alretire@sgci.com
website: www.iretire.org

ACKNOWLEDGMENTS

This edition has been "in the works" for many months. My experience is that the average reader is not aware of the intense work that goes into researching and preparing a manuscript. Even when it is a labor of love, the hours and assistance provided by others seem never ending. One thought, one detail, can result in contributions from many others. I would like to thank the following people for their insights, contributions and the time they devoted to this important workplace issue: Russell Field, Nicole Langlois, Barbara Novak, Adele Ostfield. Behind the scenes are very special people who have extended themselves greatly in the production of this book: Valerie Applebee and Pat Lee.

For permission to discuss and present an example of the Activity Vector Analysis, special thanks to Bob Sleeth at HRM Group, Inc.

As a mentor and friend, Ron Knowles has been most gracious in writing the foreword.

To Joyce for her love, patience and timely "nudging," my everlasting love.

HOW TO CONTACT US

1. Lloyd Field, or any of his colleagues at Performance House, would be pleased to respond to any questions that may occur during your use of this book. Likewise, Lloyd is available for private consultation and speaking engagements.

2. We would be pleased to receive any suggestions you may have that will enhance the spirit of Positive Employee Relations and/or specific strategies you would like us to consider for inclusion in the next edition of *Unions Are Not Inevitable!*©

3. Based on reactions from the business community, *Unions Are Not Inevitable!*© is a must-read for every supervisor and manager. Additional copies of this book are available directly from the publisher, Brock Learning Resources Inc. Volume discounts are available.

4. Lloyd Field has designed and uses several tools and assessments which are available directly through Performance House Ltd. Separate information packages are available upon request. Ask for:
   - Union Vulnerability Audit© — an assessment to accurately determine your organization's susceptibility to trade union intervention.
   - Let's Talk© — a one-on-one employee communications program.
   - AVA Profiles — a behavioral assessment that matches employee characteristics to specific job criteria.
   - Employee Perception Survey — measures the perceptions your employees have of your employee relations program.

5. For management/supervisory training, a catalogue of People Management Workshops is also available upon request. The catalogue describes many workshops related to the "people-skills" component of leadership positions. All of the workshops have been designed to reinforce the values and guiding behaviors of Positive Employee Relations. The programs are offered as in-house learning events with all the benefits of customization and scheduling around your business needs. Please request a copy directly from Performance House Ltd.

6. At least twice yearly, Brock Learning Resources schedules public seminars based on *Unions Are Not Inevitable!*© The facilitator is Lloyd Field. On-site customized presentations are also available. Please contact Jay Martin at Brock for the current public seminar schedule or to arrange an on-site presentation for your organization.

For further information, please contact:

Jay Martin
Program Director
519-725-3464
jay-brock@home.com
BROCK LEARNING
RESOURCES INC.

Lloyd M. Field, Ph.D.
President
519-746-2690
lloyd@performancehouse.com
PERFORMANCE
HOUSE LTD.